D0113055

THE RADICAL ATTACK ON BUSINESS

The radical attack on business

CHARLES PERROW
State University of New York at Stony Brook

HARCOURT BRACE JOVANOVICH, INC.
New York   Chicago   San Francisco   Atlanta

© 1972 by Harcourt Brace Jovanovich, Inc.

All rights reserved. No part of this publication may be reproduced or transmitted in any form or by any means, electronic or mechanical, including photocopy, recording, or any information storage and retrieval system, without permission in writing from the publisher.

ISBN: 0–15–575092–5

Library of Congress Catalog Card Number: 72–075076

Printed in the United States of America

Preface

The selections and my extensive commentaries in this volume do not fall neatly into any single area of academic study. The problems that are discussed are simply too ubiquitous, the issues raised too complex. But there is much here of central importance to students of economics, sociology, and business administration.

It is worth exploring the development and the ideology of the New Left's attack on liberal corporate capitalism, or monopoly capitalism, or, simply, the corporate state. Business should know what it is in for; the curious citizen should know what the uproar is about; the radical should see something of the consistency and the inconsistency, the logic and the lacunae, in his position. I cannot speak for the New Left, so for the most part I have let them speak for themselves. But as vivid and as interesting as many of the selections in this book are, they, like the New Left itself, lack a certain degree of coherence and consistency. The New Left is evolving, and there is much they must do before they can achieve a compelling, consistent interpretation of the world. Therefore, my commentaries attempt to link, explicate, and place in context the selections, as well as to demur and raise questions occasionally.

I sought selections that would spare the reader the endless (and seemingly mindless) rhetoric, dogma, revisionist revulsions, and churning and chewing of sacred texts. One characteristic of much New Left literature is that it is pithy, to the point, and colorful. This book is not "the best of the New Left" by any means, but it does contain some of the most striking and persuasive

LIBRARY
ALMA COLLEGE
ALMA, MICHIGAN

pieces available. Not all selections would be certified by a revolutionary committee. The long piece on Litton Industries from *Ramparts,* for example, hardly raises revolutionary consciousness in an explicit way—which may be why I find it so persuasive; but the article is entertaining and informative, and all the major themes are there. Nor can I claim to have examined more than a good part of the literature; these selections are not a representative sample. Such a sample would be dreary. I sought, rather, to capture the spirit and the range of the attack.

This is a sympathetic selection, and my commentaries, too, are more or less sympathetic—an attempt to give the devil his due, with some reservations. There would be no point in doing otherwise. If we are to fear the radical attack, we should see it at its best; if we are to grant it a curious hearing, let us be charitable in our choice of selections and in our commentaries; if we have sympathies in that direction, let us indulge ourselves in their best indulgences.

This book, then, presents one viewpoint. But it should be noted that of the corporate Goliaths that receive stinging criticism from the Davids of the Left here, four of the largest were invited to publish rebuttals in this volume. All of them declined to do so. But their views and actions, if not their defense of them, can easily be found in business magazines and newspapers. Moreover, there will be barbs along the way to protect the unwary reader.

I received some constructive and quite vigorous criticisms from the Left itself. Gerry Oster saved me from some errors in the chapter on imperialism, though he is convinced that many still remain; *Ramparts* editors David Horowitz and Peter Collier made pointed suggestions regarding my criticisms of the Left; and Professor Theodore Reed of Cornell University was incisive and encyclopedic in a commentary on my commentaries.

CHARLES PERROW

Contents

vii

THE RADICAL ATTACK ON BUSINESS

Introduction

"The 'New Left,'" the editors of the *Harvard Business Review* recently observed, "is a relatively small but hard core of young student revolutionaries aiming at nothing less than the destruction of U.S. society in general and the Business Establishment in particular." [1] As this collection of readings and my commentary will suggest, the distinguished editors are correct. The New Left seeks to overturn American society as it is presently structured and governed. In the few years of its existence, the New Left has come to see the destruction of American business as the particular means of that revolution.

Although it is exceedingly doubtful that the New Left will succeed, business appears to be frightened anyway (judging from the business press), and with good reason. As an executive of the General Electric Company suggests in a tense article on the subject, the charges of the New Left "are being voiced both by the New Left radicals who aim to overturn society *and* by non-Leftists who seek to improve it." [2] There is the rub: the charges against business are not only hurled by a small, hard core of revolutionaries, they are also given credence by the vastly larger group of middle-class reformers. Thus, although the business system may not be overturned, it is quite possible that it will be significantly altered.

The significance of the New Left attack is that for the first time in Amer-

1 See the editors' introduction to Gene E. Bradley's "What Businessmen Need to Know About the Student Left," *Harvard Business Review*, September–October 1968, pp. 49–60.
2 Bradley, *op. cit.*, p. 50.

ican history there has been wide dissemination and acceptance of a basic, thoroughgoing critique of the business system. The New Left—with no small help from such developments as the continuing Indochina war, scandals in the military-industrial complex, the growth of corporations into huge conglomerates, and industrial pollution of the environment—has created a climate of distrust and questioning. Should the New Left disappear tomorrow, silenced by the authorities or by their own explosive mixture of rhetoric and dynamite, the damage to the system would remain. They would leave a legacy of research, exposé, delegitimization, and, above all, a crude theory of business as a system. What was heretical in the first position paper of Students for a Democratic Society, the Port Huron Statement of 1962 (see Chapter 1), by 1967 had become the common rhetoric of *The Wall Street Journal, Business Week, Fortune,* and so on. The phrase "U.S. imperialism" could scarcely be taken seriously in 1965; it is used with considerable frequency in Congress today. The exposés of the middle 1960's are items for the agenda of John Gardner's Common Cause today; the tactics of the SDS in its community work in the same period are reflected in the various enterprises of Ralph Nader and others. Even the themes of the Women's Liberation movement now being heard by business were first expressed with urgency in the underground press.

Ideas, research, concepts, tactics, and urgency are not the only legacy of the New Left. Its views have been widely disseminated through the youth culture and especially among college students at influential universities. Three to four hundred underground papers;[3] thousands of copies of the Port Huron Statement; new college texts reflecting the radical perspective; and the assistant professors who had thrilled to, or joined, the Freedom Rides as undergraduates in the mid-1960's—all have spread the word. Radical caucuses in the professions, even medicine and law, are now commonplace.

The ups and downs of insurgent movements of the New Left, such as campus strikes, bombings, demonstrations, and confrontations, should be separated from their interpretations of the world. The former serve to publicize and activate (as well as to discredit and defuse); the latter serve to explain. The former can die out or be stamped out; the latter persist and gain in scope and intensity. In the long run, it is the explanation of such matters as wars, pollution, corporate size and power, and the role and uses of the university that radicalizes. Once the legitimacy of a system is thoroughly questioned, and that questioning becomes part of a subculture and disseminated, the system finds it very difficult to fight back. People simply do not look at the system in the same way: old information is reinterpreted (for example, the matter of economic growth or material

---

[3] James Aronson, in his *The Press and the Cold War* (Indianapolis, Ind.: Bobbs-Merrill, 1970), estimates the underground press in 1969 to have included 439 papers with a total circulation of three million.

goods); new information is rapidly disseminated and absorbed (cost over-runs or foreign investments in South Africa). If underground papers, magazines, textbooks, and television panels continue to press the new interpretations, the ebb and flow of mass marches and confrontations will be of less significance. Eventually, those who attend to the new interpretations of their world—primarily the college-educated young people—will have a hand in running that world, or at least will be close to the switches that can forever disturb its routines.

What seems remarkable today, in the early 1970's, is that it is a somewhat older generation, those already out of college when the New Left began to make an impact, that is now carrying on the patient, legal, mildly disruptive attack on business. This group is more reformist than radical, but as it grows in scope and activism, it seems likely that it will adopt more and more of the concepts of the New Left. Just as imperialism, once an epithet only of isolated and now redundant dogmatic Marxists, is now becoming a plausible interpretation of a widespread series of events and conditions, so will ideas such as "waste production" or "the corporate state" gain credence.

A few summary and introductory points should be made here, most of which will be developed in my commentaries. First, the radical attack on business is unprecedented primarily because of its comprehensive view. Such attacks are as old as American business itself, but this one is novel because this is the first time that business as a *system* has been the object of *widespread* analysis and attack. For the Marxists, business was always a system, but that narrow circle of critics was humorless and dogmatic, as well as ignored. For the liberals, the system merely needed adjusting. In the 1940's and 1950's, for example, most Leftist journals with any substantial circulation (such as *The New Republic* and *The Nation*) attacked the *sins* of business, not the system itself. Business was prone to sin; it could be expected to be under great temptation. The government had the responsibility to curb these sins; but the government, through ineptitude, greed, callousness, and conspiracy, often failed in its responsibility. The real villain in all these little exposés in left-liberal journals was government; a virtuous business was possible only if we maintained our vigilance. The New Left is not concerned with this sin or that sin, but with the whole system, which includes the domination of government by business. The system is beyond redemption. Businessmen are not evil, but, worse, they are doing their job. This is why the system must be brought down or radically changed. The view of business as a system has led to an analysis of interlocking interests and complexities and subtleties far beyond that attempted by most of the earlier attacks, and it has effectively blocked (in the view of the New Left) the possibility of a reformist posture. As the scope of the current reformers expands, they may also be led to attack the system as a whole.

The scope of the radical attack has expanded, for example, from General Motors to the universities that help to staff GM and vote its stock; to the foundations that support research for GM and generate policy statements that will influence national policy with the least long-term rupture of business interests; to the labor unions whose members have been sold out and whose leaders only scramble for the crumbs; to the liberal politicians and statesmen who would stanch a gaping, mortal wound in society with a Band-aid, suitably sterilized; and, of course, to the military. Recently *Time* magazine saw business as having made an "impressive beginning" at shouldering its share of social responsibilities. For the New Left, this is only a mask and an adjustment that compound the evil. We shall examine all these areas in detail—corporations, foundations, universities, and unions, and the new-found social responsibility.

The rhetoric of the New Left attack is also different in another way from that of past attacks; in many cases, the New Left's material is well researched. Purple prose will always be there—matching that of the corporation's antipollution rhetoric—but there are also scholarship, statistics, and careful case studies. Furthermore, the radical attack is not tied to any particular sect; radical groups come and go with bewildering speed. The attack has the character of a mass movement (even tiny masses can be critical ones, as revolutionaries know), with people and groups dropping in and out without needing to show their identity cards. It is extremely unlikely that the New Left will be captured either by orthodox Communists or repentant Weathermen. The New Left bubbles with too much change, diversity, and vigor.

What the New Left lacks, of course, is a practical, comprehensive solution. Some factions are disillusioned with the bureaucracy of socialism, but others are not; some groups are clearly unwilling to give up the benefits of technological affluence, but others would join communes. The radicals know what must come down, but not what should be left standing or what should go up. In this matter, however, they are no different from past revolutionaries, even the most successful. No major revolution has been able to experiment beforehand with models of the social system to see what is possible and desirable. The visions of revolutionaries are distorted by the times of which they are a product; the potentialities of a "free people" cannot be conjured up because there can be no free people under the old system. Thus revolutionaries call for destruction first and experimentation afterward. One may be reluctant to sign up for such an uncertain future, but if they were pressed, the New Leftists would say that the alternative is the destruction of civilization. This is not an apocalyptical movement, at least not yet, but with continuing wars, economic crises, pollution, the population explosion, and other ills, there is not much to be optimistic about. "Power to the people" is hardly a slogan on which to build a new society; more than this is needed, as I will note from time to time in my discussions. But if these selections offer no more recipes for the future than Karl Marx offered more than a century ago, that does not dim whatever splendor the reader may find in their thoroughly damning view of "liberal corporate capitalism." And if comprehensive solutions or even major reforms are to be offered, someone must first understand what the problem is. The New Left came to define the problem in the late 1960's, and it is still vigorously refining and publicizing its vision today.

In the first chapter we shall explore the beginnings of the movement and its major themes. In subsequent chapters we shall look more closely at particular areas. The final chapter offers some summary points and criticism.

CHAPTER 1

The emergent critique

It is hard to realize that the widespread radical attack on business is hardly a decade old. When the New Left emerged around 1960, their attack on the American business system was muted and reformist; corporations, they argued, should be socially responsible. By 1970, however, they had come to believe that the whole system had to be overturned. What ideas and events had caused this escalation?

For one thing, they had run up against a system so resilient, resistant, and omnipresent that no amount of energy and sacrifice on their part appeared to make more than cosmetic changes. A middle-class peace movement had been resurgent since 1958, but by 1965 the war in Vietnam had escalated. The walls of discrimination had failed to crumble after sit-ins, community organizing, the Mississippi Democratic Freedom Party, the Lowndes County, Alabama, voter-registration campaign, and the Freedom Rides with their blood and death. The poor had failed to rise up after organizing attempts in New Jersey and other non-Southern states. Not all college students had joined the clamor for campus reform.

But this explanation has its limits. Failure to produce immediate significant changes characterizes almost all social movements, yet these movements persist. Disillusionment about the responsiveness of the system and impotent anger over its ability to strike back is more characteristic of the mood of 1971 than that of 1965.

A more likely explanation for the broadening attack on business is that as disparate groups of activists working in the areas of peace, freedom, poverty, and education came together, they began to link the issues together. They all experienced the same kinds of resistance and the same resilience of the system. They looked deeper and gradually found the explanation for its perseverance: "monopoly capitalism" controlled all the major institutions of American society—the universities and schools, the regulatory agencies, foreign and military policy, the welfare system that just managed to keep the lid on insurgency, and even the labor unions, which had sold out to corporate values.

Much of the ammunition for this attack—the concepts, such as "monopoly capitalism," and the data on the subversion of free institutions—was already available in socialist literature, muckraking journalism, and the work of academics in social science and history. But the arguments were to receive new urgency, scope, and circulation from the New Left in the 1960's. In this chapter we shall illustrate this shift in radical thought from a reformist, liberal ideology to an increasing rejection of all capitalistic values.

In doing so, we shall sometimes contrast the Old Left and the New Left. It is difficult to be precise about these two groups. Generally, the Old Left is characterized by the New Left as clinging to a dogmatic form of Marxism that emerged in the latter part of the nineteenth century and the first part of this century. The Old Left reached its rhetorical peak in this country in the impotent Communist organizations of the 1930's, with their highly simplified caricatures of greedy capitalists and noble workingmen. The Old Left split over the issue of the Russian Revolution and subsequent developments under Stalin. It settled all questions of doctrine by quoting selectively from Marx and Engels. The New Left, on the other hand, neither glorifies nor denounces contemporary Russia, uses Marx as they use Mao and other present-day revolutionary theorists—as sources of ideas rather than as authorities to settle debates. The distinction between the two groups is clearest when tactics, rhetoric, and prophets are involved. In the matter of scholarship, however, the gray areas enlarge. A number of Marxist scholars writing for serious Leftist journals defy easy classification into Old or New Left. While the New Left is certainly made up primarily of young people, they draw on older scholars such as Paul Baran, Paul Sweezy, Harry Magdoff, and William A. Williams. On the other hand, the young members of the Progressive Labor party sound much like the Old Left of the 1930's. Despite these ambiguities, the distinction between Old and New Left is a useful one and will be used in this book in the loose sense of all such distinctions.

THE STIRRINGS

By the summer of 1962, a number of insurgent events had already taken place.[1] The Montgomery, Alabama, bus boycott, led by Martin Luther King,

---

[1] A useful chronology up to 1968 is provided by an Appendix in Massimo Teodori's *The New Left: A Documentary History* (Indianapolis, Ind.: Bobbs-Merrill, 1969).

Jr., had occurred in 1956; federal troops had been sent to Little Rock in 1957; a group of students at the University of California at Berkeley had organized a progressive student party called SLATE in 1958, which was to be copied at the University of Chicago, Oberlin College, the University of Michigan, Columbia University, and other campuses in the next few years. Bayard Rustin had led two civil rights marches on Washington, D.C., in 1958 and 1959. In 1960 the sit-in had been born in Greensboro, North Carolina; the Fair Play for Cuba Committee had been organized (Castro had overthrown Batista the year before); and the Student Nonviolent Coordinating Committee (SNCC) and the Students for a Democratic Society had been formed. Also in 1960 television had shown students dragged by the hair down the marble steps of the San Francisco courthouse during a demonstration against the House Un-American Activities Committee (a lurid documentary of this event produced by the Committee in cooperation with the FBI had been countered by a very different version by the American Civil Liberties Union, and both were shown at campuses throughout the country). The next year, 1961, had seen the founding of the Peace Corps, the assassination of Patrice Lumumba, the Bay of Pigs invasion, the first Freedom Ride, and the first serious American protests against the Bomb.

In 1962 some members of the tiny Students for a Democratic Society met in a union retreat camp in Port Huron, Michigan, to discuss working drafts of a statement of principles. The statement was then written up in final form by Tom Hayden in cooperation with others in the New York SDS office and titled the Port Huron Statement. It became the most significant document of the emerging New Left, with more than 100,000 copies distributed in the next five years. By 1968, SDS would be the largest and most influential radical group in the country, with more than 7,000 dues-paying members and 400 campus chapters. Later, Tom Hayden would receive some sort of fame as a defendant in the conspiracy trial growing out of the disturbances during the 1968 Democratic Convention in Chicago, and SDS itself would be fractured in the next year.

In 1962, the Vietnam War was hardly an issue, even for the New Left. The United States had a few troops there, but they were called advisers. The international issues of the day were colonialism, the Cold War, and nuclear disarmament. The domestic issues were overwhelmingly connected with civil rights, with some added concern about the concentration of economic power. An attack on business existed only in embryonic form, but it is there in the Port Huron Statement. The Introduction is reprinted first. Its literacy, its moving language, its feeling of moral outrage, and its implied dedication characterize the best writing of the 1960's.

1962

from THE PORT HURON STATEMENT [2]

Students for a Democratic Society

Introduction: agenda for a generation

We are people of this generation, bred in at least modest comfort, housed now in universities, looking uncomfortably to the world we inherit.

When we were kids the United States was the wealthiest and strongest country in the world; the only one with the atom bomb, the least scarred by modern war, an initiator of the United Nations that we thought would distribute Western influence throughout the world. Freedom and equality for each individual, government of, by, and for the people—these American values we found good, principles by which we could live as men. Many of us began maturing in complacency.

As we grew, however, our comfort was penetrated by events too troubling to dismiss. First, the permeating and victimizing fact of human degradation, symbolized by the Southern struggle against racial bigotry, compelled most of us from silence to activism. Second, the enclosing fact of the Cold War, symbolized by the presence of the Bomb, brought awareness that we ourselves and our friends, and millions of abstract "others" we knew more directly because of our common peril, might die at any time. We might deliberately ignore, or avoid, or fail to feel all other human problems, but not these two, for these were too immediate and crushing in their impact, too challenging in the demand that we as individuals take the responsibility for encounter and resolution.

While these and other problems either directly oppressed us or rankled our consciences and became our own subjective concerns, we began to see complicated and disturbing paradoxes in our surrounding America. The declaration "all men are created equal..." rang hollow before the facts of Negro life in the South and the big cities of the North. The proclaimed peaceful intentions of the United States contradicted its economic and military investments in the Cold War status quo.

We witnessed, and continue to witness, other paradoxes. With nuclear energy whole cities can easily be powered, yet the dominant nation-states seem more likely to unleash destruction greater than that incurred in all wars of human history. Although our own technology is destroying old and creating new forms

2 The Port Huron Statement was originally published in 1962 by Students for a Democratic Society, and sections have been widely reprinted in various radical readers. This selection is reprinted from the 1964 edition.

of social organization, men still tolerate meaningless work and idleness. While two-thirds of mankind suffers undernourishment, our own upper classes revel amidst superfluous abundance. Although world population is expected to double in forty years, the nations still tolerate anarchy as a major principle of international conduct and uncontrolled exploitation governs the sapping of the earth's physical resources. Although mankind desperately needs revolutionary leadership, America rests in national stalemate, its goals ambiguous and tradition-bound instead of informed and clear, its democratic system apathetic and manipulated rather than "of, by, and for the people."

Not only did tarnish appear on our image of American virtue, not only did disillusion occur when the hypocrisy of American ideals was discovered, but we began to sense that what we had originally seen as the American Golden Age was actually the decline of an era. The worldwide outbreak of revolution against colonialism and imperialism, the entrenchment of totalitarian states, the menace of war, overpopulation, international disorder, supertechnology— these trends were testing the tenacity of our own commitment to democracy and freedom and our abilities to visualize their application to a world in upheaval.

Our work is guided by the sense that we may be the last generation in the experiment with living. But we are a minority—the vast majority of our people regard the temporary equilibriums of our society and world as eternally functional parts. In this is perhaps the outstanding paradox: we ourselves are imbued with urgency, yet the message of our society is that there is no viable alternative to the present. Beneath the reassuring tones of the politicians, beneath the common opinion that America will "muddle through," beneath the stagnation of those who have closed their minds to the future, is the pervading feeling that there simply are no alternatives, that our times have witnessed the exhaustion not only of Utopias, but of any new departures as well. Feeling the press of complexity upon the emptiness of life, people are fearful of the thought that at any moment things might be thrust out of control. They fear change itself, since change might smash whatever invisible framework seems to hold back chaos for them now. For most Americans, all crusades are suspect, threatening. The fact that each individual sees apathy in his fellows perpetuates the common reluctance to organize for change. The dominant institutions are complex enough to blunt the minds of their potential critics, and entrenched enough to swiftly dissipate or entirely repel the energies of protest and reform, thus limiting human expectancies. Then, too, we are a materially improved society, and by our own improvements we seem to have weakened the case for further change.

Some would have us believe that Americans feel contentment amidst prosperity—but might it not better be called a glaze above deeply felt anxieties about their role in the new world? And if these anxieties produce a developed indifference to human affairs, do they not as well produce a yearning to believe there *is* an alternative to the present, that something *can* be done to change circumstances in the school, the workplaces, the bureaucracies, the government? It is to this latter yearning, at once the spark and engine of change, that we direct our present appeal. The search for truly democratic alternatives to the present, and a commitment to social experimentation with them, is a worthy and fulfilling human enterprise, one which moves us and, we hope, others today. On such a basis do we offer this document of our convictions and analysis: as an effort in understanding and changing the conditions of humanity in the late twentieth century, an effort rooted in the ancient, still unfulfilled conception of man attaining determining influence over his circumstances of life.

After the Introduction, the Statement gets down to particulars. It rejects both the liberal and the socialist "preachments of the past," The End-of-Ideology view proclaimed by sociologists as well as by the United Front Against Fascism of the Old Left. "There are few new prophets," said these members of a prophetic generation. Certainly, the university had failed to produce prophets. "Tragically, the university could serve as a significant source of social criticism and an initiator of new modes and molders of attitudes. . . . Students leave college somewhat more 'tolerant' than when they arrived, but basically unchallenged in their values and political orientations." (That description, however, was to change for a sizable minority of students.) The Statement analyzes the university in terms that would become more trenchant in the course of the decade:

The size and financing systems of the university enhance the permanent trusteeship of the administrative bureaucracy, their power leading to a shift within the university toward the value standards of business and the administrative mentality. Huge foundations and other private financial interests shape the under-financed colleges and universities, not only making them more commercial, but less disposed to diagnose society critically, less open to dissent.

The Congress and the Presidency are analyzed next, with the main themes being the Cold War justification of status-quo politics and the domination of Congress by Southern conservatives. Then the economic system is criticized as one of the "essential causes of the American malaise." The New Deal reforms were benign, but they obscured the real paradoxes of the economy—poverty and deprivation for millions—and the myths of the American system. "In work and leisure the individual is regulated as part of the system, a consuming unit, bombarded by hard-sell, soft-sell, lies, and semi-true appeals to his basest drives. He is always told that he is a 'free' man because of 'free enterprise.' "

There follow a paragraph and a footnote whose contents, updated from year to year, have become standard for serious tracts of the decade: the figures on the concentration of wealth and economic power in the United States. Such data were hard to come by in the 1950's; one had to rely on the figures for the 1920's and early 1930's published by the Temporary National Economic Committee in 1940. But in 1961 and 1962 a young radical, Don Villarejo, published a scholarly, detailed two-part article, "Stock Ownership and the Control of Corporations," which went considerably beyond the data and thesis of Adolf Berle and Gardiner Means in *The Modern Corporation and Private Property* (1940). And in 1962, an established economist, Robert J. Lampman, published his highly significant *The Share of the Top Wealth Holders in National Wealth, 1922–1956,* and Gabriel Kolko, a historian, published *Wealth and Power in America.* Among other things, these studies show that no movement toward greater equality of income has taken place in the United States. Such works as these, along with Michael Harrington's very significant book on poverty in America, *The Other America,* provided scholarly ammunition for a frontal attack.[3]

The remote control economy

We are subject to a remote control economy, which excludes the mass of individual "units"—the people—from basic decisions affecting the nature and organization of work, rewards, and opportunities. The modern concentration of wealth is fantastic. The wealthiest one percent of Americans own more than 80 percent of all personal shares of stock.* From World War II until the mid-Fifties, the 50 biggest corporations increased their manufacturing production from 17 to 23 percent of the national total, and the share of the largest 200 companies rose from 30 to 37 percent. To regard the various decisions of these elites as purely economic is short-sighted: their decisions affect in a momentous way the entire fabric of social life in America. Foreign investments influence political policies in underdeveloped areas—and our efforts to build a "profitable" capitalist world blind our foreign policy to mankind's needs and destiny. The drive for sales spurs phenomenal advertising efforts; the ethical drug industry, for instance, spent more than $750 million on promotions in 1960, nearly four times the amount available to all American medical schools

---

3 Don Villarejo, "Stock Ownership and the Control of Corporations," *New University Thought,* Autumn 1961 and Winter 1962; Robert J. Lampman, *The Share of the Top Wealth Holders in National Wealth, 1922–1956* (Princeton, N.J.: Princeton University Press, 1962); Gabriel Kolko, *Wealth and Power in America* (New York: Praeger, 1962); Michael Harrington, *The Other America* (New York: Macmillan, 1962). More recent research has documented the worsening position of lower-income groups in the prosperous 1960's. See the review by Leonard Ross in *The New York Times Book Review,* August 8, 1971, p. 1.

* Statistics on wealth reveal the "have" and "have not" gap at home. Only five percent of all those in the $5,000 or less bracket own any stock at all. In 1958, personally owned wealth in the U.S. stood at $1 trillion. Of this sum, $309.2 billion (30.2 percent) was owned by 1,659,000 top wealth-holders (with incomes of $60,000 or more). This elite comprised 1.04 percent of the population. Their average gross estate estimate was $182,000, as against the national average of $10,000. They held 80 percent of all corporation stock, virtually all state and local bonds, and between 10 and 33 percent of other types of property: bonds, real estate, mortgages, life insurance, unincorporated businesses, and cash. They receive 40 percent of property, income-rent, interest dividends. The size of this elite's wealth has been relatively constant: 31.6% (1922), 30.6% (1939), 29.8% (1949), 30.2% (1958).

for their educational programs. The arts, too, are organized substantially according to their commercial appeal; aesthetic values are subordinated to exchange values, and writers swiftly learn to consider the commercial market as much as the humanistic marketplace of ideas. The tendency to over-production, to gluts of surplus commodities, encourages "market research" techniques to deliberately create pseudo-needs in consumers—we learn to buy "smart" things, regardless of their utility—and introduces wasteful "planned obsolescence" as a permanent feature of business strategy. While real social needs accumulate as rapidly as profits, it becomes evident that Money, instead of dignity of character, remains a pivotal American value and Profitability, instead of social use, a pivotal standard in determining priorities of resource allocation.

Within existing arrangements, the American business community cannot be said to encourage a democratic process nationally. Economic minorities not responsible to a public in any democratic fashion make decisions of a more profound importance than even those made by Congress.

The last sentence makes a key point. As Ralph Nader was to quip nearly a decade later, it is more important to know who will be the next president of General Motors than who will be the next President of the country. In the usual attack on business, the concern is with more effective regulation, the breaking up of gigantic firms, and the corruption of government officials by business interests. In the Port Huron Statement it is simply assumed that government has little power and that capitalists, who are not responsible to anyone, have a great deal. The Statement continues:

In short, the theory of government's "countervailing" business neglects the extent to which government influence is marginal to the basic production decisions, the basic decision-making environment of society, the basic structure of distribution and allocation which is still determined by major corporations with power and wealth concentrated among the few. A conscious conspiracy —as in the case of price-rigging in the electrical industry—is by no means generally or continuously operative but power undeniably does rest in comparative insulation from the public and its political representatives.

We will hear this charge made many times again, and in some rather dramatic case studies. It is not necessary to document or to argue for a conscious conspiracy. Much of the economic analysis of the New Left in the 1960's represented an attempt to formulate the idea of a "system" independent of the conscious desires of its members, a system that had led to this form of elite control. Marx had said it long ago: the capitalists, as individuals, are not to be blamed; they are only doing what the capitalistic system demands of them. To detail that system for twentieth-century America was the purpose of the New Left.

The Statement goes on to deal with the military-industrial complex. The data—drawn from a time when we were not fighting a war—have since swelled enormously.

The military-industrial complex

The most spectacular and important creation of the authoritarian and oligopolistic structure of economic decision-making in America is the institution called "the military-industrial complex" by former President Eisenhower—the powerful congruence of interest and structure among military and business elites which affects so much of our development and destiny. Not only is ours the first generation to live with the possibility of world-wide cataclysm—it is the first to experience the actual social preparation for cataclysm, the general militarization of American society. In 1948 Congress established Universal Military Training, the first peacetime conscription. The military became a permanent institution. Four years earlier, General Motors' Charles E. Wilson had heralded the creation of what he called the "permanent war economy," the continuous use of military spending as a solution to economic problems unsolved before the post-war boom, most notably the problem of the seventeen million jobless after eight years of the New Deal. This has left a "hidden crisis" in the allocation of resources by the American economy.

Since our childhood these two trends—the rise of the military and the installation of a defense-based economy—have grown fantastically. The Department of Defense, ironically the world's largest single organization, is worth $160 billion, owns 32 million acres of America and employs half the 7.5 million persons directly dependent on the military for subsistence, has an $11 billion payroll which is larger than the net annual income of all American corporations. Defense spending in the Eisenhower era totaled $350 billion and President Kennedy entered office pledged to go even beyond the present defense allocation of 60 cents from every public dollar spent. Except for a war-induced boom immediately after "our side" bombed Hiroshima, American economic prosperity has coincided with a growing dependence on military outlay—from 1941 to 1959 America's Gross National Product of $5.2 trillion included $700 billion in goods and services purchased for the defense effort, about one-seventh of the accumulated GNP. This pattern has included the steady concentration of military spending among a few corporations. In 1961, 86 percent of Defense Department contracts were awarded without competition. The ordnance industry of 100,000 people is completely engaged in military work; in the aircraft industry, 94 percent of 750,000 workers are linked to the war economy; shipbuilding, radio and communications equipment industries commit 40 percent of their work to defense; iron and steel, petroleum, metal-stamping and machine shop products, motors and generators, tools and hardware, copper, aluminum and machine tools industries all devote at least 10 percent of their work to the same cause.

The intermingling of Big Military and Big Industry is evidenced in the 1,400 former officers working for the 100 corporations who received nearly all the $21 billion spent in procurement by the Defense Department in 1961. The overlap is most poignantly clear in the case of General Dynamics, the company which received the best 1961 contracts, employed the most retired officers (187), and is directed by a former Secretary of the Army. A *Fortune* magazine profile of General Dynamics said: "The unique group of men who run Dynamics are only incidentally in rivalry with other U.S. manufacturers, with many of whom they actually act in concert. Their chief competitor is the USSR. The core of General Dynamics' corporate philosophy is the conviction that national defense is a more or less permanent business." Little has changed since Wilson's proud declaration of the Permanent War Economy back in the 1944 days when the top 200 corporations possessed 80 percent of all active prime war-supply contracts.

Note the reliance upon published data and respectable sources of comment—such items as the number of retired officers working for General Dynamics and the quotation from *Fortune*. (*Fortune* and *The Wall Street Journal* became regular reading fare for Leftists in the decade, as did the journals of the aerospace and weapons trade.) One difference between the Old and the New Left has been the New Left's propensity to play it cool—to document its case from sources the enemy would consider irreproachable.

The Statement then gingerly and ambivalently discusses labor. Labor is the most "liberal" of the mainstream institutions, but . . . . There follows a long series of criticisms, and the general assessment that labor has no significant power in any case. Organized labor—even the working man in general—has always been a problem for the New Left, as we shall see. Even though organized labor is part of the capitalist system and has made its peace with it, the unions still offer the most direct access to the working class.

On international relations and colonialism, the Statement finds that business interests are protected by the government and the military while two-thirds of the world lives in poverty. This analysis is not particularly striking; the New Left's concern with imperialism would come later, after more revolts in underdeveloped areas, and it would be supported by more statistics on foreign investments and the link between key businessmen and foreign policy adventures.

"As democrats we are in basic opposition to the communist system," announces the Statement. In the Soviet Union, "the Communist Party has equated falsely the 'triumph of true socialism' with centralized bureaucracy. . . . Communist parties throughout the rest of the world are generally undemocratic in internal structure and mode of action." The Communist movement has failed "in every sense" to lead the movement for human emancipation. Until the sudden rise to prominence of Angela Davis in 1969, more as an articulate and fearless black and a woman than as a member of the Communist party, the party had not benefited from the insurgency of youth in the United States. But the New Left refused to consider communism or the Soviet Union as a threat to basic American liberties; the United States' response to the dynamics of Soviet society and foreign policy "has been more effective in deterring the growth of democracy than communism." Anticommunism, to the New Left, is clearly a guise under which the reactionary forces in society can gain ascendancy; there is simply no question about it, and no attempt even to document it or to convince anyone of it. In this respect the New Left made a decisive break with the Old Left—a conscious and somewhat agonizing break, it has been said.

In the summer of 1962 the New Left decided that the issue of freedom in Russia was not the burning one and they would not include at every point in their criticism of the United States a criticism of Russia; they would get on with the job of remaking the United States. This is not the generation of the 1930's, imbued with the Red Scare; it is one that looks on Russia as having just one more variant of capitalism—state capitalism. As Tom Hayden once said, "Marx, especially Marx the humanist, has much to tell us, but his conceptual tools are outmoded and his final vision implausible." Chinese communism, Cuban socialism, and North Korean communism are something else, however. For the New Left, these countries gradually became living experiments in new social systems, far more vital and effective in eliminating waste and poverty than their neighbors, India, the Latin American countries, and South Korea.

The diagnosis here, as usual, is better than the prescription. No instant recipes for the truly democratic society have been produced, but this is not surprising. No revolutionary movement in history has been guided by more than general ideals, and it would be asking a great deal to expect the New Left of 1962, or 1972, to produce a set of blueprints. Yet even today, the ideals and the rhetoric of the Port Huron Statement remain disturbingly vague, both for those who want to get on with the revolution and for those who want to see where it will all lead. The Statement makes a call for participatory democracy, vaguely defined, and one section asks "How to end the Cold War? How to increase democracy in America?" The concluding list of strategies and priorities is revolutionary only in the context of the preceding two decades: universal controlled disarmament; a fifty-year effort to industrialize all nations (without depending significantly on private enterprise); "democratic theory must confront the problems inherent in social revolutions"—a curiously ambivalent way to say that revolutions are not democratic, and revolutionary regimes that are attempting to industrialize may be "more or less authoritarian variants of socialism and collectivism"; breaking the political party stalemate in the United States; "corporations must be made publicly responsible"; and so on.

It is clear that this generic document of the New Left issues no call to tear down the social structure and wipe out the business system. But for the participants in the SDS organizing meeting that call was soon to come. What had started out as a radical critique of American society has come to sound like a modest proposal for reform. The Port Huron Statement tells us something about how far the New Left would go in the next few years.

VIETNAM

Much of the transformation of the New Left was to come because of the Vietnam War. The war prodded them to link domestic issues to American intervention in the affairs of a distant country in the name of an increasingly hollow cry for democracy. As the critique emerged, nothing could have been better calculated to demonstrate the arguments of the New Left and to gain for them a larger following and a wider audience. But one suspects the attack on business as a system would have come even without the war. There were obvious stirrings on the campuses and in the general population in the early 1960's. The New Left was active on several fronts—civil rights, nuclear testing, community organizing, and campus reforms—and it was growing steadily when President Lyndon Johnson authorized daily bombing of North Vietnam in February 1965 and announced that as many American troops would be sent in as were necessary to win the war.

Actually, in December 1964 SDS had already decided to hold an antiwar demonstration in Washington, D.C., for April 1965. They expected at most a few thousand students. To the surprise of everyone, more than 15,000 protesters appeared. Teach-ins were held that year in universities across the nation, some drawing massive crowds. The largely nonstudent Committee for a Sane Nuclear Policy (SANE, now Citizens' Organization for a Sane World), concerned with halting nuclear testing and banning the Bomb, held its own march on Washington in November 1965. The nuclear test-ban treaty of 1963 had undercut the peace movement; the bombing of North Vietnam and the reaction to the SDS march gave the movement a new impetus. SANE demanded immediate peace negotiations, while SDS demanded immediate withdrawal, an extremely radical position for the time. Nevertheless, SANE allowed the new president of SDS, Carl Oglesby, five minutes during a long afternoon of cautious liberal speeches to present the SDS position. (In 1965 many liberals thought that the bombings and the presence of 200,000 American troops might at least force negotiations, if they did not actually result in victory.) Oglesby's speech provides a second prologue to the radical attack on business. It has become a classic, and is probably the most moving and trenchant document in this book. Oglesby does not concern himself particularly with the war; he is concerned with the state of liberalism, corporate liberalism—an issue far more serious in the long run than the Vietnam War, although no doubt it was exposed by that war.

1965

TRAPPED IN A SYSTEM [4]

Carl Oglesby

Seven months ago at the April March on Washington, Paul Potter, then President of Students for a Democratic Society, stood in approximately this spot and said that we must name the system that creates and sustains the war in Vietnam—name it, describe it, analyze it, understand it, and change it.

Today I will try to name it—to suggest an analysis which, to be quite frank, may disturb some of you—and to suggest what changing it may require of us.

We are here again to protest against a growing war. Since it is a very bad war, we acquire the habit of thinking that it must be caused by very bad men. But we only conceal reality, I think, to denounce on such grounds the menacing coalition of industrial and military power, or the brutality of the blitzkrieg we are waging against Vietnam, or the ominous signs around us that heresy may soon no longer be permitted. We must simply observe, and quite plainly say, that this coalition, this blitzkrieg, and this demand for acquiescence are creatures, all of them, of a government that since 1932 has considered itself to be fundamentally *liberal*.

The original commitment in Vietnam was made by President Truman, a mainstream liberal. It was seconded by President Eisenhower, a moderate liberal. It was intensified by the late President Kennedy, a flaming liberal. Think of the men who now engineer that war—those who study the maps, give the commands, push the buttons, and tally the dead: Bundy, McNamara, Rusk, Lodge, Goldberg, the President himself.

They are not moral monsters.

4 Carl Oglesby, "Liberalism and the Corporate State," *Monthly Review*, January 1966. The speech was published first by SDS, then by the *Monthly Review*, and finally released in pamphlet form by the Radical Education Project under the title "Trapped in a System," with a new introduction by Oglesby written in January 1969. Reprinted by permission of Monthly Review Press. Copyright © 1966 by Monthly Review, Inc.

They are all honorable men.

They are all liberals.

But so, I'm sure, are many of us who are here today in protest. To understand the war, then, it seems necessary to take a closer look at this American liberalism. Maybe we are in for some surprises. Maybe we have here two quite different liberalisms: one authentically humanist, the other not so human at all.

Not long ago, I considered myself a liberal. And if someone had asked me what I meant by that, I'd perhaps have quoted Thomas Jefferson or Thomas Paine, who first made plain our nation's unprovisional commitment to human rights. But what do you think would happen if these two heroes could sit down now for a chat with President Johnson and McGeorge Bundy?

They would surely talk of the Vietnam war. Our dead revolutionaries would soon wonder why their country was fighting against what appeared to be a revolution. The living liberals would hotly deny that it is one: there are troops coming in from outside, the rebels get arms from other countries, most of the people are not on their side, and they practice terror against their own. Therefore, *not* a revolution.

What would our dead revolutionaries answer? They might say: "What fools and bandits, sirs, you make then of us. Outside help? Do you remember Lafayette? Or the 3,000 British freighters the French navy sank for our side? Or the arms and men we got from France and Spain? And what's this about terror? Did you never hear what we did to our own loyalists? Or about the thousands of rich American Tories who fled for their lives to Canada? And as for popular support, do you not know that we had less than one third of our people with us? That, in fact, the colony of New York recruited more troops for the British than for the revolution? Should we give it all back?"

Revolutions do not take place in velvet boxes. They never have. It is only the poets who make them lovely. What the National Liberation Front is fighting in Vietnam is a complex and vicious war. This war is also a revolution, as honest a revolution as you can find anywhere in history. And this is a fact which all our intricate official denials will never change.

But it doesn't make any difference to our leaders anyway. Their aim in Vietnam is really much simpler than this implies. It is to safeguard what they take to be American interests around the world against revolution or revolutionary change, which they always call Communism—as if that were that. In the case of Vietnam, this interest is, first, the principle that revolution shall not be tolerated anywhere, and second, that South Vietnam shall never sell its rice to China—or even to North Vietnam.

There is simply no such thing now, for us, as a just revolution—never mind that for two thirds of the world's people the twentieth century might as well be the Stone Age; never mind the terrible poverty and hopelessness that are the basic facts of life for most modern men; and never mind that for these millions there is now an increasingly perceptible relationship between their sorrow and our contentment.

Can we understand why the Negroes of Watts rebelled? Then why do we need a devil theory to explain the rebellion of the South Vietnamese? Can we understand the oppression in Mississippi, or the anguish that our Northern ghettos make epidemic? Then why can't we see that our proper human struggle is not with Communism or revolutionaries, but with the social desperation that drives good men to violence, both here and abroad?

To be sure, we have been most generous with our aid, and in Western Europe, a mature industrial society, that aid worked. But there are always political and financial strings. And we have never shown ourselves capable of allowing others to make those traumatic institutional changes that are often the prerequisites of progress in colonial societies. For all our official feeling for the millions who are enslaved to what we so self-righteously call the yoke of Communist tyranny, we make no real effort at all to crack through the much more vicious right-wing tyrannies that our businessmen traffic with and our nation profits from every day. And for all our cries about the international red conspiracy to take over the world, we take only pride in our 6,000 military bases on foreign soil.

We gave Rhodesia a grave look just now—but we keep on buying her chromium, which is cheap because black slave labor mines it.

We deplore the racism of Verwoerd's fascist South Africa—but our banks make big loans to that country and our private technology makes it a nuclear power.

We are saddened and puzzled by random back-page stories of revolt in this or that Latin American state—but are convinced by a few pretty photos in the Sunday supplement that things are getting better, that the world is coming our way, that change from disorder can be orderly, that our benevolence will pacify the distressed, that our might will intimidate the angry.

Optimists, may I suggest that these are quite unlikely fantasies? They are fantasies because we have lost that mysterious social desire for human equity that from time to time has given us genuine moral drive. We have become a nation of young, bright-eyed, hard-hearted, slim-waisted, bullet-headed make-out artists. A nation—may I say it?—of beardless liberals.

You say I am being hard? Only think.

This country, with its thirty-some years of liberalism, can send 200,000 young men to Vietnam to kill and die in the most dubious of wars, but it cannot get 100 voter registrars to go into Mississippi.

What do you make of it?

The financial burden of the war obliges us to cut millions from an already pathetic War on Poverty budget. But in almost the same breath, Congress appropriates $140 million for the Lockheed and Boeing companies to compete with each other on the supersonic transport project—that Disneyland creation that will cost us all about $2 billion before it's done.

What do you make of it?

Many of us have been earnestly resisting for some years now the idea of putting atomic weapons into West German hands, an action that would perpetuate the division of Europe and thus the Cold War. Now just this week we find out that, with the meagerest of security systems, West Germany has had nuclear weapons in her hands for the past six years.

What do you make of it?

Some will make of it that I overdraw the matter. Many will ask: What about the other side? To be sure, there is the bitter ugliness of Czechoslovakia,

Poland, those infamous Russian tanks in the streets of Budapest. But my anger only rises to hear some say that sorrow cancels sorrow, or that *this* one's shame deposits in *that* one's account the right to shamefulness.

And others will make of it that I sound mighty anti-American. To these, I say: Don't blame *me* for *that!* Blame those who mouthed my liberal values and broke my American heart.

Just who might they be, by the way? Let's take a brief factual inventory of the latter-day Cold War.

In 1953 our Central Intelligence Agency managed to overthrow Mossadegh in Iran, the complaint being his neutralism in the Cold War and his plans to nationalize the country's oil resources to improve his people's lives. Most evil aims, most evil man. In his place we put in General Zahedi, a World War II Nazi collaborator. New arrangements on Iran's oil gave 25 year leases on 40 percent of it to three United States firms, one of which was Gulf Oil. The CIA's leader for this coup was Kermit Roosevelt. In 1960 Kermit Roosevelt became a vice president of Gulf Oil.

In 1954, the democratically elected Arbenz of Guatemala wanted to nationalize a portion of United Fruit Company's plantations in his country, land he needed badly for a modest program of agrarian reform. His government was overthrown in a CIA-supported right-wing coup. The following year, General Walter Bedell Smith, director of the CIA when the Guatemala venture was being planned, joined the board of directors of the United Fruit Company.

Comes 1960 and Castro cries we are about to invade Cuba. The administration sneers "poppycock," and we Americans believe it. Comes 1961 and the invasion. Comes with it the awful realization that the United States government had lied.

Comes 1962 and the missile crisis, and our administration stands prepared to fight global atomic war on the curious principle that another state does not have the right to its own foreign policy.

Comes 1963 and British Guiana, where Cheddi Jagan wants independence from England and a labor law modeled on the Wagner Act. And Jay Lovestone, the AFL-CIO foreign policy chief, acting, as always, quite independently of labor's rank and file, arranges with our government to finance an eleven-week dock strike that brings Jagan down, ensuring that the state will remain *British* Guiana, and that any workingman who wants a wage better than 50¢ a day is a dupe of Communism.

Comes 1964. Two weeks after Undersecretary Thomas Mann announces that we have abandoned the *Alianza's* principle of no aid to tyrants, Brazil's Goulart is overthrown by the vicious right-winger, Ademar Barros, supported by a show of American gunboats at Rio de Janeiro. Within 24 hours, the new head of state, Mazzilli, receives a congratulatory wire from our President.

Comes 1965. The Dominican Republic. Rebellion in the streets. We scurry to the spot with 20,000 neutral marines and our neutral peacemakers—like Elsworth Bunker, Jr., Ambassador to the Organization of American States. Most of us know that our neutral marines fought openly on the side of the junta, a fact that the administration still denies. But how many also know that what was at stake was our new Caribbean sugar bowl? That this same neutral peacemaking Bunker is a board member and stock owner of the National Sugar Refining Company, a firm his father founded in the good old days, and one which has a major interest in maintaining the status quo in the Dominican Republic? Or that the President's close personal friend and advisor, our new Supreme Court Justice Abe Fortas, has sat for the past 19 years on the board of the Sucrest Company, which imports black-strap molasses from the Dominican Republic? Or that the rhetorician of corporate liberalism and the late President Kennedy's close friend, Adolf Berle, was chairman of that same board? Or that our roving ambassador Averell Harriman's brother Roland is on the board of National Sugar? Or that our former ambassador to the Dominican Republic, Joseph Farland, is a board member of the South Puerto Rico Sugar Co., which owns 275,000 acres of rich land in the Dominican Republic and is the largest employer on the island—at about one dollar a day?

Neutralists! God save the hungry people of the world from such neutralists!

We do not say these men are evil. We say, rather, that good men can be divided from their compassion by the institutional system that inherits us all. Generation in and out, we are put to use. People become instruments. Generals do not hear the screams of the bombed; sugar executives do not see the misery of the cane cutters: for to do so is to be that much *less* the general, that much *less* the executive.

The foregoing facts of recent history describe one main aspect of the estate of Western liberalism. Where is our American humanism here? What went wrong?

Let's stare our situation coldly in the face. All of us are born to the colossus of history, our American corporate system—in many ways, an awesome organism. There is one fact that describes it: with about 5 percent of the world's people, we consume about half the world's goods. We take a richness that is in good part not our own, and we put it in our pockets, our garages, our split-levels, our bellies, and our futures.

On the *face* of it, it is a crime that so few should have so much at the expense of so many. Where is the moral imagination so abused as to call this just? Perhaps many of us feel a bit uneasy in our sleep. We are not, after all, a cruel people. And perhaps we don't really need this super-dominance that deforms others. But what can we do? The investments are made. The financial ties are established. The plants abroad are built. Our system *exists*. One is swept up into it. How intolerable—to be born moral, but addicted to a stolen and maybe surplus luxury. Our goodness threatens to become counterfeit before our eyes—unless we change. But change threatens us with uncertainty —at least.

Our problem, then, is to justify this system and give its theft another name —to make kind and moral what is neither, to perform some alchemy with language that will make this injustice seem to be a most magnanimous gift.

A hard problem. But the Western democracies, in the heyday of their colonial expansionism, produced a hero worthy of the task.

Its name was free enterprise, and its partner was an *illiberal liberalism* that said to the poor and the dispossessed: What we acquire of your resources we repay in civilization. The white man's burden. But this was too poetic. So a much more hard-headed theory was produced. This theory said that colonial status is in fact a *boon* to the colonized. We give them technology and bring them into modern times.

But this deceived no one but ourselves. We were delighted with this new theory. The poor saw in it merely an admission that their claims were irrefutable. They stood up to us, without gratitude. We were shocked—but also confused, for the poor seemed again to be right. How long is it going to be the case, we wondered, that the poor will be right and the rich will be wrong?

Liberalism faced a crisis. In the face of the collapse of the European empires, how could it continue to hold together our twin need for richness and righteousness? How can we continue to sack the ports of Asia and still dream of Jesus?

The challenge was met with a most ingenious solution: the ideology of anti-Communism. This was the bind: we cannot call revolution bad, because we started that way ourselves, and because it is all too easy to see why the dispossessed should rebel. So we will call revolution *Communism*. And we will reserve for ourselves the right to say what Communism means. We take note of revolution's enormities, wrenching them where necessary from their historical context and often exaggerating them, and say: Behold, Communism is a bloodbath. We take note of those reactionaries who stole the revolution, and say: Behold, Communism is a betrayal of the people. We take note of the revolution's need to consolidate itself, and say: Behold, Communism is a tyranny.

It has been all these things, and it will be these things again, and we will never be at a loss for those tales of atrocity that comfort us so in our self-righteousness. Nuns will be raped and bureaucrats will be disemboweled. Indeed, revolution is a *fury*. For it is a letting loose of outrages pent up sometimes over centuries. But the more brutal and longer-lasting the suppression of this energy, all the more ferocious will be its explosive release.

Far from helping Americans deal with this truth, the anti-Communist ideology merely tries to disguise it so that things may stay the way they are. Thus, it depicts our presence in other lands not as a coercion, but a protection. It allows us even to say that the napalm in Vietnam is only another aspect of our humanitarian love—like those exorcisms in the Middle Ages that so often killed the patient. So we say to the Vietnamese peasant, the Cuban intellectual, the Peruvian worker: "You are better dead than red. If it hurts or if you don't understand why—sorry about that."

This is the action of *corporate liberalism*. It performs for the corporate state a function quite like what the Church once performed for the feudal state. It seeks to justify its burdens and protect it from change. As the Church exaggerated this office in the Inquisition, so with liberalism in the McCarthy time—which, if it was a reactionary phenomenon, was still made possible by our anti-Communist corporate liberalism.

Let me then speak directly to humanist liberals. If my facts are wrong, I will soon be corrected. But if they are right, then you may face a crisis of conscience. Corporatism or humanism; which? For it has come to that. Will you let your dreams be used? Will you be grudging apologists for the corporate state? Or will you help try to change it—not in the name of this or that blueprint or ism, but in the name of simple human decency and democracy and the vision that wise and brave men saw in the time of our own Revolution?

And if your commitment to human value is unconditional, then disabuse yourselves of the notion that statements will bring change, if only the right statements can be written, or that interviews with the mighty will bring change if only the mighty can be reached, or that marches will bring change if only we can make them massive enough, or that policy proposals will bring change if only we can make them responsible enough.

We are dealing now with a colossus that does not want to be changed. It will not change itself. It will not cooperate with those who want to change it. Those allies of ours in the government—are they really our allies? If they *are*, then they don't need advice, they need *constituencies;* they don't need study groups, they need a *movement.* And if they are *not*, then all the more reason for building that movement with a most relentless conviction.

There are people in this country today who are trying to build that movement, who aim at nothing less than a humanist reformation. And the humanist liberals must understand that it is this movement with which their own best hopes are most in tune. We radicals know the same history that you liberals know, and we can understand your occasional cynicism, exasperation, and even distrust. But we ask you to put these aside and help us risk a leap. Help us find enough time for the enormous work that needs doing here. Help us build. Help us shake the future in the name of plain human hope.

When his speech was republished in pamphlet form three years later, Oglesby wrote a brief introduction, apologizing for the "precious" quality of the speech. "The process of self-reeducation which the speech helped begin was subsequently to prosper," he wrote. The radicalism of SDS was then more intuitive and unformed than now, he continues, and three years later, in January 1969, the unmentionable words "imperialism" and "monopoly capitalism" could be sounded clearly. These words "have won their meanings and their status back, the perceptions of the ten-times-bigger student movement have deepened and become authentically radical, and today the priority question before us is no longer so much the clarification of our task as the making of the political instrument of its pursuit." Bold words, but unfortunately later that year some offshoots of the SDS—the Weatherman faction—found their political instrument in the form of bombings and terror, and the campus constituency went slack, either frightened or numbed. But if the political instrument failed to materialize, the analytic attack on capitalism continued.

The themes of Oglesby's 1965 speech deserve emphasis for an understanding of what is to follow. First, the war was started by liberals and pursued by them until it finally became clear that the war could not be won. The liberals were also responsible for the suppression of revolutionary movements in many underdeveloped countries. So beware the liberals, who are good men individually, perhaps, but captives of the system. The system, vaguely identified, is the corporate state, or corporate liberalism (soon to be called monopoly capitalism). Communism is not in itself the enemy of the corporate state; revolution of any kind is—whether it be by the blacks in the South or the opponents of the Saigon government in South Vietnam. The explanation of the Vietnam War is the corporate state's fear of revolution, the fear of upsetting a system where 5 percent of the world's population consumes almost half of the world's goods. A theory of imperialism had long existed in Marxist literature; the New Left was to come back to it during the Vietnam War and revise it. With this theory, the attack on business could go far beyond the "sins of business" on the domestic scene, far beyond the Port Huron call for social responsibility on the part of business.

The third and final burst of indictment and rhetoric in this chapter was published in 1965 as part of a symposium titled "Thoughts of the Young Radicals" in *The New Republic*. Aside from sharpening the themes already presented, it presents a short statement on the rallying cry of the New Left, "participatory democracy." Its main message, however, is the failure of liberalism.

Todd Gitlin, past president of SDS, calls for what West German student radical Rudi Dutschke advocated, "a long march through the institutions." Scarcely an article of liberal faith escapes Gitlin's ironic pen. One point in particular, that of the pluralistic doctrine in the social sciences, needs further comment. This view says that counterbalancing interests and institutions in society prevent one group or interest from achieving hegemony. Offsetting business are the regulatory organs of the government (which "putter harmlessly," according to Gitlin), organized labor, competing interests within business, and the legal system that affords means of redress for the average consumer or his representatives. This doctrine enjoyed great vogue in the social sciences during the 1950's, with some of the most renowned theorists demonstrating its power and citing in support Alexis de Tocqueville, the great commentator on American institutions in the early 1800's, and Émile Durkheim, a French sociologist near the end of that century.

The New Left attack on business and society received a parallel thrust from younger political scientists, sociologists, economists, and historians. The "elite" doctrines of pluralism were first questioned, then attacked. In the slow ways of academia, a scholarly confrontation emerged between those who saw society and communities as pluralistic, as representing diverse interests, and those who saw them as run by unresponsive elites. This has become the most divisive debate in the social sciences, with the antipluralists gaining considerable ground, at least in the number of their publications. A professor can now choose to teach introductory political science or sociology solely with anti-pluralist textbooks and readings. Ten years ago he had little more than C. Wright Mills and some dreadful Marxist tracts to use. The younger social scientists were, of course, shaped by the same forces that shaped the radicals, but the radical attack on the structure of capitalist society must surely have quickened interest, whetted appetites, publicized data, offered case studies, and provided an audience and a constituency.

1965

from POWER AND THE MYTH OF PROGRESS [5]

Todd Gitlin

What irritated liberals about Eisenhower's '50's was the slick assumption that the essential problems had been solved. That delusion was crippled by John F. Kennedy's rallying cry to "get the country moving again," and buried by Lyndon Johnson's mighty sermons on the Great Society. The upshot is a new orthodoxy: There are problems, but solutions are on their way. If the dissidents would only shoulder their load, we could get there a lot faster and with less aggravation all around.

. . .

The basic liberal misapprehension about America is that power is dispersed among competing institutions which balance each other. The national interest, or the "best for all concerned," is supposed to emerge from the orderly conflict among government, business, unions, interest groups, on down to the PTA. Individual liberty is supposed to be guaranteed because there is always room for one more interest.

But the brute reality is that for most Americans the reins of power—control over elemental life decisions—are remote. Most of us are reduced to apathy, sensing that the world is indifferent to us.

Political free enterprise is as illusory as the economic, largely *because* the economic model is a fraud. The dual engines of industrialization and war have created a tightly planned corporate complex that dominates the economy. Its power extends over work, information and policy, colossal in degree and unchallenged in kind. The New Deal institutions intended to circumscribe that power do so marginally if at all. The unions, remote from their members,

[5] Todd Gitlin, "Power and the Myth of Progress," *The New Republic*, December 25, 1965, pp. 19–21. This was originally part of a symposium, "Thoughts of the Young Radicals," sponsored by *The New Republic*. Reprinted by permission of *The New Republic*, © 1965 Harrison-Blaine of New Jersey, Inc.

remain largely unable or unwilling to do much more than bargain for incremental dollars and cents. The regulatory commissions putter harmlessly. Progressive taxation is eaten away by regressive exceptions. After each price showdown, government quietly yields another prerogative to the offending companies—and uses its tough-on-business image to clamp down all the harder on wages. Capital export restraints are not allowed to interfere with the business of exploitative investment abroad.

Much of the sham of pluralism stems from the unchallenged domination of the values of the marketplace, the fact that profit still motivates production, communication, education. If the sheer bulk of goods is all-important, who needs democracy? How can the New Deal prevail against the Fast Deal?

Yet it would be a mistake to cast government in the role of hapless bystander, for it too is a mechanism of irresponsible power, almost as free of democratic control as are the corporations, and as comfortably respectful of business as business is of it. Cementing the alliance at the top is the postwar marriage of the defense plants and the Pentagon, necessary to each for its own reasons. Comsat and the supersonic transport and commodity subsidies are not isolated boondoggles, but part of a pattern of industry-government symbiosis.

. . .

Material equality would be one valid criterion of progress. But the liberal assumption of upward mobility conceals the fact that the poor *as a class* are going nowhere. Of course, if you draw an arbitrary income line (even allowing for inflation) and count the number of families subsisting below it, the measure declines over the years. But if equality is your standard, the more relevant index is the distance between the actual and the fair. Thirty years ago the poorest fifth of the population earned 4.1 percent of national income. Last year the poorest fifth earned 4.6 percent. At that rate, equality is nearly a literal millennium away.

. . .

So deep lie the distempers of the society that they are barely scratched by the traditional liberal instruments of change: gradual legislation and the ballot-box. The liberal faith in additive progress mistakes quantity for quality, or, where it hazards innovation (as in the civil rights bills and the war on poverty), fails to come to grips with powerlessness, inequality, human waste.

It is not simply that choices turn out to be echoes, though this is certainly true. Worse, elections have been irrelevant because the public issues of control —foreign policy, militarism, economic power, decentralization—have been defined *out* of politics by an elite's appeals to free enterprise and exclusive expertise. Then too, the personalized consequences of mass impotence—boredom, conformity, inconsequentiality, violence, indifference—are mostly immune to changes in nominal power.

The same blindness arises as liberalism addresses the hungry majority of the world. To the anger of the peasant it offers only the chimera of "orderly change"—and, that failing, napalm. Legitimately horrified at the price some revolutionaries are willing to pay for economic development, it brands them indistinguishable, treating the name "Communist" as the end rather than the beginning of political discourse. Vietnam is thus no tragic mistake: it is the logic of American "law and order."

The New Left is said to be longer on critique than on prescription. The charge is rather accurate on its face, but we have had good reason to be tentative and skeptical about blueprints. For one thing, we have learned that blueprints tend to freeze. But rigid agnosticism too can be and is being transcended. Values and experience generate certain guidelines.

1. Power must be shared among those affected, and resources guaranteed to make this possible. This formula is quite precise. It means, for example, that slums should be rebuilt according to plans adopted by the residents, with capital provided from public funds and labor from the neighborhood. Welfare programs should be supervised by the recipients, until welfare becomes superfluous because a decent income is guaranteed for all who will not or cannot work. The mass media should be opened up to all comers, with no restrictions except a bias toward dissent. Political candidates should be publicly subsidized. The university's curricular and extracurricular decisions should be up to students and faculty alone. The great corporations should, somehow, be made responsible to workers and consumers. (Here we are in special need of fresh thinking and honest experimentation.) New political institutions are needed to localize and distribute as much power as possible: police forces elected by residents; neighborhood courts with authority over the quality of goods, the availability of loans, the behavior of municipal, state and federal agencies, etc.; computerized referenda on national issues like war and compulsory health insurance; and so on.

2. The institutional props of racism must be extirpated. This would entail not just the vigorous enforcement of existing laws and the Constitution but the guarantee of income, the razing of the ghetto by its unemployed and the founding of new, integrated communities, the provision of land and crop allotments for sharecroppers and small farmers, the extension of a serious federal presence in the vigilante South, fair jury legislation, and more along these lines.

3. America must put down the big stick and take self-determination seriously. Revolution must at least be tolerated if not embraced—then we may earn the right to be critical. Foreign investments must be withdrawn unless invited by governments committed to their people. Disarmament is imperative, and this means rapprochement with China. Overall, whatever progress the comfortable make must not be at the expense of the miserable.

But a great deal depends on how change takes place. The top-down facsimiles of these proposals would amount to little, if anything. Far more than any particular program, America needs a movement dedicated to remaking America at the roots. The solid and decisive changes must be the burden of people who see the need and organize, wherever they are, to demand and create a society that would honor men. *Only* the experience of movement confronting institutional power can generate the issues now submerged in rhetoric and helplessness. . . .

A "movement confronting institutional power" is what now presents itself. This is the credo of the New Left that the General Electric executive attacks in his *Harvard Business Review* article and that numerous publications such as *Fortune, The Wall Street Journal,* and *Time* warn of. It seems unlikely that this movement will be snuffed out by repressive measures, by the tapering off of the Vietnam War or the winding down of campus protests, by the excesses of groups like the Weathermen, or by the sniping of ghetto residents.

This prologue has presented the ideology and the rhetoric of the New Left; but what about their facts? What case studies do these radicals draw on? What information hardens the certitude of their world view? What evidence supports their position? The next chapters will look at specific institutional areas, starting with giant corporations, to show what the politically involved but alienated young are reading and thinking today.

CHAPTER 2

Where it's at: the corporation

The following sardonic, witty, and lengthy bit of muckraking by David Horowitz and Reese Erlich for *Ramparts* magazine might be seen as having more ulterior motives than the exposé of two very prominent industrial statesmen, Roy Ash and Tex Thornton. Underplayed, but ever present, are the following themes: the interdependency of the business and governmental elite; the easy way in which those who have high positions in Washington, or connections with those who do, get things done and make decisions informally, without public discussion or accountability; the accounting system by which in the larger sense the taxpayer finances the growth, profits, and power of people with the right connections; the relationship between imperialism, business, and government; and the growth of what is called domestic imperialism, under which sections of the American population are treated much as Negroes in Africa or Asians in the Far East. These are some elements of the New Left attack on business. It is not merely that business sins; it is not even important that Ash and Thornton had apparently engaged in illegal and unprincipled activities while at Hughes Aircraft. Caught up in the business system, even principled, honorable men such as Clark Clifford must operate this way.[1] The ever-present image of a power elite of businessmen, government officials, and military men underlies this article and the New Left's attack. The elite need not consciously conspire; conspiracies are immaterial if a system exists. Later this chapter will try to detail more explicitly what the New Left means by the system; here is the system at work.

1 See the critical profile of Clark Clifford in the August 24, 1968, issue of *Ramparts*.

1968

BIG BROTHER AS A HOLDING COMPANY [2]

David Horowitz and Reese Erlich

It's a sign of the times

"According to our computer," says Robert Allan Jr., head of Litton Industries' Greek project, "there's less than 800 weeks before the present trend will be irreversible.... The need for food and the lack of capacity of technology in ... underdeveloped nations will be overwhelming.... It's time that we got to work on it." To listen to Litton executives and to read their annual reports, one might suppose that Litton was some enormous social welfare agency rather than a multibillion-dollar defense contractor. In reality, it is both of these and more.

Litton Industries produces S&H Green Stamps and Stouffer Foods, missile guidance systems and nuclear attack submarines. It runs important programs of the War on Poverty at home. And abroad it recently secured an $800 million contract—to which Mr. Allan's statement referred—with the Greek military junta for the economic development of the whole geographical region of Western Peloponnesus and Crete. Litton is the perfect example of the new corporation extending itself beyond the limits that have divided the private oligarchies of business from the realms of responsibility traditionally reserved to government.

Already a new crop of names has appeared to describe this development, among them "New Industrial State" and "Contract State," as well as the older and more restricted term, "Military-Industrial Complex." The shape of the new social and economic system that is emerging from behind these labels is as distant from the classical image of "free enterprise" capitalism as is Allan's statement from anything that one might expect to hear from a Calvin Coolidge, much less a Henry Ford.

Among the corporate bearers of this brave new American future, Litton stands out as something of a paradigm and archetype foreshadowing the shape of things to come. It is not just the new corporation, but the Now Corporation. It has gathered about itself the full mystique of modernity: advanced technology, the "systems engineering" approach (a product of military contracting), electronics and space. And the mystique has paid off phenomenally well, with a corporate growth rate which *Business Week* says may well be the fastest in the history of U.S. business.

2 David Horowitz and Reese Erlich, "Big Brother as a Holding Company," *Ramparts*, November 1968, pp. 44–52. Copyright Ramparts Magazine, Inc., 1968. Reprinted by permission of the editors.

In 1953, when a group headed by Charles "Tex" Thornton bought Litton, then a small electronics firm, for $1.5 million, the company showed $3 million in sales. This year its worth has grown to a fantastic $1.8 *billion* level, making it the 44th largest industrial corporation in the U.S., ranking ahead of such traditional giants as Alcoa Aluminum, Coca-Cola and Dow Chemical. The aura of futuristic competence that surrounds and powers Litton's conglomerate explosion is reinforced by the higher circles of the business world: *Fortune*, the *Social Register* of the business establishment, describes Litton as "the very symbol of all that is modern in U.S. management" and calls its guiding captains "as brilliant a group as can be found at the head of any corporation in the world."

It is perhaps natural that the guiding forces of American society, frustrated by the nation's stubborn social ills which appear to be insoluble by traditional means, should turn to the methodology of military-space development as the Way to Get Things Done. Unable to confront the real moral and political dimensions of its economic and social crisis, the American leadership defines the crisis as basically a technical problem and is immensely comforted thereby: the technical problem is large, to be sure, but it is one that can be handled without any serious reassessment of American values and institutions—and without the social upheaval that might be necessary to restructure them. If engineers employed by private corporations on contract to the government can put men on the moon, it is reasoned, surely they can cure the social and economic crisis at home.

The social engineering approach to race and poverty is merely the logical extension of the pervasive liberal doctrine of pragmatic America and the "end of ideology." As John F. Kennedy, whom many look on as the last national statesman to bear the torch of idealism, affirmed in his famous Yale address in 1962: "What is at stake is not some grand warfare of rival ideologies which will sweep the country with passion, but the practical management of a modern economy. What we need is ... more basic discussion of the sophisticated and technical issues involved in keeping a great economic machinery moving ahead."

The domestic upheavals in the years following President Kennedy's address have torn to shreds the mythology of the crisis-free welfare state. But the mythology of salvation through the application of technology by the Great Partnership between government and the private corporations has not only survived, it has risen to a new intensity of apocalyptic promise. The theme recurs across the political spectrum, though Democrats may call it a domestic Marshall Plan while Republicans and Wallacites more candidly emphasize Incentives to Business. And if the extension of the contract state means further entrance of a military-social-industrial complex into governance of American society, maybe it is just the right outfit for the job.

Litton Industries was the first corporation to take over one of the poverty program's multimillion-dollar job corps camps—whose large urban centers are now run completely by private enterprise—and was an early promoter of the "military systems" approach for other areas of national policy. As the idea has caught on, proposals have proliferated. General Bernard Adolph Schriever, special Administration consultant on housing and urban development programs, has already suggested that aerospace's management process be applied to these programs, and aerospace industrial teams have begun pushing for contracts in such areas as urban traffic management and water conservation (California's waste disposal program is in the process of being handed over to Aerojet-General). Litton, for its part, has offered to contract whole local school systems, promising to put them on a sound footing and to run them smoothly and economically—a logical step since it is already a major textbook publisher and runs a college of its own in Michigan. It is a proposal that may well appeal to harried parents and tax-ridden homeowners.

Litton Industries has been *the* corporate success story of the postwar period just because it is the perfect product of the times, custom-made to fit the outlines of the new order. For the same reason, it is a perfect image of the economic developments of this period: the vast expansion of the military budget during the Cold War and the largest corporate merger wave in U.S. history.

While the notion of a military-industrial complex has gained currency in recent years, the *technological* underpinning of the new intimacy between government and business has gone largely unnoticed. Yet fully 70 per cent of all research and development being done in the United States today (about $16 billion worth), is paid for by the federal government, whereas a little more than 20 years ago it supported almost none at all. The significance of this for the civilian economy was spelled out recently by Litton's number two man, Roy Ash, in explaining his company's relation to the military sector. Since "almost all new products have their first application in military uses," said Ash, "we always want at least 25 per cent of our business in defense and space."

Ash's statement and the facts behind it reflect the final collapse of the cornerstone of old-fashioned capitalism. In the old days private corporations would develop technological innovations at their own expense, risking the outlay with a view to being rewarded by future returns from the competitive marketplace. This was the very essence of entrepreneurship. However, technical research has now become extremely expensive, and because of the gentlemanly pace of competition among the monopolistic giants of the American economy, these corporations are no longer forced by fear of rivals to risk such investments. So they have become accustomed to getting the government to pick up the tab before they move. These corporations have grown economically lazy, in part because *they* really *can* live better on the largess of the so-called welfare state. One of the factors that has made it possible for them to pry such huge sums of research money out of the government has been the unprecedented increase in the concentration of economic—and with it, political—power in the last decade.

This tremendous concentration movement in the economy has been spearheaded by the advance of the "conglomerate" corporations, formed by the acquisition of companies operating in diverse markets. Litton is the star of this movement, with enterprises in 18 distinct industrial categories.

To an uninitiated observer of the conglomerate phenomenon, Litton's fantastic rise has a distinctly mystifying air about it, like some kind of psychic levitation. For despite all the hullabaloo about new technologies and go-go management, Litton can point to no revolutionary innovation which has benefited the civilian economy and represents a tangible basis for its surging nonmilitary growth (about two-thirds of Litton's present sales, according to Roy Ash, are in civilian fields). One has only to think of Xerox and Polaroid, where jet-powered corporate growth and revolutionizing technology have gone hand in hand, to bring the contrast into focus. It is not that Litton produces nothing innovative or useful (if inertial guidance systems for missiles and fighter planes can be considered useful), but rather that nothing Litton has marketed seems to warrant its unparalleled record of corporate expansion. Indeed, most of Litton's technological innovations were already being developed in the 70 and more businesses which Litton has acquired—*before* they became part of the parent firm.

Yet to be mystified by this is merely to confuse what Thorstein Veblen called the "business system" with the industrial system—that is, to mistake the system of developing and implementing technologies to meet human needs for the system of making a buck off them. Litton's success is a function almost entirely of a brilliant, if sleight of hand, business strategy, with the U.S. government as silent partner. If the constituents of its success seem somewhat insubstantial to the ordinary man, the cash it has made is real. And in the "business system," it is the cash that counts.

To mastermind such a success in the business world, as in the theater, one must learn to live in an attenuated universe where the fictitious is more tangible than the real. At a very early age, Tex Thornton, the brains behind Litton, learned just that.

Growing up with Tex

"Tex Thornton—good abilities along a few lines but not a good all round man; is unprincipled, ruthless and is universally disliked; cannot be trusted."

> FROM a confidential memo prepared by a member of the prestigious Wall Street accounting firm of Haskins & Sells; marked as an exhibit in the Steele vs. Litton case.

Tex Thornton is the paradigm new corporate manager of the paradigm new corporation. His career follows the now well trodden path from civilian Washington to the military to the corporate elite.

Thirty years ago Tex Thornton was a $1400-a-year clerk in Washington; today he is a university trustee, a member of the President's Advisory Commission on Civil Disorders (the Kerner Commission) and head of its special Advisory Panel on Private Enterprise. He was one of a handful of nominees considered to succeed Robert McNamara as secretary of Defense, and according to a Washington Post columnist he is—with typical military-industrial bipartisanship—presently being considered by Richard Nixon for that job. He has already achieved the coveted seat next to the President at White House business meetings. In addition to being chairman of the board of Litton, he is an "interlocking director" of such giants as TWA, Lehman Corporation, General Mills, the Western Bancorporation (a bank holding company for the Bank of America interests) and Union Oil. Needless to say, in Thornton's new circles being a millionaire is not at all unusual, but he has already made $80 million and is aiming for the status of centimillionaire. If the market for Litton stock holds up, he will soon make it. Tex Thornton has come a long way, and the Horatio Alger award he received in 1964 was shrewdly given.

Soon after Tex was born in a small north central Texas town his father ran off, leaving his mother to drill him in the manly art of finance. When he was just twelve, she was already encouraging him to use his earnings from odd jobs to buy land, instead of frittering his money away like a kid. He eventually accumulated nearly 40 acres. By the time Tex was fourteen, every store in town would accept his personal check. And he was all of nineteen when he launched his first real business venture: a combination gas station and Chrysler-Plymouth dealership.

Later, setting his sights always higher, he enrolled in Texas Technological College, starting first in engineering, but switching quickly to business administration—after all, the engineer works for the businessman. He quit Texas Tech in his junior year and took off for Washington to check out the action in the School of Life. In Washington he returned to college and got his Bachelor of Commercial Science in 1937. His first job was as a clerk in the Department of the Interior.

For four years Tex was unable to find that combination of business-military-political influence which he needed to power his ascent. When he did find it, its name was Robert Lovett, Wall Street banker and assistant secretary of War. Lovett was not just a run-of-the-mill Wall Street banker, either; he was destined to become—in the euphemism of such a scholar as Arthur Schlesinger Jr.—one of the co-chairmen of the American establishment. Highly impressed with the twenty-eight-year-old Tex, Lovett suggested that he join the Army (it was pre–Pearl Harbor 1941) as a second lieutenant. Apparently a brilliant officer, Thornton received his first promotion within 48 hours. A series of such jet-assisted takeoffs made him one of the youngest colonels in the U.S. Army, at one point with as many as 2800 *officers* working for him around the world. Like the present secretary of Defense, Clark Clifford, whose military career had a striking resemblance to Thornton's [see *Ramparts*, August 24, 1968], Tex never left his desk. Yet the War Department honored him with a Legion of Merit, a Commendation Ribbon with two oakleaf clusters, along with a Distinguished Service Medal that Tex still wears on his lapel. "It's the kind of thing a guy would wear," observes one of his detractors, "if he wanted you to think he had been a big combat hero during the war."

It was at this point that Tex's instinct for the Combination manifested itself. The federal government, with an assist from banker Lovett, had gathered, as if for Tex's own benefit, an array of managerial talent which, if offered in the right package on the business market, could command a premium price. So Tex organized nine of his subordinates into a team—later known as the Whiz Kids—and offered it to Henry Ford II with price tags of around $10,000 a year each on the nine, and $16,000 on himself, the commanding officer. With

Lovett's blessing, Tex sold his package. Ford did not do too badly on the deal, gaining four future divisional bosses and two presidents of the company, including Robert Strange McNamara who was later to become—on Robert Lovett's nomination—secretary of Defense.

At thirty-two Tex had become director of planning for one of the giants of U.S. industry. Within only a few years, however, Thornton's ambition brought him into collision with his superiors at Ford. So he offered his services to Hughes Aircraft. Apparently, Thornton was not exactly welcomed with open arms. Noah Dietrich, then financial head of the company, strongly objected to hiring him. But with the help of two of Tex's old Army buddies, Generals George and Eaker, who were on the board, Dietrich was overruled. As assistant general manager Tex took command of operations and hired his future right-hand man, Roy Ash—a Bank of America statistician with no accountancy training—to be assistant comptroller. Ash had been one of Thornton's subordinates during the war.

Hughes' business, especially with the newly independent Air Force, boomed. In 1948, Hughes did a total of $2 million in sales. By 1953, when Thornton left Hughes, the figure was $200 million. The biggest boost came from the Korean War and an exclusive contract to produce a special Fire Control System (a device to regulate the firing of aircraft guns). The contract with the government for the control system was on a "fixed price, redeterminable" basis; that is, a price was agreed on at the outset which could be "redetermined" if costs increased. Based on the ongoing costs of material, Hughes received periodic "progress payments."

Thornton and Ash were very anxious to have Hughes Aircraft make a profit on this contract—a little too anxious, it would seem. According to sworn court testimony which convinced the jury in the case of Steele vs. Litton Industries (although the judge suspended the verdict on a legal point), and a number of other suits and counter-suits, the following picture emerges:

Hughes Aircraft's accounting department was unable to keep track of the costs under the fire control contract and began falsifying the affidavits they were required to submit to the government regularly, stating the current costs. Thornton and Ash found out about this, but far from stopping the procedure, they encouraged it. James O. White, one of the company's accountants, gave the following testimony:

Q: In substance, did somebody tell you that Mr. Thornton had said that, "We want to file false affidavits"?

A: In substance, yes.

Q: Who was this?

A: Ash.

Q: What did he say?

A: He said, "Tex wants to get the money and we're to do it any way we can to get it."

Another means of cheating the government was artfully described as "midnight requisitions." Clerical personnel were called in after-hours and on weekends and told to fill out millions of dollars worth of phony requisitions. Again James White's testimony explains:

"They [the requisitions] were filled out by people who had no knowledge of the facts, who had not used the parts, who had not withdrawn them from stores. They were put into the records as though they had. They were made to look as though they had been proper. They were backdated. They were made to look as though they had been handled by factory people instead of office people, dirtied, in other words, to make them look old and genuine as having come through the shop. They were complete forgeries."

Eventually a group of five CPA's revolted and refused to continue these procedures for fear of losing their certificates. When they told Thornton they would resign, he told them to be quiet and be "good company men." They went to General Harold George, nominally head of the company, but his position was that, "This is something . . . generally indulged in by other military contractors," and he "didn't think there was anything out of order."

The CPA's resigned after taking their case to the Hughes directors. But Secretary of the Air Force Harold Talbott had already learned of the indiscreet management at Hughes and had given Howard Hughes himself an ultimatum: "Either change your management or sell the company. By God, I'll give you 90 days."

On September 1, 1953, Howard Hughes locked Thornton and Ash out of their offices. By February of 1954, Hughes Aircraft had paid back some $43 million to the Air Force which had been "misappropriated" during the stay of Thornton and Ash.

The lockout at Hughes was Tex Thornton's lucky day. For at the same time as he was being kicked out, there was a massive walkout of disgruntled top engineers and executives, men who went on to found such stars of the conglomerate aerospace field as TRW and Teledyne. Tex managed not only to lose himself in the exciting crowd but also to take some talent with him. Emmett Steele, with an ingratiating personality and invaluable contacts in the Pentagon, was to become his sales manager, and Hugh Jamieson his top engineer.

Meanwhile, Charles V. Litton, owner of Litton Industries, having suffered a family tragedy, was ready to sell his small electronics firm. And Thornton and his team were on the lookout for just such a deal. However, Litton apparently regarded Thornton as untrustworthy and was reluctant to sell to him. At one point he even broke off negotiations. According to Litton, it was Jamieson and Steele who finally convinced him to sell. (This was a key point in the breach of promise suits which the two later brought against Tex for allegedly defrauding them of their original shares of founders' stock. Jamieson, who had agreed to testify in Steele's case as well, suddenly settled out of court for a sum estimated at anywhere from $3 million to $20 million.)

With Litton ready to sell, all that Tex needed was cash to consummate the deal, and that meant a trip back to Robert Lovett's milieu and the giant investment banking house of Lehman. Joe Thomas, Lehman's partner and a fellow Texan, provided $1.5 million to buy Litton, in exchange for 75,000 of the original 575,000 shares. Common stock cost Lehman's investors ten cents a share. During the next decade and a half it sold for as much as $150. It was no doubt one of the best deals the Lehmans had cut since they helped finance the slave South's cotton crop during the Civil War.

Numbers games

"...it was obviously only a question of time before some smart fellows would start building companies not around the logical progression of a business but around what would beef up the numbers."
"ADAM SMITH," *The Money Game*

When Tex Thornton and company took over Litton, it was essentially a laboratory production office, a very modest enterprise. After four years under the new management, Litton's annual sales had risen from $3 million to $100 million—and that was just the beginning.

The traditional conception of the growth of a business brings to mind images of the firm selling more of its products, creating new ones, and building new plants to produce more to sell. Only a fraction of Litton's growth, in fact, was achieved in this way. Of the $97 million increase during Tex's first four years, for example, sales from Charlie Litton's original firm accounted for only $11 million. The rest of the increase in sales resulted from the acquisition of some 17 previously existing companies and their incorporation into a new overall financial superstructure: "Litton Industries, Inc." As Thornton explains, "We had to grow fast. There wasn't time to learn a business, train people, develop markets.... We bought time, a market, a product line, plant, research team, sales force. It would have taken years to duplicate this from scratch."

Buying, not building, was the formula of Litton's growth. To understand how a small firm with limited resources *can* buy itself into bigness, one must understand how corporate growth can feed on itself. For the very act of merger creates new power to merge on an even larger scale through its effect on the value of the corporation's stock.

The value of the stock and therefore of the corporation is not determined by adding up the values of tangible assets: cash reserves, inventories, equipment, plant and so forth. The value of the stock is determined by what people are willing to pay for it, and they will pay more now if they expect its value to rise in the future. Of course these are not just expectations of expectations, but are ultimately derived from an assessment of the potential for real growth of corporate assets and earnings.

Expectations, however, are by nature intuitive, and intuition can be influenced by all kinds of intangible factors. Jack Dreyfus, head of one of the biggest mutual funds on Wall Street, once commented wryly on the subjective "glamour factors" which have gone into making the stock of corporations like Litton highly valued on the market, by offering his own prescription for such a success:

Take a nice little company that's been making shoelaces for 40 years and sells at a respectable six-times-earnings ratio. Change the name from Shoelaces Inc. to Electronics and Silicon Furth-Burners. In today's market, the words "electronics" and "silicon" are worth 15 times earnings. However, the real play comes from the word "furth-burners," which no one understands. A word that no one understands entitles you to double your entire score. Therefore, we have six times earnings for the shoelace business and 15 times earnings for electronics and silicon, or a total of 21 times earnings. Multiply this by two for furth-burners and we now have a score of 42 times earnings for the new company.

The key to conglomerate growth is the fact that a company's stock can be—and ordinarily is—the "money" that is used to purchase another corporation. So a smart businessman can make the process come full circle. By successfully creating a glamorous "growth image" on the stock market that excites expectations of real future growth, he can drive the value of his stock up. This then gives him new "money" with which to buy *real* assets in the form of another corporation: in other words, his business can grow in fact and not just on paper, thereby confirming the expectations he aroused and further strengthening the image. And so the circle becomes a spiral of increasing growth.

It is small wonder, then, that creating a glamour image is a major preoccupation of conglomerate managements like Litton's. Indeed, Litton was a pioneer in converting the traditionally staid Annual Report to Stockholders into a high-class Advertisement for Myself. Litton's reports look more like catalogues from Pasadena's Huntington Museum of Art than informational materials from a major industrial corporation. Abraham J. Briloff described it in the *Financial Analysts Journal:*

Litton's 1967 report is, as you undoubtedly know, a most beautiful document . . . which symbolizes the ethics of 20th century commercial life in the New Industrial State . . . distorted in my view is the series of graphs most beautifully set to type at page 55 of the annual report. . . . The curves which the eye is invited to make are optical illusions capable of inducing inappropriate investment decisions.

Another art which is employed in the production of a glamour image is creative accounting. This important technique of the Big Growth game is made possible by the looseness of the principles under which firms are audited. The usual methods are not as crude as those that were used at Hughes Aircraft, but their effects can be pretty significant.

As the pseudonymous "Adam Smith" notes in *The Money Game,*

Numbers imply precision, so it's a bit hard to get used to the idea that a company's net profit could vary by 100 per cent depending on which bunch of accountants you call in, especially when the market is going to take that earnings number and create trends, growth rates, and little flashing lights in computers from it. And all this without any kind of skulduggery you could get sent to jail for.

An explanation for this legal generosity was given by the real Adam Smith, the 18th century prophet of the free enterprise system. The very purpose of government, he wrote, was "to secure wealth, and to defend the rich from the poor."

The spread between one set of figures and another can be the difference between a real glamour stock and a merely good performer, as evidenced by Litton's 1967 report, which with one flick of the accounting wrist boosted the figure for the increase in the corporation's earnings over the previous year from 15 to 26 per cent. This was accomplished by ignoring the pre-merger earnings of newly-acquired companies when estimating the increase. And this is only one of the gambits available to merger oriented firms. As "Adam Smith" observes,

If you are busy buying and selling companies, every time they pass through your accounting firm you get the chance to try to describe artistically some of the assets as earnings, to capitalize costs that have previously been expensed, and in general to create what Wall Street is looking for, which is a neat pattern of constantly growing earnings.

Conglomerates are so obviously based on highly speculative, not to say shady, principles that even *The Wall Street Journal* has been prompted to take off its gold-rimmed rose-colored glasses for an instant and ask a few probing questions about them: how much of their growth is based on improved products and efficiencies and how much reflects the attractive arithmetic of acquisition and the temptations of empire building? ... Can they be managed efficiently?

This last question has an especially poignant ring for Litton's super-managers. In 1968, Litton's second quarter report admitted a disastrous 30 per cent earnings drop (Litton's stock price plummeted nearly 50 per cent at the news), reflecting managerial errors so gross that not even the most creative accounting techniques could cover them up.

The mistakes affected several of Litton's divisions, including its business furniture, Royfax duplicators, Monroe calculators, and its Royal typewriter line. But the biggest error of all provided the clue to the overall pattern of Litton's debacle. The Litton shipyard, which had been accustomed to a rich diet of cost-plus contracts at the government trough ("Your chances of losing money" under such contracts, admits a Litton executive, "are not too great"), had for the first time bid competitively on a package basis for the construction of automated merchant vessels—a *civilian* contract under which you don't get to come back for more money if you can't make it at the agreed-upon price. The result of this market test was that Litton underestimated the costs, submitted a bid that was too low, and instead of netting a profit, had to write off a loss of $8 million.

In what must rank as the understatement of the year, *Fortune*, after noting that the key to Litton's setback was its inability to stand the test of the relatively competitive civilian market, observed: "The requirements for profitability in government work are less exacting than those of the private marketplace." They certainly are.

Under government contracts there is a decided lack of competitive strictures. Little or no capital is risked by the corporation. If it makes errors of judgment, timing, cost analysis and so forth, there are no competitors to take advantage of its mistakes. And it has an enormously understanding buyer. If costs are underestimated, they can always be adjusted up through contract renegotiation. One former Litton executive with responsibilities in this area estimated that as a matter of *normal* practice, Litton in the course of production and development renegotiated its contracts to one and a half times the original price—a nice margin for inept planning and mismanagement.

In short, its vulnerable, soap-bubble growth strategy could never have carried Litton so far had it not possessed the ability, though a small firm at the outset, to get a front-line position in the prime military contract game and latch on to that secret fuel which alone can launch space age corporations towards the moon: the financial largess of the state.

Contracting national security

... the creation of the U.S. Air Force as a separate military service ... may have had more important consequences for U.S. industry than any other event in recent decades."

Fortune, September 1968

The high point of Litton's close connections in Washington was reached during the reign of Tex Thornton's one time subordinate, Robert McNamara, as secretary of Defense. Thornton, who was often a breakfast guest at the Pentagon, claims never to have talked business with the secretary during those visits. But, as the executive of another corporation in the contract field observed in a *Ramparts* interview, "A clever man would merely let it be known that he was having breakfast with McNamara every other morning. When talking to procurement officers and the like, he wouldn't even have to mention McNamara's name."

The subtle but far-reaching significance of good connections was pointed out by the leading student of the military-industrial complex, Professor H. L. Nieburg: "Officials in the lower reaches of the government bureaucracy (both civilian and military) charged with administration of contracts, find themselves dealing with private corporate officials who often were their own former bosses and continue as companions of present bosses and congressional leaders who watchdog the agencies. A contract negotiator or supervisor must deal with men who can determine his career prospects; through contacts, these industrial contractors may cause him to be passed over or transferred to a minor position in some remote bureaucratic corner, sometimes with a ceremonial drumming before a congressional committee."

Among Litton's vice presidents are Joseph Imirie, a former undersecretary of the Air Force, and John H. Rubel, a former assistant secretary of Defense (a key member of the McNamara team). But what may be Litton's most important connection is Tex's close friendship with George Mahon, chairman of the vital House Appropriations Committee. Mahon's Texas district lies near Thornton's home town, and Tex has been friendly with him since the Whiz Kid days at Ford. According to the previously quoted executive, Mahon "is a very dedicated public servant, but he doesn't know how to handle the power he has. This friendship [between Mahon and Thornton] has had more to do with the growth of Litton's military contracts than any other factor. Tex has played Mahon like a fiddle."

But political strings are only half the story. More than anything else, it is the defense contracting system itself, as it evolved after World War II, which has created the new and sinister relationship between the giant corporations and the state.

Following the profiteering scandals of World War I, which revealed that American business had milked the American taxpayer by "sliding" price policies on military contracts, and had spent the lives of many American soldiers by producing cheap, shoddy equipment, the practice of competitive bidding on government contracts was instituted to simulate the open market. The two armed services developed their own "in-house" design and production capabilities which served to measure and check outside performances. Under the pressures of the Second World War, contracting procedures on aircraft, ordnance and ammunition reverted to the cost-plus basis which had inspired the earlier scandals. Then a series of developments after the war produced the current unprecedented state of affairs.

First, as part of a movement heralded as a return to "free enterprise," plants, factories and facilities built by the government during the war were either sold to private corporations, usually at a fraction of their original cost, or were leased at nominal fees to contractors, to use for military contracts. This largely deprived the government of the performance "yardstick" of its in-house facilities.

Second, the Air Force was established as an independent military service. Naturally, it did not have the already built in-house capabilities of the other two services, so it hired out the entire process of designing, producing and even maintaining weapons systems, instead of presenting its own designs to contractors for production. This necessitated a cost-plus contractual basis, since no prearranged price could be fixed for so indeterminate a process. In addition, the Air Force's prime contracting corporations, now responsible for complete weapons systems, had to establish, in the words of one Congressional Report, "procurement organizations and methods which proximate those of the government." These prime contractors were thus in a position to force subcontracting small companies out of business, acquire their proprietary information, make or break geographical regions and decide a host of other critical issues of national import, without even the quasi-democratic checks imposed on the federal bureaucracy. No wonder H. L. Nieburg has warned of the ominous erosion of public control by the giant aerospace companies and has dubbed the whole relationship "the contract state."

Once established, prime systems contracting quickly spread to the other services. A losing battle with the Air Force for responsibility for missile program development taught the Army that its extensive in-house capabilities and technical independence were a distinct disadvantage. For in the political struggle over missile development, the Air Force's corporate prime contractors constituted a powerful lobby in Congress against which all the in-house expertise of the Army was of no avail. A quick learner when the future of its bureaucracy is at stake, the Army began to disband its in-house facilities and to surrender its jurisdictional and discretionary capacities to private industry and the latter's impressive political power. For any corporation in advanced technologies on the way up, prime contracting soon became the indispensable order of the day.

From the outset, the new Tex Thornton team at Litton had its eyes on the really big electronic equipment and systems markets. They were determined not to be pikers and they knew their way up the federal escalator, but they needed a break. In 1954, a team of Litton scientists headed by Dr. Henry Singleton appeared ready to give them one. He outlined a project for miniaturizing an inertial navigator and guidance system. Perfecting such a system was of paramount importance to the military, for it would be the only kind of navigational system that could not be electronically jammed. Further, a missile guided by such a navigator would not emit signals that would disclose its whereabouts. The military had already set out the objectives of such a system and various working devices had been produced, but they all weighed from 500 to 1000 pounds, too heavy for aircraft and missiles. Thus, Singleton was proposing an innovation that would revolutionize the field.

All that was needed to attempt to develop the system was capital. Of course the Litton management, well oriented towards the new age, had no intention of putting up their own money, or of raising it through old-fashioned loans or investors. For to raise capital in that way would entail risks and obligations. What Litton really needed was a banker who would not seek repayment of capital (with interest) if the investment bore no fruit, and if the project should come through, who would not insist on reaping any return on his investment. Could there *be* such a banker? Litton thought so.

With nothing but a wooden mock-up of the proposed navigator and a ten-cents-a-mile expense account for its station wagon, the Litton sales team set out to sell a miniaturized inertial navigation system to the Army Air Corps. In 1956, they finally convinced the purchasing agents at Fort Huachuca, Arizona, to finance the development of a prototype. For its proposal, Litton got a fixed-price redeterminable contract for $214,902.

With the Fort Huachuca contract safely tucked away in their display kits, Litton salesmen then made the rounds of various other government agencies and aerospace firms, stressing the advantages of getting in on the ground floor with contracts for the navigators while the opportunity lasted. In 1957,

Litton contracted to produce for Grumman, the chief Navy aircraft supplier, 68 of the navigators for Navy planes. By 1959, this contract was worth some $7,400,000. In subsequent months, Litton used its new foot in the door with Grumman to sell them additional items, until their total contracts amounted to a full $10 million.

According to the Steele case testimony of John McDonald, then head of Litton's electronics division's contract negotiations, Litton's engineers did successfully achieve the new revolutionary design. But Litton never delivered the prototype navigator to the Army, which had originally paid for it; instead, it used the design to fulfill its contract with Grumman Aircraft. All the Army got was a bagful of disassembled parts. In 1960, the Army purchasing officials canceled Litton's contract "for the convenience of the government."

As for Litton, it had won for itself a tremendous future contracting position for electronics and guidance systems in missiles, planes and even ships, on which all the federal giveaways on costs and profits would be multiplied a thousandfold. No longer a little laboratory but a real comer in the field, Litton was now ready for a really golden opportunity: a major subcontract for the guidance system of the F-104 Starfighter jet. And when Germany decided to incorporate 700 F-104's into its postwar Luftwaffe, Litton bought two German companies just to produce the guidance systems for their version of the plane. Unfortunately, the Luftwaffe's Starfighter turned out to be, in the words of *Business Week*, "an essentially American product that now bears the blackest name in the history of German aviation." At least 83 of the planes crashed, killing 42 pilots and forcing Litton to modify the guidance system. Some time later a further modified version of Litton's navigator was installed in America's new fighter plane, the ill-fated F-111, McNamara's notorious pet project and one of the costliest boondoggles of all time. The prime Navy contractor for that plane: Grumman Aircraft.

Contracting a modern industry

"The aerospace industry, with its intimate contacts in the Department of Defense, is making its move now to take over the entire maritime industry in the United States. Unless the maritime industry recognizes its real enemy, the military-industrial power of the aerospace industry will succeed."

FROM a full page ad in *The New York Times*, October 24, 1966, placed by the chairman of the board of the now defunct Sapphire Steamship Lines.

The American maritime industry had been ailing badly since World War II. Even the captive business of the U.S. Navy and a big federal subsidy on nonmilitary business (paying the difference, up to 50 per cent, between U.S. shipbuilders' inflated prices and those of foreign rivals) couldn't sustain sales. The Swedes and the Japanese had surpassed them technologically, and protective government assistance had merely allowed the gap to widen. So in the early 1960's, the U.S. Navy, which bought 80 per cent of the industry's output anyway, decided to act.

The Navy—then the last holdout—decided to adopt the Air Force's "total package" or "weapons system" approach: a single shipyard would be given a supercontract to design a ship and build a fleet of them. The extraordinary scope of the order would require the contractor to build a new shipyard with modern assembly line features unavailable in then current U.S. shipyards. And because the contract was for a total package, the contractor would have to plan everything from the skills of the crew to the maintenance requirements.

Of course no one in the maritime industry at that time was even remotely equipped to handle this kind of operation. In essence, it was a plan to vault over these moribund corporations, arriving in one jump at a new technological level by turning the shipbuilding business over to the only corporations who were already equipped for the "systems" approach: in a word, aerospace. And among the aerospace corporations, those fortunate enough to have had a head start in the maritime field would naturally be ahead of the game.

The Navy did not announce its decision to adopt this new approach until after 1963. But long before the announcement came, Litton somehow managed to get a sniff of what was in the wind. As Roy Ash explained, "We saw some developments coming and thought we could be a part of them. One thing we foresaw was an expansion of the practice—it was already established in the Air Force and for Navy aircraft—of turning to industry for help in developing total weapons systems." So in 1961, Litton picked up Ingalls, an ailing shipyard with $60 million in annual sales, for $8 million and an agreement to pay $9 million in debts to the Navy. Ingalls got a number of contracts over the next few years—for one amphibious assault ship here, six cargo ships there.

Then in November 1965, the big deal went up for grabs: McNamara announced approval of a large integrated system of Fast Deployment Logistics (FDL) ships. These "floating warehouses"—perhaps as many as 30 of them— would be stationed strategically around the world, ready to move quickly into "trouble spots" to back up U.S. troops with ammunition, C-rations, tanks, etc. The FDL was the first ship to be handled under the Navy's new weapons system approach.

Several shipbuilding companies were in the initial bidding for the contracts, but they all either dropped out or were eliminated. The final stage of bidding included three aerospace giants: Litton, General Dynamics and Lockheed. Each got $5 million in contracts to finish plans for the FDL and the yard. Of course each would need a site for its yard. According to *The Wall Street Journal*, climate ruled out New England and the steep cost of steel and highly unionized labor made the West Coast undesirable. That left the U.S. domestic colony of cheap labor: the South.

Litton, of course, luckily already had a location in the South, in Pascagoula, Mississippi: Ingalls shipyard, to be exact. But they still needed to find a way to finance the new yard, which according to informed sources at the time would cost $100 million to build. And this time the federal government was not putting up the money. But there are state governments too. Already the largest employer in Mississippi, Litton went straight to the state capital and threatened to take their new yard to Tampa, Florida, if they did not get cooperation. Mississippi quickly agreed to build the most modern shipyard in the world and hand it back to Ingalls on lease at a minimal price. Governor Johnson called a special legislative session in order to pass a $130 million bond issue (the extra $30 million was interest). In October 1967, the bond issue was approved by Mississippi voters.

Of course the people of Mississippi would "own" the leased-out shipyard, though they would not reap the profits from or control its operation. For their $130 million investment they would get an estimated 12,000 jobs, at Pascagoula wages and under special "long-term" union contracts ("yellow dog" is such an old-fashioned phrase). Litton also rewarded its Mississippi friends by writing into its contract the latest in sophisticated legal loopholes to help the shipyard bosses keep blacks out of the good jobs for as long as possible.

Yet, despite all this stage setting, Litton still had not been awarded the contract. So they set 200 experts to work on a winning design, under complicated and difficult new CF-CD (Contract Formulation; Contract Definition) procedures that had been worked out by McNamara's assistant secretary of Defense, John H. Rubel.

Once again, Litton was in luck: in the interim Rubel had shuttled over from the Defense Department to head the Litton team working on the bid. Having helped toss the plum in the air, he was right on the spot to catch it. Unfortunately, however, just as Litton won its $2 billion prize, the project hit a snag. Congress refused, first in 1967 and again this year, to appropriate the money for the FDL's. In the Senate debate even Richard Russell, chairman of the Armed Services Committee, expressed concern that the ocean-going bases might contribute to "an impression that the U.S. has assumed the function of policing the world and can be thought to be at least considering intervention in any kind of strife or commotion occurring in any nation of the world." Of course, an embittered Litton backer might note that military land bases may have a special place in Senator Russell's heart, since he has blessed the construction of 19 of them in his home state.

But do not fear for Litton; it is an unwritten law of the contract state that what the Navy brings to birth it does not allow to die. The Navy will see that Litton, its answer to the decrepitude of the U.S. maritime industry, is well taken care of. Since the first congressional slash, the Navy has already salved Litton's wounds with at least $1.2 billion in new contracts.

And Litton's now modernized shipbuilding enterprise, which has already become the largest producer of automated cargo ships in the world, can still, like the older maritime companies, mark up its price to civilian buyers 50 per cent above the prevailing world market price and have the difference paid by U.S. taxpayers—through the nose. Litton's relationship with the Navy was summed up quite well by Senator Stuart Symington: "... Litton has got the whole bag now."

Part Two of the Litton story begins by using John Kenneth Galbraith, whom the article describes as "the New Monopolistic State's most urbane, unabashed and best-selling apologist," as a foil for attacking some myths about corporate enterprise. Contrary to Galbraith's defense of size as a

"general servant of technology, not the special servant of profits," Horowitz and Erlich point out that authoritative studies indicate that a high concentration of power and facilities is not needed for efficient production and distribution in most industries; that large organizations generally decentralize production and distribution while centralizing financial and political power; and that Litton's success is not due to acquiring technologically advanced firms and giving them new resources. Furthermore, a large proportion of the significant inventions have not come from large industrial laboratories, and even when they occasionally do, these advances often seem to result in spite of, rather than because of, the policies of large laboratories. Finally, the government funds some 60 percent of the research and development investments made by private firms, and two-thirds of the remaining 40 percent is ultimately charged off as overhead on government contracts. "So it seems," say the authors, "that the real entrepreneur is the government, who is not only extraordinarily openhanded about putting up the investment, but agreeably lighthearted about not reaping the profits on it. So agreeable, in fact, that it goes on to buy the product that it financed, at a healthy profit to the surrogate developer." The major device involved here is the military contract, but such contracts also provide facilities and expertise (paid for by the taxpayer) that the firm uses to penetrate civilian industries such as shipbuilding, the welfare industry (in the areas of job training and public education), and the rich area of foreign economic development.

1968

from LITTON INDUSTRIES: PROVING POVERTY PAYS[3]

. . .

...Neither military policy nor the Defense bureaucracy is divorced from the rest of the national political structure, and the political power gained by the successful prime contractors in the military field has become an important basis for extending their field of operation to other areas where the federal government exercises responsibility and allocates its huge budget.

With an eye to the immense dominions of largess still to be granted by the sovereign power, Litton has been careful to keep its representatives at court

3 From David Horowitz and Reese Erlich, "Litton Industries: Proving Poverty Pays," Ramparts, December 14–25, 1968, pp. 44–49. Copyright Ramparts Magazine, Inc., 1968. Reprinted by permission of the editors.

and to keep a foot in every available political door. Among its executives and directors are Defense Department secretaries and military generals, highly influential Democrats and equally important Republicans, liberal Humphrey supporters and the chief financial backer of Ronald Reagan—in short, the whole spectrum of legitimized political power (and potential contract dispensation). With its expansive political network as a foundation, Litton has been in the forefront of the move to extend systems contracting to nonmilitary fields. Litton was the first private contractor to take over responsibility for a War on Poverty Job Corps project and the first corporation to apply the systems approach to the economic development program of an entire geographical region (in Greece), and its distinctive mode of operation in these instances provides an ominous portent of things to come. Litton's career follows what may turn out to be the most natural line of development for the huge and continuously growing conglomerate corporations as they overflow the traditional limits which have contained them.

Contracting development

"Litton is a world-wide organization dedicated to utilizing the discoveries of modern science by converting them into useful goods and services—products that bolster the Free World's vital economic base and defend the inflexible ideal of human freedom."
                    Litton Industries' annual report to stockholders, 1963

On April 21, 1967, a sudden coup d'etat in Greece sent a shudder through Europe. The coup, carried out by junior officers to forestall an impending liberal electoral victory, represented a shift so far to the right that the conservative monarchy was eventually thrown into opposition and the king virtually deposed. The epithet "fascist" was thrown in the face of the regime as it quickly filled the jails with thousands of political prisoners. And for the first time in non-Iberian Europe since World War II, the term rang true. The governments of Norway and Denmark immediately tried to have the Greek junta kicked out of NATO, and later out of the Council of Europe. Other West European governments signified their disapproval but reserved action. Even Washington, whose military and intelligence agencies were implicated in the coup, held back any immediate support. Then, three weeks after the overthrow, when the new regime was still unstable and the adverse worldwide reaction held out the possibility that the junta might disintegrate and fall, a gesture of support was made by one of the largest U.S. corporations, one with a reputation for having powerful connections in the White House and the Pentagon.

That corporation was Litton Industries. The gesture was the agreement by Litton to be prime contractor on a "development" program for Greece.

In keeping with Litton's usual strategy, the agreement was on a cost-plus basis, with Litton agreeing to procure $840 million in capital for Greece over a 12-year period. In return, the military junta agreed to repay Litton its costs plus 11 per cent, plus a commission of about two per cent on all capital that Litton succeeded in steering to Greece. For readers whose minds are fixated on the concept of private enterprise as in some sense free or competitive, the significance of this kind of contract might be spelled out once again. Litton itself risks nothing. Every month Litton files invoices for its costs, and in 15 days it gets back everything it has paid out plus a profit of 11 per cent. As explained by Robert M. Allan Jr., president of Litton International Development Corporation and head of Litton's program in Greece, "The return on investment here, of course, is very large because we don't have any basic investment. Our real investment is our good name which of course is the most valuable thing we own." Litton's good name (and contacts) were indeed attractive assets for the military regime.

Another was Litton's promotional expertise, which was promptly directed to the vital task of convincing Americans—particularly very important Americans—of the virtues of iron rule in Athens. The key figure in Litton's PR work for the junta is Barney Oldfield, Litton International's chief public information officer, who, according to spokesmen for the Greek resistance, runs the projunta propaganda campaign both in Athens and in the United States. Oldfield, who was an Air Force colonel before going to Litton, got his PR training as chief public information officer for NATO in Europe and has excellent Pentagon and Republican connections.

To the uninitiated, it might seem strange that the former chief PR man for NATO—a military alliance allegedly formed to defend freedom—should suddenly become a salesman for a totalitarian dictatorship in Greece, but Oldfield's behavior is certainly within the norms laid down by Washington. Thus on May 17, 1968, a year after the coup (and a good deal of Litton politicking), Washington softened its attitude towards the junta. Secretary of Defense Clark Clifford went before the Senate Foreign Relations Committee to ask support for an administration proposal for $661 million in military aid to the dictatorships of Korea, Turkey, Iran, Taiwan and Greece. Of the latter, Clifford said: "The obligations imposed on us by the NATO alliance are far more important than the kind of government they have in Greece or what we think of it."

One of Litton's most important services to the junta prior to its reception into the Free World fold was performed by Litton's president, Tex Thornton, six months earlier in September 1967. Following a meeting of the governors of the World Bank in Rio de Janeiro, Costas Thanos, a high Greek official whom Columbia University has accused of plagiarizing his Ph.D. thesis, and Demetrius Galanis, governor of the Bank of Greece, traveled to New York for a planned banquet with American bankers. At the urging of the U.S. State Department, however, the American bankers decided not to attend. Thanos then flew to Washington and requested meetings with Vice President Humphrey; Secretary of the Treasury Fowler; Congressman Mendel Rivers, chairman of the House Armed Services Committee; and Speaker of the House John Mc-Cormack. The Greeks wanted to talk to these powerful American politicians about increased foreign aid and a resumption of full military assistance. However, all four men declined to meet Thanos and Galanis, again because of a negative sign from the State Department. Faced with this crisis, the Greeks naturally turned to their powerful ally, Litton.

Tex Thornton immediately flew to Washington in his private plane, ostensibly to attend a meeting of the President's Advisory Commission on Civil Disorders, of which he was a member, but also to pull some of Litton's golden political strings. Within days, the doors of the four politicians were opened to the representatives of the Greek colonels, while the State Department fumed.

While Thornton's behind-the-scenes maneuvering was building up pressure for an eventual resumption of military aid to the Greek regime, the junta's first real break came with the announcement of a $12.5 million loan from the World Bank. This was the first solid evidence of external financial support for the regime. (After the coup, the European Economic Community—more popularly known as the Common Market—which had in 1962 made available $125 million in loans to Greece, refused the ordinarily automatic extension of time allowed for drawing the funds. Having used less than half of the total, Greece lost a $70 million credit.) It happens that the World Bank loan was one of the first issued under its new president, Tex Thornton's old breakfast chum Robert McNamara. So this might look like a classic case of friendly persuasion. In fact, however, most observers discount Litton's role.

Ironically it is Litton itself which, rather than issuing demure protestations of innocence, has sought to create the impression—among those who don't already know better—that it was not only responsible for the loan, but that if the Greek junta wants any more loans from the World Bank it will have to go through the Beverly Hills conglomerate. When you are marketing a reputation for prowess and success, Don Juanism can be a valued accusation.

Foreign capital, representing foreign confidence, was obviously a high priority for the Greek junta. One full page ad which the junta ran in *The New York Times* was headed: "Greece: Ideal Country For Investors." The ad underscored the stability of the internal political situation as a major encouragement to investment, in contrast to the turbulent days of Greek democracy. This was echoed in a speech two months later by Litton's Robert Allan. According to Allan, there were four basic ingredients of national growth in Litton's view: capital, know-how, incentive and "stability of environment." As Allan explained, "If a government will restrain itself from outbursts which create long pauses among investors, and potential investors ... then we have a working partnership."

Allan's speech went on to attack such opponents of the Greek junta as actress Melina Mercouri and former Cabinet Minister Andreas Papandreou, who were described as "an aging actress without a play" and "an agitating professor out of work." "Their country," Allan declaimed, "which owes its very existence to soldiers who fought for its survival, they say is now in poor hands because the same men rule it." (Actually it was the Communist-led guerrillas who liberated Greece in World War II.)

Readers may be wondering if this kind of double-think is reserved by Litton executives for public occasions and formal addresses. Partly to find out, *Ramparts* went down to Beverly Hills to interview Robert Allan, who describes himself as working "for the Greek people." By the time *Ramparts* spoke with Allan, several authenticated descriptions of the terror in Greece and the torture of political prisoners had already been smuggled out of that country and circulated in the international press. Writing of one of the island prisons five months after the coup, *Newsweek* observed:

Tradition has it that the Emperor Tiberius, one of the cruelest Roman rulers, refused out of simple humanity to imprison any of his subjects on the treeless, waterless Aegean island of Yioura. No such scruples, however, inhibit the present military rulers of Greece who, soon after their coup last April, filled Yioura's cellblocks and ten camps with 6500 of their fellow citizens.

Alluding to similar reports documenting the torture of Greek prisoners, Allan went into a monologue right out of 1984: "I satisfied myself that most of these prisoners in Greece are living on an island, the way you and I'd live on Catalina. They're free to come and go as they wish. A lot of fresh air and a lot of sunshine, but no communication. It isn't the way that you and I would like to see something done, but they couldn't stand any more riots. The whole nation was just going into chaos, and this was their way of answering it. I've also tried to my best ability to determine what went on, and as far as I could determine, there was no more torture or beatings than they would have in a normal police station anywhere in the world . . . which, God knows, none of us like, but do go on."

The reason that Litton likes the military junta, as Allan freely admits, is because the junta "provided the atmosphere in which things can get done," and in particular an atmosphere in which Litton could do them: prior to the coup, the Litton contract had been turned down by several Greek parliaments. The very structure and strategy of Litton as a business enterprise gravitates toward the military and the state, and toward authoritarian regimes. The Litton-Greece contract has been followed up by parallel schemes for Portugal and Turkey. In conversation, Allan's thoughts drift toward the dictatorships of Nicaragua, Indonesia and Taiwan, as examples of countries where he'd like to try the "Greek approach."

This gravitation toward the state is a function of the systems approach, as is the particular preference for the state's authoritarian forms. The primary features of the systems approach are its dependence on state financing and its need to override the sovereignty of the people. So while one might think that the overall economic development of Crete and the Western Peloponnesus was the proper concern of the people who live in the area and of a representative government of the people, under the Greek-Litton arrangement it is Litton who draws up the overall development plan. "In Greece," explains Tex Thornton, "our objective is not to single out one economic activity, but to apply the systems approach to building a future for that historic nation."

What specifically did Litton's space-age systems-oriented management propose for launching Greece out of its morass of poverty and underdevelopment and into the modern era? "Our primary thrust," Allan explained, "is to develop tourism." If tourism were indeed a lever of development, rather than one of the chief syndromes of economic dependence and underdevelopment, then the West Indies, Spain and Greece itself would long ago have become industrial nations. Old-fashioned imperialism begins to look economically progressive compared to what Litton is proposing! The old imperialists at least dug a mine, built a port (financed by the colony's taxes) and ran a road or a railway from the mine to the port. What Litton has in mind, according to one business magazine, are "hotels, roads leading to hotels, the airport where hotel guests can land, supplies of food and water, handicraft manufacture [for tourist trading posts, no doubt], recreation facilities," etc. In other words, a Disneyland economy with an ample supply of colorful locals to service the pavilions and their visitors. Naturally, Litton's Stouffer Division will supply the hotels.

Perhaps the worst aspect of this is that Allan knows Litton's plan is a bitter prescription for the Greeks. In person he will admit that it won't really meet the long-term needs of the Greek economy. But if there is something offensive about the transformation of the crucible of Western civilization into another Honolulu, then again, worse things could happen. "I don't approve of it, and I hope Greece won't have it happen," Allan told *Ramparts*, "but gee, Honolulu in ten years has gone from here to here [raising his hand over his head] as far as volume of input is concerned."

In addition to the Honolulu complex, Litton has plans for "agricultural development." These feature a system of artesian wells which Allan says would save about $72 million over the cost of a planned system of irrigation dams. Litton also has assigned its computers to wrestle with the problem of the price of brussels sprouts in the West German market, and it is talking of making Crete a major producer of this basic foodstuff. Finally, an international developer from Wichita, Kansas, has submitted a plan to Litton proposing the construction of 300 townhouses, at a cost of $7000 each, in the Western Peloponnesus. The average Greek—for whom the houses, needless to say, are not planned—would have to spend his entire annual income for more than 15 years to buy such an item.

If Litton succeeds in its "development" plans, it is evident that the result will be merely to extend the economic and social blight which has characterized Greece's postwar dependence on the United States and on U.S. investment in tourism, oil refining (Esso-Pappas) and Coca-Cola. However, there are signs that Litton may not be succeeding even in this modest endeavor. Under the terms of the original contract of May 1967, Litton had committed itself, as a starter, to attracting $60 million in foreign capital to Greece by May 1969. With two-thirds of the period gone, Litton has attracted only $3.5 million, or about six per cent of its projected goal. Most of this investment represents Litton's own capital; none of it is in industrial or agricultural projects. Not only has Litton failed to attract any substantial capital (or to invest much of its own), even the research and feasibility studies were not prepared by its own high-powered managerial talent. According to highly placed sources, Litton has been digging up old economic feasibility studies prepared by academics (including the arch-opponent of the military regime, Andreas Papandreou), Greek government economists and economic consultants.

All this led to rumors that the junta would not renew the contract with Litton in May. To scotch these rumors, Litton announced plans for a $3 million

German brewery, a $350,000 electronics assembly plant (a Litton subsidiary), a $3.8 million Stouffer hotel in Crete and a multimillion dollar tourist complex in the Western Peloponnesus. But while speculation developed as to whether these plans would materialize, Litton was dramatically upstaged by another entrant onto the scene, the newly-wed Aristotle Onassis.

Ten days after Washington had resumed delivery of major military equipment to Greece, thus offering its imprimatur for the regime and a new guarantee of its stability, Onassis announced his own systems approach: a $400-million investment package (the largest ever made in Greece) in tourist facilities, an airport in Athens, an aluminum processing plant (in conjunction with Reynolds) with a companion thermoelectric power plant, a shipyard, and an oil refinery which, according to initial reports, would be "bound to make more money than all the action in Las Vegas." So it seems that for all his private plane trips and brussels sprouts, Tex Thornton may have been out-hustled by a local boy.

If Onassis has upstaged Litton it is not simply on the basis of national solidarity. The Greek government finds Onassis important because he deals in the kind of old-line imperial enterprises that are part of the basic economy— he owns one of the world's great tanker fleets and will soon be producing his own oil. In contrast, Litton's major thrust is in advanced technologies and knowledge industries geared to markets in highly developed environments. So all it could really attempt in Greece was to exploit the government without exploiting the economy, and there is just not enough loose money around in the country to sustain such an arrangement. The opportunities of under-development were enticing, but Litton was ill-equipped to profit from them.

The perfect situation for Litton would be an underdeveloped area with an overdeveloped government which would be less discerning about results than the colonels. An impossible dream?

Not at all. Litton had already found it—at home.

Contracting poverty

"The input—the raw material—that is fed into this machine is people. The output is people. It is the function of this machine to transform these people." That is the philosophy of "education" held by John H. Rubel, vice president of Litton's Economic Development Division, as expressed in a letter to Sargent Shriver. Rubel, formerly assistant secretary of Defense under Robert Mc-Namara, is credited with having convinced Shriver to award Job Corps contracts to private enterprise rather than strictly to educational institutions. Of course, it was only fair that Litton should get one of the first contracts: the Parks Job Corps Center in Pleasanton, California.

Litton's predictably titled Educational Systems Division includes many valuable properties, such as the American Book, D. Van Nostrand and Chapman-Reinhold publishing companies. They also serve as program administrators for Oakland Community College in Bloomfield Hills, Michigan. Its most important enterprise, however, is the Parks Center, because the Job Corps is the opening wedge for Litton's entrance into the potential treasure houses of social welfare and education.

Litton's public relations department celebrates the Parks Job Corps camp as a free enterprise success story. Recently, Park placed its 5000th "graduate" in a job; the center has thus placed more of its graduates than any other Job Corps camp in the country. Of course, the PR men neglect to mention that the number one "employer," accounting for roughly 40 per cent of Parks' graduates, is the U.S. military.

Litton administrators consider Viet-Nam a highly desirable placement for their predominantly black corpsmen. The waiting room of the placement office, where each graduate of the nine-month course goes to inquire about future employment, is plastered with posters urging, nondenominationally, enlistment in the Army, Navy, Air Force or Marines. A life-size cardboard cutout of a sharp looking black soldier salutes the graduate as he steps in the door. Piles of brochures invite him to learn "The Secret of Getting Ahead in Today's Action Army." And lest the message be forgotten, on the way out a flashing sign reminds him: DESIRABLE LOCATION—YOUR U.S. ARMY—TRAINING GUARANTEED WITH BIG BUSINESS—YOUR CHOICE OF SCHOOLS—STEADY ADVANCEMENT.

Of course where enticement fails, there is always induction. Every week an IBM print-out announces the names of those at the Parks Center who have turned eighteen. Each one must then register for the draft with a Litton employee, conveniently certified by the local Hayward board. Upon graduation, Litton notifies the corpsman's draft board of his new educational achievements. (Litton arranges for the majority of its enrollees at Parks to receive a high school equivalency diploma, which makes those who had been deferred due to low scores on the Army mental aptitude exam eligible for retesting.) Al Cassell, the head of placement at the Parks Center, explained: "We get draft notices by the hundreds every day. We furnish the draft board with information relative to the training level achieved by the young man. . . . We take him to Hayward and have him retested. . . . If he passes . . . the Hayward testing center notifies his local board, and they in turn will usually draft him."

Even if the corpsman does not improve his score on the test, his new high school diploma might well make him eligible for induction. At one time, in a kind of reciprocal trade arrangement, Litton kept a Job Corps recruiter at the frequently embattled Oakland Induction Center in California. Many ineligible draftees, led to believe that they would become qualified for a high paying job in industry, enrolled in the program only to find themselves returned full circle at the end of the course. Two sergeants from Hayward go out to the Parks Job Corps Center every day. No other prospective employers have permanent recruiters there.

Vernon Alden, president of Ohio University, envisioned the Job Corps as a place that would "offer a new environment where hopes can be lifted and skills developed free from the shackles of oppressive and antagonistic surroundings." So much for visions.

Litton's Job Corps center, located on an unused Navy base, is surrounded by a barbed wire fence with checkpoints manned by Litton-employed guards. The 2000 corpsmen sleep in open bay Army barracks, wear green uniforms, march to their meals at the mess hall, and are hauled off to the brig when they misbehave. The young men arriving at Parks are not exactly prepared for such an environment. Most of them have been signed up by the Litton recruiters who are stationed throughout the poverty areas of the nation advertising the wealth of opportunity in California. Since Litton's contract with the Office of Economic Opportunity (OEO) depends on a sufficient number of enrollees, the recruiters use every possible means to lure them. Of course, they give the standard come-on: training for a good-paying job, the equivalent of a high school diploma, $30-a-month spending money, a $50-a-month bonus upon graduation for time completed, and a chance to get away from home. There is also exotic talk of pools and girls, private rooms with TV's—even draft deferments!

If getting them there is half the battle for Litton, keeping them there is the other half. When a new enrollee decides that life was better back home, even though home may have been a decaying urban slum, his request to leave is met with hostility by Litton officials. He is told that he cannot leave for at least 90 days for any reason other than a death in the immediate family. Moreover, if he wants to quit at any time prior to the end of his nine-month course, he must pay his own way home, often halfway across the country.

Those who protest this policy too loudly are "quieted" by muscular counselors or hauled off to the brig. Some become desperate. A psychiatric social worker at Parks reported that he had been assigned to work with a young boy from Dallas, Texas, who had sliced his arm open in an attempt to get out. But even with all of Litton's tenacity, 55 per cent drop out before the end of the course.

Justice at Camp Parks is supposed to be administered by a Center Review Board (CRB) comprised of corpsmen and Litton people. But by disciplinary counselor Lindsay Johnson's own admission, the board is his rubber stamp: "I have a good working relationship with the CRB," he notes. "They do whatever I tell them to."

While Job Corps discipline is harsh, it is not really like the Army's. As one Parks teacher told *Ramparts*, "It isn't feasible to take these kids off the streets ... and put them in the equivalent of boot camp, especially since the counselors aren't armed." Rather, Litton does try, in its own words, to "rehabilitate the entire social perspective" of the corpsmen, including particularly their work ethics and attitude toward authority. As Pat Coughlin, Parks' program coordinator for occupational training, told us, "If the boss tells [the corpsman] to pick up a broom and sweep the floor, he's got to learn not to tell the boss what to do with the broom."

If the physical surroundings at the Parks Center are grim and the general atmosphere intimidating, the educational operation is laughable. The Basic Education program is intended to bring the corpsman's reading and arithmetic skills up to a level appropriate to the specific job skills in which he is to be trained. The curriculum materials for the reading course, developed by Litton, are somewhat unusual. The pre-test, which determines the student's reading level before he takes the course, and the post-test, which determines his level upon completion of the course, are identical. In addition, the actual teaching materials used during the course and those used to measure any improvement contain the same text and exercises as do the pre-test and post-test. Of course, this setup merely passes off the repeatedly coached memorization of a particular passage as the ability to read. But schemes like this enable Litton to present impressive statistical evidence "documenting" their expertise in educating underprivileged youth—a cruel but profitable joke. When a Parks teacher complained that all the enrollees were only learning how to improve their scores on one particular test, the head of Litton's curriculum development at Parks replied, "We're not doing anything here that college fraternities don't do for their members." True enough. Still, no college fraternity has yet been awarded a $25 million government contract to educate ghetto youth.

Aside from such relatively subtle deceptions, there is doubt about the simple veracity of the figures used in the statistics Litton has put out about Parks. According to Professor William Austin, former president of the Parks Federation of Teachers and Counselors, "Public relations officers kept putting out fake figures.... One would hear about this number of corpsmen being placed in job positions and this number of corpsmen demonstrating academic success by various grade levels.... All of it was nonsense.... There was so much pressure on supervisors to produce figures that in general people just faked them.... Fifty per cent or more of the corpsmen didn't make it to class ... if a corpsman quit after having completed just one module out of 15 in the total training, he would be considered a 'graduate.' "

Austin feels that educating the corpsmen is not Litton's primary concern. "The corpsmen didn't mean a damn thing," Austin reported. "There was a lot of very expensive equipment around which nobody had any idea how to use...."

Along with its display of educational ingenuity in the management of the Job Corps Center, Litton has exhibited those lucrative skills which have made it a leader among defense contractors. It subcontracts to its own divisions as a means of maximizing profits while minimizing service. Litton originally received from OEO a $12.8 million cost-plus contract with a fixed but redeterminable fee for running the Job Corps Center. It then decided to buy unnecessary textbooks from the American Book Publishing Company, a member of Litton Educational Systems. A General Accounting Office (GAO) investigation later showed that $337,000 worth of American Book Publishing Company textbooks lined closet shelves at Parks. According to a copyrighted story in the Denver Post," "Among the books it bought for Job Corpsmen, many of whom could barely read, were textbooks on the theory of relativity, the stock market and the slide rule."

This same GAO report noted that there was, in the words of the San Francisco Chronicle,

a devastating picture of high costs, waste and disciplinary problems at a Job Corps Center [Parks] in California. After two years of operation the estimated cost of the Center had jumped from $12.8 million to $25.5 million, the dropout rate was 55 per cent and only eight per cent of the enrollees were placed in jobs related to their training.

Given what is known about Parks, it is not surprising that a great deal of racism is exhibited there. One new employee, upon arriving at the gate, was met by a guard who hailed him with, "So you're another one coming out here to help these dumb niggers." But far more unnerving was the surrealistic scene—straight out of *Invisible Man*—when a Litton executive flew over Parks in his private plane dropping dollar bills to the corpsmen assembled below. Litton officials amused themselves by watching the young men trample each other in a frantic effort to grab the money. A former Litton employee remarked that the object of the "airlift" was to "see how fast the niggers could run."

Litton, in keeping with a gentleman's agreement with officials of the semi-suburban towns near Camp Parks, has forbidden corpsmen to enter them. Young men from the Parks Center have reported that whenever they ventured into one of the neighboring communities, they were returned to Parks by local police, although they had created no disturbances. Litton's idea of community relations is to keep the cages locked during the week and to bus the corpsmen on weekends to "hospitality houses" in the nearby cities of San Francisco and Oakland.

According to Professor Austin, living conditions and sanitary facilities at Parks were at times worse than those in the big city ghettos the corpsmen came from. At one point, hygiene conditions in the dormitories were so bad that Austin approached public health people at the University of California to ask what could be done. The answer seemed to be "nothing," because the center was located on a military base leased to a private company, and no one knew if county health officials had any right to enter the base.

If Litton was running Parks so poorly, why didn't the government step in and enforce its contract? The answer is that in the spring of 1967, the OEO did try to enforce part of its contract with Litton. The teachers union at Parks had been refused a room to meet in at the center after working hours, a denial which violated both the National Labor Relations Act and Job Corps bulletin 67–12. Despite the intervention of W. P. Kelly, a director of the Job Corps; Richard Groulx, an executive of the Alameda County Central Labor Council; and several arbitrators from the OEO office in Washington, Litton was able not only to refuse to meet with anyone, but also to fire the president, two vice presidents and the secretary-treasurer of the teachers union for "disloyalty to the company." The last OEO arbitrator, Hyman Bookbinder, commended to Groulx and union officials that the OEO was unable to enforce the terms of its contract with Litton.

During the teachers' strike at Parks that resulted from Litton's action, Senators Robert Kennedy, Joseph Clark and George Murphy of the Senate Subcommittee on Employment, Manpower and Poverty, were in San Francisco on a nationwide tour of the Poverty Program. The senators curiously reversed their original plan to visit Parks, and showed no interest in discussing the situation there with Parks teachers and corpsmen. Cynics said it was possibly because Litton was one of the largest contributors to the Democratic Party, of which Kennedy and Clark were members.

In a recent paper, Professor Austin observed, "Job Corps facilities have been a popular form of educational experimentation for these companies, allowing them to train their staffs and develop materials on taxpayers' dollars. The real profits will come, it is hoped, from supplying the physical plant, audiovisual equipment, curriculum materials and "experts" to educational programs in large cities.

Companies like Litton are planning to subcontract a city's *complete* school system, claiming to be able to meet whatever contractual standards are set more "efficiently" than local school boards could. This will be a tempting offer to the often hard-pressed, bewildered city officials whose school systems have been bogged down by almost total impotence. And for the community, dumping the whole complex educational crisis into the lap of Litton's "experts" would seem a blessed relief.

· · · ·

The Parks Center was closed when President Nixon shut down the national training centers, but it had put a little change in Litton's pockets and Litton had done well by its investment in any case. More important, Litton could now use its questionable statistics with city officials across the country in the effort to convince them that business can handle public education cheaper and more efficiently. As unsatisfactory as the schools are, it would hardly seem an improvement to have companies such as Litton run them.

After many well-publicized scandals about defense contracting boondoggles and use of government money to bail out apparently incompetent firms such as Lockheed Aircraft, the federal government is revising its procedures. Indeed, President Nixon has appointed Tex Thornton to do the job. He should know about submitting fraudulent requisitions and filing false reports, according to the charges made against him in federal court.

Now that the wisdom of unregulated technological change and gadgetry is being widely questioned because of the dangers of pollution, it is reassuring to know that Roy Ash, too, sits on government panels and is close to President Nixon. For example, it seems reasonable to assume that some subsidiaries of Litton Industries had sought roles in the huge SST contracts. In this connection a prediction made by Roy Ash in 1967 is apt. He noted that corporations should be "hothouses for fulminating innovations. . . . The flow of new products and services—from pop-top cans to supersonic transports—will accelerate and the beneficiary will be the U.S. public." [4] The examples are, at the least, appropriate. Because nonreturnable but nonbiodegradable pop-top cans are presently littering the environment and overflowing the garbage dumps, and because the supersonic transport threatens to become an ecological disaster while it whittles a couple of hours from the flight time to Europe for those who can afford the ticket, the beneficiary is not likely to be the American public, as Ash claims, but only firms such as Litton Industries.

Litton is a new, aggressive, and imaginative corporation with a slick

4 Quoted in "A *Fortune* Forum on the Changing Business Scene," *Fortune*, March 1967, p. 153.

image and an announced concern for social problems of all sorts. In contrast, the following profile by Jerry DeMuth, a Chicago newspaper reporter, takes a close look at an old, sluggish (but very profitable), conservative corporation, the fourth largest industrial corporation in the United States— General Electric. DeMuth's article draws no conclusions, except in its final short paragraph, and presents no explicit analysis. It is simply an inventory of some of the actions of General Electric. The prose is drab, but the message is clear and important: GE has managed, despite government regulatory agencies, the Justice Department, labor unions, and so on, to control its environment in its own interests. In recent years General Electric has been a defendant in an average of almost five antitrust suits annually. The pluralistic devices of judicial suits and regulatory actions appear to have had no appreciable effect on GE. Social scientists have well researched the ineffectiveness of regulatory agencies.[5] Their almost invariable conclusion has been that regulatory agencies have been captured by the dominant firms in the very industry that they seek to regulate; this view conforms to the sins-of-business analysis. A somewhat newer theme, which emerges from historical studies, is that large firms have welcomed and encouraged regulatory legislation in order to minimize competition and to increase stability and predictability;[6] this view reflects the systems view of the New Left.

GE: PROFILE OF A CORPORATION[7]

Jerry DeMuth

Early in 1960, when the big price-fixing indictments against General Electric were made, Ralph J. Cordiner, GE board chairman, called the resulting publicity a "blow upon the company's good name. But this situation will pass," he added, "as have other unfortunate situations."

There have been many other such "unfortunate situations." GE's record in-

---

5 See, for example, Murry Edleman, *The Symbolic Uses of Politics* (Urbana: University of Illinois Press, 1967). Various reports on federal regulatory agencies by Ralph Nader and his investigating teams have given much more publicity to a matter that political scientists have well understood for several decades.

6 These are the "revisionists" in history, one of whose leading members is Gabriel Kolko. See his *The Triumph of Conservatism: A Reinterpretation of American History, 1900–1916* (Chicago: Quadrangle Books, 1967).

7 Jerry DeMuth, "GE: Profile of a Corporation," *Dissent*, July–August 1967, pp. 502–12.

cludes, besides price-fixing and other antitrust activities, anti-union efforts and ties with the right wing.

GE was a defendant in an antitrust case as far back as 1911, when the company was only 19 years old. Since that time it has been a defendant in 64 additional government antitrust cases, 49 of them in the last 10 years. The Justice Department referred to "GE's proclivity for persistent and frequent involvement in antitrust violations" in early January 1962, when it unsuccessfully asked for a court order to forbid GE's fixing of prices.

Price-fixers since 1911

Back in 1911 a federal court held that GE had violated the Sherman Antitrust Act by fixing prices and eliminating competition with respect to light bulbs by concealing its stock ownership of ostensibly independent companies and using tie-in contracts and other agreements. GE then gained control of a patent from two Viennese scientists and fixed prices and divided markets under cross-licensing agreements. But this still wasn't good enough for the company.

In 1932 a GE engineer's report told how GE had reduced the life of its flashlight bulbs by one third, so that they would last as long as two instead of three batteries. Then he added, "We have been continuing our studies and efforts to bring about the use of one battery life lamps.... If this were done, we estimate that it would result in increasing our flashlight business approximately 60 per cent."

A former GE vice-president, T. K. Quinn, admitted that "from the beginning of the electric lamp industry, freedom of enterprise in manufacture and sale has been restricted by GE. The effect has been to keep prices and profits up and investment down."

No wonder, then, that light-bulb profits carried the whole company during the Depression, even enabling GE to pay dividends, although the volume of bulb sales was only about 10 per cent of the GE total sales volume.

In 1959 TVA authorities protested GE's high prices on turbines and showed that, even excluding labor costs, prices were higher than the competing British product. GE lowered its turbine prices but immediately raised the prices of its light bulbs.

GE was convicted of monopolizing electric bulbs in 1949. Suits against the company, totaling $104 million, were eventually settled for $1.395 million.

On April 4, 1937, GE, Allis-Chalmers, Westinghouse, and two other firms were ordered by the Federal Trade Commission to "cease and desist" from acting to maintain uniform turbine generator prices. As the convictions of the same companies less than seven years ago for similar charges showed, GE did not "cease and desist."

GE resumed price-fixing on what has perhaps been its most ambitious scale around 1954. In 1953 GE boycotted price-fixing, which had begun when OPA was discontinued after World War II, because some companies were undercutting others. GE resumed its rigging in 1954, a year in which sales had slumped. In 1955, although GE's sales continued to drop, the company earned a profit of $212,613 million.

Price-fixing was GE's private face. In an article in the July 1954 issue of *American Magazine*, Philip D. Reed, chairman of the board, revealed GE's public face. Writing of a talk with a cab driver, Reed said, "I told him that in any modern business you must move forward, take risks, and yes, stick out your neck if you want to lead rather than follow in your field. At my company," he emphasized, "we see 10 golden years ahead."

Those golden years were cut short in 1960, when GE was named as defendant in 37 antitrust suits. The government charged that GE and other companies worked out common prices, split up markets, and set up systems for rigging bids under which the companies involved took turns at making the low bid.

George E. Burens testified at Senate Trust and Antimonopoly Subcommittee hearings that in 1954 GE president Robert Paxton had suggested he meet with officials from Cutler-Hammer of Milwaukee to discuss prices. Paxton, who had referred to price-fixing as "optimum prices," resigned from the company in February 1961 because of "ill-health." Burens also said that Henry Van Erben, executive vice-president, told him the "only way to operate the apparatus business was to meet with competitors and set prices."

In August 1956 GE executives, including company vice-president W. F. Oswalt and executives from other electric manufacturing companies, moved into separate cabins at Camp Keystone, North Bay, Ontario. A messenger carried communications between them and when all was over, prices on heavy electrical control equipment increased by 10 per cent.

In 1958 there were eight meetings between executives and in 1959, 35 meetings. They used code names, assumed names, pay telephones, plain envelopes, and never contacted each other at company headquarters.

From 1951 to 1959 prices on generators, for example, rose 50 per cent. The Senate Small Business Committee announced that on one contract in 1959 GE had charged the Navy $82 per unit of carbon packing while a small company in Hackensack, New Jersey, had charged $15, representing an overcharge of 446 per cent.

In the summer of 1959 a grand jury in Philadelphia began investigating price-fixing. The following February indictments against GE began. In 1962 the company's sales totaled close to $5 billion, and GE, which had already been fined $437,500, agreed to pay the government $7.470 million in damages. From 1962 to 1964 GE paid out over $150 million in damage suits filed by electric utility companies as a result of the 1960 indictments.

Earlier, Ralph Cordiner, who once served as head of the Commerce Department's Business Advisory Council, had said, "We don't think anybody's been damaged." And in the 1960 GE Annual Report, dated February 17, 1961, Cordiner wrote in his "Report on the Antitrust Cases": "Your management believes that purchasers of electrical apparatus have received fair value by any reasonable standards." Several weeks earlier, Cordiner had been named the National Association of Manufacturers' Man of the Year.

GE demoted, shifted, or cut the pay of 48 employees involved in antitrust violations, including 16 who were indicted and fined a total of $53,500. However, GE did not discipline its $125,000-a-year vice-president William S. Ginn, who was one of three GE officials to spend 30 days in jail. Ginn, who was director of a boys' club in Schenectady and chairman of a campaign to build a new Jesuit seminary in Lenox, Mass., left GE of his own accord to become president of Baldwin-Lima-Hamilton Corp. at approximately $70,000 a year. A second indicted GE official became president of ITT Europe, Inc., and European general manager of ITT; a third became president of an earth-moving equipment company; a fourth became vice-president of a car-leasing company, and a fifth official a division manager of the Philco Corporation.

Identical bids continued. On December 14, 1960, less than a week after GE, Westinghouse, and others had pleaded guilty (with no contest) to price-fixing charges in federal court, TVA opened identical bids of $1,680.12 for lightning arresters from GE and Westinghouse. On January 5, 1961, TVA opened another set of identical bids for lightning arresters from GE and Westinghouse as well as identical bids of $2,208 for instrument transformers from the two firms. On January 12, both GE and Westinghouse bid $604.80 on current transformers, and on January 20 both bid $1,276 on overcurrent ground relays. On January 30, GE and *five* other firms all bid $4,274.50 on bus-type insulators, and in April GE and four other firms submitted identical bids on 11 different types of watt-hour meters to the city of Cleveland. Not only were bids continuing to be identical, but some prices were also rising identically.

"Sure, collusion was illegal, but it wasn't unethical," an "old GE hand" was quoted saying in the April 1961 issue of *Fortune.*

Industries sue GE

Not only the Justice Department has initiated suits against GE. A suit filed in May 1933 by Tectron Radio Corp. charged that GE, RCA, and Westinghouse had restricted Tectron's use of its own radio tubes, and through conspiracy to monopolize trade the three firms had acquired control of over 4,000 patents. (During that year the Justice Department ordered GE to divest itself of its controlling stock in RCA and ordered GE company director Owen Young to resign as director of RCA.)

The Save Electric Company of Toledo, Ohio, also brought suit against GE and in February 1934 a federal judge ruled for Save Electric Co., declaring that GE's light-bulb patents were invalid. In March 1954 Save Electric Company brought another suit against GE, charging that $7 million had been lost in profits due to conspiracy and monopoly in light-bulb manufacturing.

In 1934 the Electric Machinery Manufacturing Company brought suit against GE for violating 15 of its patents covering operation and control of synchronous motors for a period of more than 10 years. In February 1936 a federal judge found GE guilty and ordered the company to pay court costs plus part of its profits. The amount GE eventually paid has not been disclosed, but it ran into the millions.

In November 1940 the United Lens Corporation of Detroit filed a suit against GE in Philadelphia for infringements of its patents on two filament headlight bulbs. In August 1944 Duro-Test Corporation and its subsidiary Tungsten

Products Corporation instituted a trade monopoly suit against GE. The suit charged GE with controlling 90 per cent of electric lamps manufactured in the United States and asked that GE be rejoined and restore former prices. The suit was settled out of court by a compromise, according to Duro-Test attorneys.

In the same year that GE's profits were falling and the company resumed price fixing, the career of Ronald Reagan was also failing.

A new career for Ronald Reagan

At one point Ronald Reagan was $18,000 in debt and had resorted to emceeing a Las Vegas night-club act in a desperate attempt to make money. Revue, an MCA subsidiary, suggested a weekly dramatic program to GE, which was then looking for a new television show. Reagan would emcee the program, star in six of the plays each year, and spend a few weeks each year making personal appearance tours for GE.

GE Theater ran from 1954 to 1962, and Reagan visited all 135 GE plants during that time and spoke before innumerable civic groups. After the first year, Reagan was accompanied by George Dalen, an ex-FBI agent, who was put in charge of the tours and promotion for GE Theater. Reagan's tours changed. His Hollywood gossip shifted to dire talk of the "attempted take-over of the industry by the Communists." He spoke of the GE union that "suffers from Communist infiltration amounting to outright domination" and warned his audiences of "the swiftly rising tide of collectivism that threatens to inundate what remains of our free economy."

Now Reagan no longer spoke only before GE employees. Soon his tours were scheduled for three years in advance, with speaking engagements at Chamber of Commerce banquets, national conventions, high-school assemblies, executive clubs, and so on. Reagan recruited members for Young Americans for Freedom, helped plan Los Angeles Project Alert, appeared with Fred Schwarz's Christian Anti-Communist Crusade, made an anti-Medicare recording for the AMA, and was campaign chairman for John Birch Society supporter Lloyd Wright in the 1962 California GOP primary. He also was a featured speaker with Arkansas Governor Orval Faubus and Dr. George Benson of Harding College at a joint meeting of the Arkansas Chamber of Commerce and the Associated Industries of Arkansas.

He kept attacking Social Security, federal aid to education, public housing, foreign aid, federal farm programs, and public power; and he called for the repeal of the income tax which he claimed was "spawned by Karl Marx." Reagan was always a representative of GE. They never indicated, he said, "I was singing the wrong song and should switch tunes."

The right-wing politics of Reagan and GE even carried over to GE Theater. In March 1962, for example, Reagan starred in a two-part program on Marion Miller, an FBI agent on whose testimony before HUAC right-wingers have capitalized (including her charges that the American Friends Service Committee was a belt line of the Communist conspiracy).

But the meeting at which Reagan shared the speakers' platform with George Benson was not the company's only contact with Harding College.

GE's ties with Harding College

Harding College operates the National Education Program, with Benson as president and the same board of trustees as that of the college. NEP is mostly known for its film "Communism on the Map," produced by Bircher Glenn A. Green and widely used by the Birch Society, which contends that the only remaining non-Communist countries in the world are West Germany, Formosa, Switzerland, and the United States. NEP is under the supervision of Howard Bennett, a retired GE executive. While with GE, Bennett originated a plan to teach the "fundamental facts" about America's private enterprise system to GE's 280,000 employees and traveled from plant to plant setting up educational programs.

In a letter written March 25, 1961, in response to an inquiry to NEP, Bennett replied: "The General Electric Company uses the NEP films extensively in their many plants." He then gave a list of industrialists who recommend NEP, which included Ralph Cordiner and five other GE officials.

"It is a pleasure to endorse, without reservation, the National Education Program," G. Roy Fugal, GE's manager of employment practices, wrote that same year on GE stationery.

GE has also given money to Howard Kershner's Christian Freedom Foundation and to the Southern States' Industrial Council, a group that has fought organized labor, protects Southern wage differentials, and opposes anything federally supported. Lemuel Boulware, who developed GE's labor policies, is a leading contributor to Americans for Constitutional Action and the Intercollegiate Society of Individualists. GE official Russel E. White is a member of the senior advisory board of the American Security Council, which was organized in 1955 to provide information on "Communist and other statist activities" and keeps a file on tens of thousands of Americans for industries to use.

In 1964 GE built a special communications network system for the two private planes of Barry Goldwater and William Miller so they could be in fast contact with their Washington headquarters, and Ralph Cordiner headed a committee to raise funds for Goldwater's campaign. More recently, John T. McCarty of GE has been active in the New York Conservative party.

Cooperating with Nazi rearmament

GE's cooperation with the Far Right extended to Germany, where the company worked closely with the firm of Nazi war criminal Alfred Krupp, who was to serve six years of a 12-year sentence for using concentration-camp slave labor in his factories. In August 1940, while Nazi planes were bombing London and British planes were bombing Germany in retaliation, including the Krupp armament plants in Essen, GE was indicted by the federal government for conspiring with the Krupp corporation. GE was charged with and in October 1948 found guilty of conspiring with Krupp from 1928 to 1940 to achieve and maintain control of trade and commerce, to fix prices, eliminate competition, pool patents to restrict production, maintain a monopoly, and to impose restraints, limitations, and restrictions upon trade and commerce in hard metals. Although the Justice Department had asked for jail terms, arguing that fines were considered a license fee to be charged off as the cost of illegal business acts, GE, its two subsidiaries, and the three company officers involved were only fined a total of $36,000.

John Henry Lewin, Assistant to the Attorney General in the Antitrust Division, charged that GE's agreement with Krupp was "directly responsible for the disadvantage at which this country finds itself in comparison with its enemies" in the use and production of hard metals, mainly tungsten carbide.

The price of one hard-metal compound, according to the government, was $48 a pound. After Krupp and GE agreed that GE would set the price in the U.S., the cost sky-rocketed to $453 a pound, and at the time of the suit the price was still around $205 a pound. Two months after the government indictment, the price dropped to about $40 a pound.

Jay Jeffries, a GE vice-president and chairman of the board of the Carboloy Co., a GE subsidiary which manufactured the hard metals, stated that the $453-a-pound price tag wasn't excessive. But a letter by a GE engineer in GE's files said that the metal cost $8 a pound to produce. He suggested setting the price at $50 a pound for a "satisfactory profit."

Under terms of the agreement, GE would not compete with Krupp while Krupp controlled GE's licensing of additional manufacturers of the hard-metal compounds in the U.S. and collected royalties from GE. Krupp shipped the compounds to the U.S. until 1936, selling at the high prices set by GE, but the rest of the arrangement wasn't broken off until GE sent a cable to its international representative in Berlin on December 16, 1940.

Correspondence shows how GE referred business to Krupp. On August 8, 1939, GE advised a firm that "we are not in a position to make offers on Carboloy to the Russians." On April 8, 1940, a GE official wrote that the firm couldn't sell the hard metals to China. "You'll have to take your business to Germany," he advised.

Agreements extend to five continents

On January 18, 1945, while the Krupp indictments had been postponed until after the war, the Justice Department filed suit against GE and International GE, charging them with having made agreements, since 1919, with six companies in England, France, Belgium, Germany, Italy, and Japan to divide the world into marketing areas, eliminate competition, and exchange patents and trade processes on an exclusive basis. Wendell Berge, Assistant Attorney General in charge of the Antitrust Division, said that some agreements were still in effect during the war and that "without them the capacity to produce electrical equipment here would have been greater when the present war started." A vice-president of IGE explained that GE feared "a general lowering of prices of these products in this country" if there were competition.

Nine months later the government filed another antitrust suit against GE and Westinghouse and two of their subsidiaries, aiming, in Berge's words, at "extensive cartel activities" in Asia, Africa, South America, and Australia which had begun in 1931. GE, Berge explained, with Westinghouse and leading German, British, and Swiss manufacturers, conspired to form a cartel organization which acted as "a bid depository." The secretary of the cartel would decide to whom business was to be allocated. Prices were fixed, Berge said, and the company which was permitted to win the bid paid "compensation" that was divided among the members who did not receive the contract.

Although GE had illegal agreements with companies in countries the U.S. and its allies were fighting, two of GE's leading officials, C. E. Wilson and Ralph Cordiner, served as vice-chairmen of the War Production Board from 1942 to 1944. And while GE had seen nothing wrong with its cooperation with Krupp, even when the United States was at war with Nazi Germany, the company suddenly became very patriotic when Sen. Joseph McCarthy ran his investigations of alleged Communists.

Cooperation with McCarthy

When McCarthy shifted his investigation to industry, he began with GE, explaining on November 13, 1953, "Frankly, I hope that General Electric decides to can any employee who pleads the Fifth Amendment before this committee." After five days of hearings the company announced, on December 9, that it would "discharge from its employ all admitted Communists, spies, and saboteurs and will suspend employees who refuse to testify under oath on such matters when queried in public hearings conducted by government authority." With this policy, GE became the first non-governmental or non-institutional employer to have a "loyalty" program. McCarthy called GE's policy "fine" and said that the company "certainly should be commended" for it.

By March 1954 GE vice-president Lemuel Boulware was able to boast before the Senate Internal Security Subcommittee that the company had suspended 17 employees who had taken the Fifth Amendment. Back in the mid-1940s, while under government indictment for the Krupp conspiracy, Jay Jeffries, GE and Carboloy official, defining what he considered un-American, said that labor leaders had "un-American objectives." This was the beginning of GE's present labor policies, which were developed by Lemuel Boulware and have become known as "Boulwarism." Boulware considered both major GE unions, the IUE and UE, "collectivist-minded." GE wanted, president Robert Paxton explained in February 1959, "responsible union leaders who will not only avoid unwarranted strikes and slowdowns, but will also be constructive in their economic and political teachings."

The birth of Boulwarism

Boulware's policy was established in 1947, following a strike in which GE had attempted to hold firm with a 10¢-an-hour pay raise to UE members. GM and Westinghouse both had agreed to 18½¢, and finally GE was forced to fall into line. GE, which had abolished a pension plan in 1935 when the Social Security Act was adopted, was also forced to reestablish a pension plan for workers. GE, however, reduces its pension payments when Social Security payments begin or increase and has steadily reduced its own payments to the pension fund.

Workers' support of the 1946 strike and of the union caught GE by surprise. GE was also taken aback and frightened by the criticism it received during the strike from mayors, merchants, and editors, and by the clergymen who even had walked the workers' picket lines.

Boulwarism was developed so that GE would not have to give in to union demands again. In 1947 GE also abolished its bonus plan for employees, which had been established in the 1930's in an attempt to stem the tide of unionism. However, GE continued its bonus plan for executives. Under this plan company president C. E. Wilson, for example, in 1946 received a bonus of $90,000 above his base salary of $108,000.

"We decide what is fair," Boulware himself explained of his policy, "and stick to it. We don't go in for haggling." An NLRB trial examiner reported:

> It [GE] disparagingly refers to the "ask-and-bid" or "auction" form of bargaining as a "flea-bitten eastern type of cunning and dishonest but pointless haggling." Such bargaining ... only serves, it says, to mislead employees into believing that union officials are useful in ways they are not, thus falsely enhancing the union's prestige while diminishing that of the employer and encouraging employee support of union shows of strength.

"General Electric seeks nothing less than to maintain total management control over the bargaining process," wrote Prof. Salvatore J. Bella of the University of Notre Dame in an unpublished study, "Boulwarism and Collective Bargaining at General Electric." Under Boulwarism, Bella pointed out, the power of unions decreased while the number of unionized workers increased and unions had to retreat on their demands and sometimes capitulate totally to the firm.

Because of GE's decentralization and the fact that it manufactures such a wide variety of products, strikes have little power. Also, less than half of GE's 250,000 employees are unionized with 70,000 in IUE, 10,000 in UE, and the remainder in some 100 other bargaining units. GE has also been able to play competing unions, IUE and UE, against each other to its own benefit.

In 1957, before Boulware retired, GE brought in Jack S. Parker as Boulware's successor and retained Boulware as Parker's consultant to provide continuity in labor policy. During that year, IUE tried to reach an overall automation agreement with GE. In April, GE agreed to study the problem and then to discuss it with the union, but by July IUE was still waiting. IUE wrote to the company, and GE replied by saying there wasn't anything to talk about. In August, GE finally agreed to hold a meeting on automation, but that meeting was never held.

GE refuses to change policies

In April 1963 an NLRB trial examiner upheld IUE's unfair labor charge that Boulwarism was a "take it or leave it policy" and in December 1964 the NLRB itself upheld the trial examiner's report and found GE guilty of unfair labor practices. After the NLRB trial examiner issued his ruling, GE vice-president Virgil Day declared that GE "will approach and conduct this year's negotiations with over 100 unions in the same spirit and with the same approach as in the past years' negotiations."

The IUE, UAW, and Steelworkers filed charges of bad-faith bargaining in 1963 against GE. These charges were still pending before the NLRB as of February 1967.

NLRB trial examiner Arthur Leff found that even before negotiations began GE was discrediting union leaders and presenting its case directly to its employees. After negotiations began, GE put into effect for non-union workers the wages and benefits contained in its offer to IUE, although in the past GE had never given non-union workers benefits offered to union members until after a new union contract had been signed. But in 1960, before negotiations had begun, the company had told plant managers: "Show how employees not represented by unions get their wages and benefit improvements without possible delay of waiting for union acceptance."

GE also, in Leff's words, "rejected, ignored, or brushed aside" requests for cost or other information relating to holiday and vacation proposals, income extension aid, supplementary unemployment benefits, pensions, and insurance. Under the National Labor Relations Act companies are obligated to make pension and insurance costs available to the union but, out of six requests, GE only fulfilled two, and those only after the strike had ended.

At a meeting on September 27, 1960, GE's union relations manager, Moore, told the IUE president, "You'll get the information when we get it, or if we feel we should get it for you." When the union asked Moore how many workers would benefit from income extension aid, Moore gave his reply: "Somewhere between zero and 100 per cent." Leff stated that although GE was not talkative with union leaders, it was talkative with its employees. GE, he found, "advanced arguments not only more full but different from those presented to the union negotiators at the bargaining table" and "criticized to employees the Union's demands before first discussing them with the Union."

GE communicated with workers at plant meetings, through supervisors, and by means of plant newspapers, reports, bulletins, leaflets, letters, press releases—and newspaper, radio, and television advertisements. (GE conveniently owns radio and television stations in Schenectady.) In Waterford, letters were even sent to the homes of neighbors of GE employees. The communications, Leff found, reached "flood proportions."

GE threatens workers

At the Augusta, Ga., plant, GE refused to reinstate 20 striking employees and hired replacements for them. At the Waterford plant, employees were told by letter that "a strike would wipe out indefinitely all of the 75 new jobs created ... since ... 1958. It would also bring about a direct reversal of promotions, and result in a great many downgradings in reassignment.

At Lynn, GE's largest and oldest plant, foremen warned workers that the plant might be closed down if there was a strike. The company explained to supervisors that "the Company has more and more in recent years looked to the South and the West for its growth and expansion."

GE also bargained directly with employees and union locals and in some cases offered terms and conditions different than those offered in national negotiations. Leff concluded:

There can be little doubt from the totality of its conduct that the Respondent [GE] was determined ... merely to go through the motions of bargaining in the conference room and to rely entirely on the effectiveness of its direct "sales" approach to employees to resolve the bargaining issues in its favor.... Respondent virtually stated as much....

On December 16, 1964, the NLRB found GE guilty of unfair labor practices and issued 11 orders to the company, including to rehire the Augusta workers, supply the union with the information it had requested, and to refrain from bargaining with locals or offering locals separate terms.

In May 1965 when workers at the Wayneboro, Virginia, GE plant voted to join UE, GE challenged the vote in an attempt to prevent the NLRB from certifying UE as the collective bargaining agent. The NLRB dismissed GE's objections in September and certified UE, but GE still told the union in a letter that "it cannot recognize or bargain with UE." Late in 1966 the NLRB ruled in favor of UE for the third time, this time ordering GE to bargain with UE. GE then appealed the ruling to the Circuit Court of Appeals.

In early 1964 GE even threatened to shut down its Schenectady plant unless the union agreed to shift 3,000 employees from piece rates to day rates.

The resulting pay cut would have averaged $60 a week per worker. The plant employed 5,000, and 3,700 additional workers in Schenectady depended upon those 5,000 jobs.

The union did not agree, and GE began cutting pay on its own on July 13. In October GE and the union, UE, finally reached an agreement whereby workers would be given "transition" pay for four years so they could adjust and the company would begin a new incentive plan under which 250 workers would return to piece work in the next five years.

To make sure that employees at the Schenectady plant worked just as hard for less pay, GE installed what it termed "a modern industrial tool, closed circuit television." A television monitor was placed in the office of the general foreman who kept in touch with foremen by a direct telephone hook-up.

GE's effort in Schenectady, company vice-president Donald E. Craig explained, was an attempt to prove "we could be able to do everything in Schenectady we could do in the South."

The South has been an especially attractive spot for GE since the mid-1950's; the company, of course, has long been attracted to such low-wage areas. At the end of World War II, for example, GE abandoned a number of war plants and spent over $91 million building seven new plants in small-town low-wage areas.

In June 1953 Ralph Cordiner announced that the South would soon become a major center of GE's operations. Two years later, when GE opened its twelfth Southern plant, Raymond W. Smith, GE general manager, said, "It is in this area that great future growth is forecast."

In 1958 Cordiner and 18 other GE directors toured the South. Speaking in Atlanta, Cordiner explained why the South was becoming a major area for GE. "Right-to-work legislation very definitely is a factor," he said, "in deciding where General Electric plants are built. General Electric has a very firm stand in favor of right-to-work laws because we are interested in the rights of individuals."

The individuals whose rights General Electric is interested in are its own officials and major stock-holders, not the American worker or the American consumer. Profiteering is still the most important GE product.

Sources

Issues of the *IUE News* and *UE News*.

Information from the files of ADL and Group Research.

Reports from the NLRB and the Department of Justice.

Correspondence with some of the firms involved in antitrust suits against GE.

More than 80 stories from *The New York Times* since 1930; more than 70 articles from *America, American Magazine, Business Week, Christian Century, Dun's Review, Fortune, Life, Nation, New Republic, Newsweek, New Yorker, New York Sun, Saturday Evening Post, Scientific American, Time, U.S. News & World Report*, and *Vital Speeches*.

The American Ultras, by Irwin Suall, New York, 1962.

Where's the Rest of Me, by Ronald Reagan, New York, 1965.
Gentlemen Conspirators, by John G. Fuller, New York, 1962.
Society and Man, by Meyer Weinberg and O. Shabat, Englewood Cliffs, 1965.
The Public Plunderers, by James B. Carey, Washington, D.C., 1961.

Jerry DeMuth's piece is a catalog of the sins of one business, but, more important, it indicates the inability of existing methods of social control to stem the rapaciousness of the corporation and illustrates the close link between the corporation's interests and politics and government. But all this is presented more by the force of illustrative events than by the logic of the system of corporate control; any systemic logic is implicit. At the other extreme, one can assume the logic of the system and count it as demonstrated with examples of corporate interlocks and tentacles that reach out to other institutions in society. This is the position taken in the following three brief splashes, originating with the Liberation News Service (which disseminates news releases to subscribing radical publications). The first piece makes a more general point about GE than DeMuth does because it starts with an explicit radical assumption about the coherence and the goals of the system.

1970

GE: ELECTRIC OCTOPUS [8]

Liberation News Service

147,000 workers are on strike against General Electric. There are at least that many reasons why GE should be defeated.

General Electric is run by nineteen men, all white, all but one Anglo-Saxon Protestants. They hold more than half the company's voting stock and hire the chief executives and managers. They are some of the most powerful men in the world, heads of the fourth largest industrial corporation in the U.S. (Only General Motors, Standard Oil of New Jersey and Ford are bigger.) These men usually see the inside of a GE plant only on the yearly guided tour; they can't tell the difference between a relay and a rectifier. They don't care about

8 Liberation News Service #223, January 7, 1970, p. 7.

producing anything in particular, but only about extracting profit from everything in general. General Electric is only one of the profit-making schemes that they control.

For example, take GE Director Gilbert Humphrey, one of the nineteen. He is also board chairman of the Cleveland-based quarter-billion dollar Hanna Mining Corporation. Or take Directors Neil McElroy and George Love; they also run Detroit's Chrysler Corporation, the fifth biggest U.S. corporation. There are about 75 other corporations that GE directors control. Whether you inspect bottles at Coca-Cola, blast ore for Hanna, make buttonholes in a Stevens sweatshop, or stamp out dashboards for Chrysler, the profits from your time and energy go into the same set of pockets. The major companies are wired together at the top. Chrysler cars use GE lightbulbs; GE's company fleet uses Chrysler cars. Coca-Cola has the concession in GE lunchrooms; Hanna's tungsten mines supply filaments for GE lamps. Hanna owns part of Chrysler. And so on. But that's just the beginning.

The nineteen men who run GE are powerful voices in the White House and the Pentagon. Four GE directors were at the top of the military establishment when the Viet Nam war was being planned. Thomas S. Gates and Neil H. McElroy were Secretaries of Defense under Eisenhower, Robert T. Stevens was Secretary of the Army and Fred J. Borch was a member of the Defense Industry Advisory Board. General Electric keeps close ties with the Pentagon through the 89 retired colonels and generals who now work for GE.

General Electric has used its power in the national military establishment to advance its interests. In 1954 President Eisenhower said that the American military had to intervene in Asia so that the U.S. could control "the tin and tungsten of Indochina" (Viet Nam, Laos and Cambodia). GE is a heavy tungsten user and Hanna Mining Co. produces a lot of tungsten. Another GE director, Edmund W. Littlefield, is head of Utah Mining and Construction Company, which also produces tungsten; further, his company built the jet runways in Thailand and Laos that are used for bombing raids on Viet Nam. The bombers' engines and their machine guns are part of GE's war production.

General Electric's power to make national policy pays the company very well. General Electric was stagnating in 1964, with profits scarcely higher than in 1960. Then came the 1965 escalation of a war that GE helped plan, and GE's balance sheet took a great leap forward. Average annual profits since 1965 have been 43% higher than they were in the five years before. General Electric war contracts have more than doubled since 1965, for a total of $6.5 billion in five years. This year, with war sales of $1.6 billion, GE is the number two military contractor.

General Electric directors are on the governing boards of at least eleven major American universities and colleges, including Stanford, Harvard and Princeton. General Electric men control the faculty and curriculum to see that potential GE stagehands in the form of brainwashed company-loving engineers, technicians and managers are turned out in every graduating class.

General Electric is part of the worldwide U.S. system of imperialism. The men at the top turn a profit on everything from cars to cornflakes, from dime stores to life insurance in twenty-five countries. . . .

About the time this story appeared in early 1970, board rooms and stock-holders' meetings were being invaded by middle-class liberals, who were concerned with civil rights, pollution, and consumerism. (These liberals are a major source for the enlarged audience that the radical attack on business reaches.) At that time the Liberation News Service printed the following short item.

1970

GE'S MANUAL FOR CORPORATE FRONT-LINERS[9]

Liberation News Service

An internal memo prepared by GE dealing with confrontations shows that the central office has whole departments devoted to producing the non-commital bullshit they come out with at the bargaining table.

Take for example, this list of directions for a Company spokesman facing a confrontation:

a. use the appropriate digest of positive Company attitudes and accomplishments.
b. avoid conferring legitimacy on a demand that may or may not have merit.
c. avoid any specific commitment that could prejudice subsequent assessment and consideration of the demand.
d. avoid being responsive to the demand itself.

GE feels that they are in for heavy weather. The introduction to the memo sets the problem out thus:

There is a growing likelihood that industry in general and General Electric in particular face a mounting wave of confrontations similar to those directed against church and campus.

9 Liberation News Service #229, January 28, 1970, p. 13.

GE goes on to state their objective in solving the problem:

Identify sites and subjects of likely confrontation with the company. Prepare management for a standard operating procedure of reaction that will maintain a favorable corporate image with minority groups and with the public at large without compromising future corporate actions or decisions and without provoking escalation of the conflict.

Later in the memo GE states:

The currently mounting attack upon ... the military-industrial complex is stage-setting for a new period of political attack upon virtually every aspect of corporate management.

The radical press publishes a running commentary on big business, reinforcing the image presented in the preceding articles. The next brief item about General Motors, also furnished by the Liberation News Service, appeared in *The Guardian*, a New Left weekly newspaper published in New York. Note that in a very short space it covers the familiar major topics: production for waste rather than for human needs, the profit system, imperialism, and the power elite.

1971

CAR IS KING [10]

In America, the car is king. More people have jobs related to the auto industry than any other industry in the American economy.

Some 30% of the nation's consumption of sheet, bar and strip steel goes for the manufacture of automobiles; the auto industry consumes 70% of the rubber, 50% of the lead, 45% of the malleable iron, 35% of the zinc, 12% of the nickel, 11% of the aluminum and 9% of the copper used in this country. The major share of oil and gas consumption also goes to automobiles.

The car is designed for profit. Expensive to buy, expensive to maintain, expensive to park and expensive to repair, the auto is America's biggest

10 Liberation News Service, as reprinted in *The Guardian*, January 9, 1971.

profit-maker. New cars cost the public over $30 billion each year. Repairs on America's 100 million autos total more than $20 billion.

Auto production is woven into the nation's entire fabric. Many of the resources for production and use of autos must be obtained from third world countries: 80% of the rubber used in the U.S. comes from Southeast Asia, where the U.S. is fighting to defend and expand its access to such resources as rubber and oil.

Interlocking directorship

There is an interlocking directorship of corporations in the various sections of the auto industry and in nearly all other important sectors of the economy. The directors of GM, for example, sit on the boards of three major oil companies and four major steel companies. The auto giants also have enormous defense contracts. GM alone has a yearly business of more than $580 million in government military contracts.

GM and other giant corporations need the U.S. government bureaucracy and military to secure the expansion and control over third world countries to insure them a continual supply of crucial resources, as well as to provide markets for their products and cheaper labor than what they can get at home.

IS BUSINESS ALL–POWERFUL?

The subsequent chapters of this book will explore the manner in which the New Left sees business as controlling foreign policy; the universities as the source of personnel, information, and ideologies for business; the working-man as ready but unable to join the attack; and the much-heralded response of business to the current social crisis. In this chapter we have been content to look at a few giant firms through the lenses of the New Left, but some problems intrude to cloud the vision.

If business is so powerful, so protected by interlocking directorates, so immune to the thrusts of the courts and the consumer, why is its road sometimes so rocky? How could the Ford Motor Company manage to lose a healthy $200 million on the Edsel if "Car Is King" and advertising is irresistible? The answer might be that even large corporations can make mistakes and display vanity. Besides, Ford did not miss a dividend even if workers did lose their jobs. What, then, about General Dynamics, which had to write off some $425 million worth of civilian jet aircraft losses in the early 1960's? The business system was apparently not working too well then because the loss occurred despite the fact that the president of

General Dynamics was Frank Pace, a former Director of the Budget and a former Secretary of the Army. The answer might be that these were losses in the civilian market, and Pace and his successors did manage to secure sufficient government contracts to allow General Dynamics to survive and prosper. In fact, it prospered well enough to sustain additional losses and to become involved in various government-contract scandals without going under.

Is the civilian marketplace then a more relentless taskmaster than the government? Is the discipline of competition present in the production of civilian goods? It is interesting that Horowitz and Erlich note that when Litton went into private, competitive markets, its incompetence was revealed. And we see signs of earnest competition all about us, even to the extent of a flourishing business in industrial espionage. GE exists, but there also is a Westinghouse. If business is so powerful, why have all markets and regions not been divided up and wasteful competition eliminated? Why, indeed, has business not walked off with everything in one splendid demonstration of how a centrally controlled, well-run, all-embracing system might function?

These are the arguments that liberals, moderates, and conservatives alike present to the New Left, and they do not find satisfactory responses; indeed, one suspects that many members of the New Left do not take such arguments seriously. They explain conflict within the capitalist elite as the emergence of the "contradictions of capitalism" that Marx predicted so long ago would bring capitalism down. More than that is needed. While short pieces, such as those from the Liberation News Service, project an all-powerful corporation going its own way, the more thoughtful inquiries suggest something like the following:

First, the system of monopoly capitalism is not monolithic. There are diverse interests within business and industry based on different functions (such as manufacturing and banking), geographical regions, foreign trade interests, substitution of products and materials, claims on the government for subsidies and internal trade restrictions, and so on. There are also restraints, however minimal, placed on the power of business and industry by organized labor, consumers, and public officials.

Second, monopoly capitalism is a system; the parts must fit together no matter how imperfectly. A substantial portion of the population must have enough income to consume the products of industry; enough people must be sufficiently educated and healthy to work in industry; there must be enough civil order to permit stable production and short-run forecasting. Corporations have an interest in seeing that large numbers of people are decently fed, housed, educated, and entertained. Though run by business, the system still must use most of the population.

Third, the system is dynamic, evolving, and only imperfectly rationalized and centralized. Banking interests in the West are challenging those in the

East, and the outcome is not predetermined. New conglomerates that have burst regional and broad product bounds are challenging the established giants. The action of President Nixon's chief trustbusting official, Richard McLaren, has been interpreted as an attempt to stem the power of the new conglomerates. But he focused on those that threatened to upset regional balances and power structures, or those that attempted to link diverse industries. He did not attack the agglomeration of power *per se,* but only the way in which established interests might be affected.

More central to the evolving order of the system is the growth of financial power. There is a debate in the New Left over whether the established theoreticians of American capitalism, Paul Baran and Paul Sweezy, who held that industrial interests dominated, are now out of date since the hearings on the banking system conducted by Representative Wright Patman revealed that fiscal institutions are providing the integrating force of the capitalist system. Two young radicals, Robert Fitch and Mary Oppenheimer, have drawn on the hearings and other material to present a brilliant, complex, well-documented analysis titled "Who Rules the Corporations?" They conclude that finance capitalism has moved to the center of the stage since the Second World War. At least one other radical has challenged their interpretation, resulting in a bitter, but still scholarly, exchange in one of the New Left periodicals.[11]

Finally, the argument of the nonradicals that competition does exist and that corporations are disciplined by it seems to be true, but inconsequential. Competition does not often appear to produce greater efficiency, only more waste; it does not often affect major decisions, as we shall soon see; and it does not appear to weed out incompetent firms, as the following remarks will suggest.

Few of the 100 largest corporations drop into a lower bracket over time; few of the 500 largest ever leave that prestigious category except through merger. The stability of the system is awesome. Financial losses in one year—few enough at that—are soon made up. Corporations in the most volatile of industries—defense and aerospace—have their ups and downs, but there was considerable evidence, even before the recent loan to Lockheed, that the United States government would act to prevent large and even moderate-sized defense firms from actually going under. Few executives are on welfare, and no large defense suppliers have been forced to close their doors. Even if a company should be forced into bankruptcy, that would only consist of a massive reorganization and mergers, not the disappearance of plants, equipment, profitable subsidiaries, and so on.

---

11 See Paul Baran and Paul Sweezy, *Monopoly Capitalism* (New York: Monthly Review Press, 1966) for the established Left critique of capitalism. See Robert Fitch and Mary Oppenheimer, "Who Rules the Corporations?" *Socialist Revolution,* 1:4, 5, 6 (July–August, September–October, November–December 1970) for the critique, and James O'Connor's comment and Robert Fitch's reply in 2:1 (January–February 1971).

The most recent public notice of the stability of giant firms involved Lockheed Aircraft, which for seven of the past eleven years has been the nation's number one military contractor. The news concerned a congressionally approved decision to provide federal guarantees for a loan of $250 million to Lockheed so that it could proceed with development of its commercial Tri-Star jet, in competition with Boeing and McDonnell-Douglas. The story, as told by Robert Fitch in *Ramparts* magazine, is so complex as to defy adequate summary; but even an outline is revealing of the way in which American capitalism is and is not monolithic, and of how and at what level competition really operates.[12]

First, "even when not asking for a federal subsidy, Lockheed has been hard to love," Fitch states. Its Electra had to be withdrawn from the commercial market because of defects. Its expensive F-104 Starfighter, forced on West Germany, killed more than sixty German pilots in more than 180 crashes, leading to an economic and political crisis in West Germany. Its C-5A military transport plane had a cost overrun of more than $2 billion, bringing the total cost to twice as much as all the federal poverty programs, three times as much as all federal expenditures on public health programs, fifty times more than the federal funds available for urban mass transit. Even so, the wings of the plane kept falling off. Following triumphant announcements that all the "technical difficulties" had been solved, all the operational planes were grounded in October 1971, when the engine of one of them fell off while the plane sat on a runway. It is hard to beat that kind of record.

Why, then, the commercial Tri-Star jet, a 400-m.p.h. turboprop intended to compete with 600 m.p.h. pure jets? And why, in June 1969, did twenty-four banks lend Lockheed $400 million at the lowest rate, which is reserved for firms that are the best risks, when the news of delays, cost overruns, and wings falling off were on the front pages of newspapers? They did so because banks make a great deal of money from financing and leasing aircraft to airlines, and banks have substantial interests in the airlines. Notes Fitch, "most of the airplanes flown by the five major U.S. airlines are actually owned by the big New York banks and insurance companies." First National City Bank, for example, owns more than 100 airplanes valued at more than $1 billion, giving it the third biggest air force in the world, after the Russian and American governments, according to the executive vice president of the bank.

What do the banks do with airplanes? They lease them to the airlines, and as a result of accelerated depreciation allowances and the 7 percent investment tax credit, they take in a return of 56 percent on their investment in the first year. This rate drops to a mere 20 percent by the tenth year. (This estimate comes from the business magazine, *Forbes*.) The new jets cause the

12 Robert Fitch, "Lockheed: Dinosaur on a Hot Tin Roof," *Ramparts*, September 1971, pp. 45–50 ff.

airlines financial suffering because of their overcapacity. As a senior vice president of TWA said of the giant 747's when they were introduced, "An industry that had a rational control over its own technology would not introduce the 747 at this time because there is no need for it." First National City Bank owns twelve of these behemoths. The airlines have little choice because the banks own a substantial piece of the airlines.

But banks compete in some substantial respects. This competition extends to engine makers (GE versus Rolls-Royce), airframe companies (Lockheed versus Boeing), thousands of subcontractors, and airlines. For example, David Packard, Deputy Secretary of Defense, is a director of General Dynamics, which is the main subcontractor of McDonnell-Douglas. McDonnell-Douglas builds the DC-10, which competes with Lockheed's Tri-Star. General Dynamics also competes with Lockheed directly in shipbuilding contracts. Packard opposed guaranteeing the loan to Lockheed and apparently favored merging it with one of the two remaining large airframe companies. Also opposed to the loan were most of the large firms in the military-industrial complex, and so were many of the banks, since a merger to a stronger company would safeguard their initial loans. However, for Packard's boss, President Nixon, Lockheed was vital to the prosperity of Southern California, where Nixon has many political debts, especially after the SST debacle. His former law firm services Eastern Air Lines, which has made a $75 million nonrefundable down payment on the Tri-Star, and various other connections would dispose him to favor a government guarantee for the loan to Lockheed. The system, then, is not of a piece.

Most complicated of all was the problem of the British-built engine. Rolls-Royce had gone bankrupt before Lockheed threatened bankruptcy, thereby leaving Lockheed with the prospect of having "the world's largest glider." But in a complex maneuver, engineered by the powerful Lord Cowdray, Rolls-Royce was nationalized by England's Conservative government, along with all its bad debts and astronomical expenditures ("enabling all British taxpayers to share in them democratically," notes Fitch). One division was left un-nationalized—the jet engines division—which receives government subsidies of £2 million a week. This decision had European complications, since German, French, and Dutch interests are producing a direct competitor of the Tri-Star. Once again Britain appeared to Europe to be politically and economically tied to the United States rather than to its neighbors across the Channel. The Cowdray interests are closely interlocked with American investment houses, and the two governments shared the welfare payments to this incompetent client.

Fitch digs deeper into the corporate interests and those of the "political errand-runners" in the government, from Nixon down to lowly members of the House of Representatives. (He is especially hard on liberal New York Senator Jacob Javits, who also introduced a bill to bail out the Penn Central Railroad after its debacle.) What Fitch has done is to paint the complex and fascinating picture of high finance and dependent industry in the United States. Much of the picture is necessarily based on conjecture and innuendo, but he makes more sense of this fiasco than most accounts I have seen. Yet all he can conclude from the manifold evidence of competition and conflict among the financial and business elite is that despite the criticisms directed at Lockheed, the elite needs such companies to make the system run smoothly. "Lockheed does provide the weapons necessary to suppress the external proletariat, while providing employment opportunities for the proletariat at home." That charge hardly nails down the case for business as a system. Fitch admits that it might be necessary to dissolve Lockheed and transfer its task to worthier firms, but if so, he says, it would be done in such a way as to buttress "the financial framework of the defense industry as a whole" and to preserve its "pattern of operation." Thus, either way— bail-out or bankruptcy—the thesis of business as a system is upheld. We have in Fitch's article a cogent analysis of the Lockheed affair and considerable evidence for the thesis that the banks are behind the surplus capacity of the airline industry and indifferent to the incompetence of airplane manufacturers. This in itself tells us more than a conventional sins-of-business commentary on the issue, but it still does not really allow us to grasp the limits or parameters of the system.

Perhaps this is asking too much of the New Left at this time. After all, they hardly have access to the crucial data; there are not that many scholars concerned with such issues; the system is changing continually, making a detached, historical analysis difficult; and the system is not of a piece—large social systems seldom exhibit more than an imperfect meshing of critical parts, and many pieces are left strewn around. All this makes the task of the radical scholar and publicist difficult, but even as direct action and confrontation appear to wane, the search for an understanding of the system intensifies.

COMPETITION AND ELITES

An adequate examination of the issue of competition among the members of the elite would indicate that it is kept within bounds, that it results in waste and inefficiency instead of technological progress in production for use, and that it does not threaten the basic interests of the elite. It is obvious, at least to this student of business structure and goals, that firms do compete, that managers are usually judged on their ability to enable the firm to compete successfully, and that long hours, ulcers, espionage, and considerable talent go into the process of doing so. For example, competition among the oil companies starts at the busy intersection, and the service station manager who does not do well will suffer. Farther up the ladder, there is intense competition in advertising, some in research and development, and some in the logistics of moving oil around the world through many stages of production and distribution. Men's careers depend in part on how well they perform these tasks. At the top, the officers of the firms carefully watch the sales and profit figures of the industry and of their own firm, and they suffer or rejoice as the case may be. One cannot deny that competition exists even among the giants in this concentrated industry.

But the competition is kept within bounds. Price wars are comparatively few, and they are usually set off by small, independent oil firms and dealers testing the giants. Larger oil companies often own pieces of one another through direct or indirect means.[13] Furthermore, the vast sums spent on advertising and gimmicks are efforts that produce no real goods or services that consumers can use. Technological innovation is not conspicuous in this or in most other concentrated industries. Finally, the areas in which real competition does not exist are the most revealing. It is not in the basic interests of the giants to disagree about pricing; about the need for oil import quotas, which keep domestic prices high; about oil depletion allowances; about the emphasis on the private automobile rather than mass transit; about U.S. foreign policy toward oil-rich nations; about the internal affairs of oil-producing countries; or about the need to diffuse the attack on the pollution caused by oil spills and by the highly inefficient piston engine in automobiles. Indeed, it is not even necessary that the giants confer on such matters; their common, noncompetitive interests are clear. Disagreement and competition, then, are limited to certain areas in which the consequences are not likely to be great, except for consumers.[14]

In a similar manner, competition among Boeing, McDonnell-Douglas, and Lockheed is intense at contract time, but none of these firms would argue that larger jets should not be built because passenger demand is not increasing fast enough. The financial houses that are allowed by government policies of taxation to profit from financing new aircraft are not likely to argue that the nation's capital resources and tax incentives are being misused. The airlines manage to get fare increases on the basis of their poor profits. Cities use tax dollars to build more and larger airports and airport facilities. United, Eastern, and the other airlines spend a great deal on advertising and decor to "compete," but this is not the kind of competition that benefits the consumer.

For the New Left all this is probably quite obvious, but if its analysis is to have an impact on liberals and moderates who see competition all about

---

13 The basic critical work on the oil industry is Robert Engler's *The Politics of Oil* (New York: Macmillan, 1961), in which many of these charges are fully documented.
14 See the discussion of this issue in terms of the failure of organizational theory to understand the impact of organizations on society in Charles Perrow, *Complex Organizations: A Critical Essay* (Glenview, Ill.: Scott, Foresman, 1972), Chapter 5.

them, it must be spelled out in obvious terms. Otherwise, the story of Lockheed or Penn Central, and numerous other seamy chapters in the history of business, will be only that much more muckraking, on an unanalytical par with books such as *America, Inc.*, which only call for better regulation.[15] That the firms are "all wired together at the top," as the Liberation News Service notes with reference to GE and other industrial and manufacturing interests, is only the beginning of analysis.

What is true of business and industry is equally true of government. Liberals and moderates are correct in saying that, just as there are competing interests regarding tariffs, there are also hawks and doves in government, Republican or Democratic. But the doves do not advocate that no military support should be given to American interests abroad, only that it has gone too far in Vietnam. The doves argue that the threat posed by leftist governments in Latin America is not great enough to justify dispatching American troops or American support for rightist coups. But the doves in the power elite do not define the very presence of United States interests in Latin America as imperialistic, and they are not ready to question the legitimacy of massive United States interests abroad. There is little dissensus within the elite on these matters, only on specific tactics and particular wars.

This point should not come as a surprise. Considerable scholarship has been devoted to showing the common origins, interests, and career lines of the elites that control business and industry, government, the military, and the foundations and universities. According to Richard Barnet, the vast majority of the top national security officials in government (notably in the Defense Department, the State Department, the Cabinet, and the White House staff) are connected with large corporations or with the law firms and banking houses that service them. The traffic between the economic and governmental power centers is heavy.[16] A man like Robert S. McNamara, for example, could start his career in the military under Tex Thornton; go to an important private corporation, the Ford Motor Company; become Secretary of Defense; and then go on to head the World Bank, which protects and oversees American foreign investments and guides the development of noncommunist nations. After a stay in this post, he could easily become a university president (as did one of his Defense Department lieutenants, Charles Hitch, who became president of the giant University of California) or a foundation head, or he could move back into government or business. The backgrounds and careers of such men do not dispose them to encourage ruinous competition when they head corporations or award them contracts.

15 Morton Mintz and Jerry S. Cohen, *America, Inc.: Who Owns and Operates the United States?* (New York: Dial Press, 1971).
16 Richard Barnet, *The Economy of Death* (New York: Atheneum, 1969); G. William Domhoff, *Who Rules America?* (Englewood Cliffs, N.J.: Prentice-Hall, 1967), and *The Higher Circles* (New York: Random House, 1970).

But this pattern of reciprocity raises perhaps the thorniest of all the issues the New Left faces: who is to run the country? Instead of financiers, businessmen, lawyers, and all the highly placed and specialized experts, should we expect plumbers, machinists, assembly-line workers, school teachers, and welfare mothers to make the complex decisions required by a complex economy existing in a complex world? As later chapters will show, the New Left argues that college professors are co-opted by the elite, that labor unions are captives of business, and that large foundations are the tools of elite strategies. Where else could the decision-making elite come from, other than from the well-born, well-educated, well-financed upper class? Members of this elite are socialized at an early age into the world of power and bigness—the world of big business, big government, and big decisions. They receive the best educations, and they waste the least time on the nagging problems of everyday existence. They know how the system runs and how to run it. Was the Soviet system any better for the fact that Stalin was a Georgian peasant?

Direct democracy could not exist in a country of this size and complexity. Even few members of the New Left are willing to consider self-sufficient communes as the answer; these are at best experiments in interpersonal relations, not in societal governance. Even if America's affluence were equitably distributed and waste production were eliminated, a vast bureaucracy would have to administer the country, and at the top would be something we would have to call an elite. As one radical notes: "The requirements of a planned society bring into being a vast administrative apparatus which exercises considerable authority in all areas of life. The problem of bureaucracy is one of the internal contradictions of socialist society." [17] This is an internal contradiction almost as serious as those so often cited as existing in capitalism.

Solutions are hard to come by, but the New Left would argue that unless the problem is posed in uncompromising terms, there will be no search for solutions. The conventional explanations are losing ground as the critique of the New Left gains ground through its increased scope and sophistication. It is no longer enough to attribute our problems to human nature, to the observable fact that all industrialized societies have similar problems, to the ignorance and laziness of the lower orders, to the biblical maxim that the poor will always be with us, to the greed of rulers, or to the failure of mechanisms of regulation. The analyses of the New Left destroy these easy excuses. By detailing how the system actually operates, its writers raise the possibility of finding alternatives that those who cite the conventional explanations would not consider.

This, I believe, is the main contribution of the New Left and will be the basis for its lasting impact: in trying to analyze how the system actually

---

17 Irwin Silber, *The Guardian*, January 9, 1971, p. 6.

works, they will discredit piecemeal and ephemeral attempts at reform and allow us to explore strategies and alternative forms of governance that our present understanding cannot encompass. It is too early to formulate alternatives and the strategies that would bring them into being; we must first understand the actuality. The liberals have not grasped it sufficiently, and the Old Left has buried it in outmoded dogma and rhetoric.

The rest of this book will be devoted to a tour of some of our established institutions to see how the New Left is attempting to understand the system. We turn first to imperialism—the inexorable impulse of an economic system that is compelled to find foreign markets for its surplus and to gain access to the raw materials of the globe.

CHAPTER 3

Imperialism

The attack on the business system reaches its culmination in the cry of "imperialism." Whatever the business system has done to the nonaffluent one-third of our nation is trivial compared to what it has done to two-thirds of the world. In the name of democracy and free enterprise, argues the New Left, the United States has waged imperialist wars, subjugated power-less peoples, stripped them of their resources, and covered the noncommu-nist world with military bases, advisers, and ruling juntas. Imperialism is the necessary product of capitalism when it reaches that advanced stage where domestic markets and domestic raw materials no longer are sufficient. Without imperialism, capitalism would be torn apart by the contradiction of enormous productivity and profits with no places to sell the goods or reinvest the profits.

There is more than a century's worth of scholarship and polemics dealing with the various types of imperialism, the necessity for it in capitalist countries, and the consequences of it. This chapter ignores the history of that debate, which still goes on. It deals only with economic imperialism, only with imperialism on the part of the United States, and, of necessity, ignores many of the complexities and subtleties. I have avoided all the absurd blanket statements that attempt to explain all foreign involvement and even domestic policies in terms of the rape of the world by United States business concerns and have utilized only serious articles that present concrete evidence. Even so, this chapter constitutes a hasty tour of this essential part of the New Left attack.

The attack on business must include a charge of imperialism. If business is a system that reaches into every phase of our national life, it must reach into our international life as well. Business must profoundly influence our foreign policy, even if it does not make it outright. Otherwise, business would have to be seen as just one of many powerful influence groups in the United States, rather than as the controlling group. For this reason, the conventional explanations for our economic, political, and military foreign policies must be discredited. It is not godless communism that menaces us and requires military operations and support for dictators and right-wing politicians. We are not attempting merely to promote worldwide trade and prosperity in the interest of the health of all peoples. We are not protecting weak countries from economic exploitation by communist nations. We are not arming countries to put down criminal elements that threaten the existence of their free institutions. If any of these justifications for our foreign policies were to be accepted, business would be merely playing its allotted role, along with other groups, in carrying out a foreign policy set by our elected political leaders. There would be no business system dominating our nation.

Nor can the New Left accept a liberal view of the roots of our foreign policy. This view might say that, yes, fear of communism has been excessive and we have made many mistakes, but these were "honest" mistakes, understandable in a country that so fears collectivism. Business itself does get involved in some unfortunate adventures here and there that are settled by shows of force or arm-twisting diplomacy, and it well might exploit some underdeveloped nations at times, since the temptation is great. But this only argues for tighter government control over the foreign activity of business and for the rapid development of underdeveloped nations through our aid so that they are not so vulnerable to the United States' or to any other country's business interests.

This is the sins-of-business viewpoint. Business, like any other powerful interest group, can get out of hand. It is the job of government to regulate these interests, and it has not done a very good job. To argue that business interests dominate our foreign policy and that the policy is largely one of aggressive imperialism, however, is to move to a radical position. At first glance, the imperialist viewpoint is a difficult position to hold, in view of the many arguments against it.

These arguments can be quickly stated. Exports from the United States are small—they amount to less than 5 percent of the gross national product. The great bulk of these exports and of our foreign investments involve the developed areas of Europe and Canada, rather than areas where we are fighting wars or supporting dictators and supplying arms. American investment abroad is considerably less than 10 percent of domestic investment. Could we really control the economies of nations with so little of our own funds, especially when most of the investment goes into strong European countries? How could this small figure support a view of exploitation of other countries and warrant some 6,000 military presences or bases abroad, a huge defense budget, the activities of the CIA, and numerous small and large combat operations since the Second World War? In relation to our total economy, the investment of American business in an area such as Vietnam is so minuscule that to mention it in the same breath with a war lasting more than eight years, resulting in close to 50,000 American combat deaths, and costing $30 billion a year at its peak seems simply ludicrous.

Furthermore, the greatest need of the underdeveloped areas is for capital. A country cannot industrialize without it, and industrialization is the surest way to solve major problems such as overpopulation, famine, and malnutrition. The United States is pouring capital into developing countries; it moves in massive amounts from our business firms, banks, and government agencies into many of the underdeveloped areas in the Free World. Furthermore, the United States government takes money from its own taxpayers to buy technical assistance and send it abroad. The United States has Peace Corps and Food for Peace programs and sends social scientists to work on land reform, disease control, schools, and government planning. The American businessman, as well as the general public, pays for all this. In addition, huge foundations are heavily involved in financing programs aimed at development; even the churches are still there, saving lives first and souls where they can. We are our brother's keeper; many a business-oriented conservative politician would like nothing better than to see this whole complex of programs and aid dumped. Can this be imperialism?

Exactly so! says the New Left. It is perhaps a tribute to the New Left's resourcefulness that all this activity can be neatly explained in terms of the business system and its motivating logic. Of course, in large part the radicals are drawing on Lenin, Engels, Hobson, and others as well as on present-day orthodox socialists and Marxists. But they have used such sources well, opened up the topic to more shades of interpretation, and done some detailed homework.

WELFARE IMPERIALISM

Let us start with the last argument—our generosity, as demonstrated by the Agency for International Development, Food for Peace, and technical and university assistance of all kinds. It is here that the New Left (in contrast to the Old Left) has made the greatest contribution to the imperialism argument. Again, their prime target seems to be the liberals. The motives of conservatives are obvious enough, while the liberal line constitutes a more serious challenge to the New Left's position because the liberals argue that reform is all that is needed. Their argument draws deployable energy away from the more radical attack.

We will focus on Latin America, for, as George Ball once put it, there is a natural division of labor in the West that puts Africa into the hands of the Common Market and Latin America into the hands of the United States.[1] The job of developing the underdeveloped countries is, of course, too large for one country alone. The first selection is part of a pamphlet published in 1968 by the North American Congress on Latin America, a small but resourceful group of scholars and publicists. The authors are two well-established New Leftists, Steve Weissman and John Gerassi. The title, "The Vietnamization of Latin America," suggests again the crucial role that the Vietnam War has played in galvanizing and radicalizing the thinking of the New Left. Much of that part of the pamphlet that is not printed here draws a parallel between the decades of struggle the Vietnamese people waged first against the French colonial regime and now the American regime, and the struggle going on in Latin America. As Ché Guevara said in 1967, there must be "two, three, many Vietnams."

For several years we have been winning the war in Vietnam, according to our government, and in the last decade we have been winning the war against bandits and revolutionaries in Latin America. In 1966, Weissman and Gerassi note, President Johnson could cry jubilantly, "We're winning militarily in Vietnam." In the same year, Secretary of Defense Robert McNamara took pride in the fact that "U.S.-trained units of Venezuela's armed forces and police have spearheaded a government campaign both in the cities and in the countryside . . . U.S.-trained and supported Peruvian army and air force units have played prominent roles in this counter-guerrilla campaign. In Colombia, U.S. training, support, and equipment, including several medium helicopters, have materially aided the Colombia armed forces to establish government control in the rural insurgent areas." Johnson's Assistant for National Security Affairs, Walt W. Rostow, felt confident a few months later that the "Romantic revolutionaries who have long disturbed world order are passing from the scene." He claimed they were being overtaken not only by United States troops on the ground, but more generally "by history and by increasingly pervasive attitudes of pragmatism and moderation." But only two months after Rostow's pronouncement, *The New York Times* could report that "an epidemic of guerrilla fighting is sweeping over Latin America." This fighting continues today, even as the Vietnam War does.

What do these two areas, Vietnam and Latin America, have in common, beyond the fact that both exhibit a depressing inability to fulfill the prophecies of American leaders? The New Left argues that they are both enduring the welfare imperialism of the United States, and this article presents that argument.

---

[1] Quoted in Herbert I. Schiller, *Mass Communications and American Empire* (New York: Augustus M. Kelley, 1969), p. 16.

1968

from THE VIETNAMIZATION
OF LATIN AMERICA [2]

Steve Weissman and John Gerassi

Of course, few Liberals support outright interventions. Most refuse to see themselves as supporters of imperialism. Some, who call themselves the sophisticated ones, accept the inevitability of a global "sphere of influence" dichotomy between the great powers. They refer to this inevitability as "the responsibility of power." But even they are well-intentioned and, like all well-intentioned Americans, claim that some good can come out of the evil imperialism. If only power is used wisely, argue these Liberals and Social Democrats, the poor can still profit from our richness. Thus, they wage campaigns against the shipment of arms to underdeveloped lands, insist that the U.S. instead send social aid. They want to export the New Deal, the welfare state. They are welfare imperialists.

But it is precisely these liberal commitments, precisely this welfare imperialism which creates the setting, sets up the conditions, and generates the attitudes for old-style military and economic imperialism. The best example is Vietnam, where, after the collapse of the French, the U.S. moved in not as a policeman but as a social worker. As John McDermott explained in *The Nation* (July 25, 1966):

> The Americans had influenced the choice of Diem in the first place. They gave technical and dollar support to a revamping of the entire Vietnamese educational system from elementary schools through the university and technical institute level. This included both teacher training and the rewriting of textbooks. They gave technical assistance in revising the banking and currency system and in framing general economic and monetary policies. The United States Operations Mission (USOM—the AID Mission) undertook planning and dollar support for the reconstruction and development of the entire Vietnamese transportation and communications network—railroads, canals, highways, civil aviation, coastal transport, radio and television, and the telephone system. They assisted in planning and executing the various agricultural programs, including crop diversification, land reclama-

---

2 Steve Weissman and John Gerassi, "The Vietnamization of Latin America," in Massimo Teodori, ed., *The New Left: A Documentary History* (Indianapolis, Ind.: Bobbs-Merrill, 1969), pp. 266–69. Originally published in pamphlet form by the North American Congress for Latin America in 1968. Reprinted by permission of Brandt & Brandt.

tion, land reform, agricultural extension and mass peasant regroupment (the Refugee Resettlement, Land Development, Agroville and later Strategic Hamlet Programs). Finally, they exerted extremely strong influence over the nation's two largest economic activities (exclusive of farming)—military operations and the import business.

Half a million U.S. soldiers have caused us to forget this earlier escalation. But military intervention was a natural follow-up. The U.S. aid apparatus had overwhelmed the Vietnamese government and destroyed its independence. American welfare imperialism had disrupted the Vietnamese economy, politics and culture. And the success—not the failure—of the U.S. development program set off such changes in Vietnamese society and institutions that the resulting social and political disorder overcame American efforts to establish stability. There was just no way for the peasantry to fit into the new U.S.-made society in Saigon. Hence from 1954 to 1961, while U.S. aid to Vietnam amounted to $1,544 million, only $42 million (less than 3 percent) went into rural projects (and at that, the figures include education and health from which the peasants did not really benefit).

The Vietnamese peasants, unable to partake in the high-consumption urban economy, became more and more isolated, more and more prone to reject the American way of life, hence more and more repressed. Thus, U.S. social democracy created an enemy out of a people who were generally unpolitical, uncommitted, and unsophisticated. What's more, the process was inevitable for even if America had wanted to help the peasantry, the mechanism for doing so simply didn't exist.

This is even truer in Latin America, where AID officials must work with and through an already established U.S. presence—American corporations, totally and naturally geared to meet the demands of urban consumers. Under such conditions, U.S. aid programs can only increase the gap between the urban consumer (including the so-called rising "middle sectors") and the poor, unintegrated campesinos, who generally make up the majority.

As that gap continues to widen, both American investors and U.S. AID expectantly focus more, for both profits and political showmanship, on visible returns. What has happened to public utilities is indicative. In Latin America, three North American firms—International Telephone and Telegraph, American and Foreign Power, and Brazilian Light, Power and Traction companies—have long exercised a virtual monopoly over all public utilities. In recent years, however, profits have dwindled while political costs have risen. Highly visible, dependent upon politically determined rates, and in direct daily contact with ordinary people, the public utilities became a natural target for nationalists. As a result, the companies felt reluctant to invest money on new equipment and instead began to withdraw.

With the Alliance for Progress, this withdrawal was speeded up. The three companies ended up with over $1 billion of Alliance funds, investing much of it into higher paying sectors of the economy. In Argentina, for example, AMFORP poured its sell-out wealth into consumer industry, in housing (with the Rockefeller-owned IBEC), and in money-lending (at 18 percent on 90 to 180 day notes). Meanwhile, their poorly equipped, overpriced, costly-to-operate facilities became the property of the local governments, turning them into symbols of the inefficiency of government involvement in the economy. Whereas, one of the industrial investments, the PASA Petroleum complex, which was made possible only through an Alliance for Progress "extended risk guarantee" loan by the Agency for International Development, became "the largest privately financed project in a developing country. It is important to the future of private enterprise in Argentina, and to the United States, that it not fail" (Hearings on Foreign Assistance, 1964).

It certainly is important to the U.S.—and to private enterprise in Argentina. But it is not important, on the contrary it is another form of subjugation, to the poor of Argentina. That project will increase the poverty of the population of such provinces as Salta and Tucumán. There, where the poor don't have cars or oil heaters or factories to work in, petroleum products are meaningless. The project itself will augment their isolation. Like the peasants of Vietnam, the disenfranchized sugar growers of Salta will learn to view the city, the bureaucrats, and eventually the Americans as their enemy. They will join Ché Guevara in revolution.

They will do so anyway because no social democratic or liberal government, no local oligarchy or local entrepreneur class can cope with the problems of the poor. Their profit-oriented or pay-as-you-go type of structure, no matter how well-meaning, does not embody the mechanism capable of dealing with lower classes. Rebellion therefore becomes natural. With the U.S. involved on the side of modernization, i.e., the establishment, the poor's fight necessarily becomes long and costly. Yet it all started with well-meaning liberals who wanted to help, who looked upon Food for Peace as altruistic, upon Foundation help as generous, upon church group volunteers as dedicated, upon civic action programs as forward looking, upon academic "objective" research programs as constructive.

In Vietnam it is now too late. If the U.S. aggression there is to end, it will be only because the Vietnamese people will have forced the U.S. to get out. Well-motivated Americans now oppose that aggression. But it started in 1954. Such Americans should have opposed U.S. aid then. Instead, they tried to turn Diem into a nationalist. They campaigned for social measures. They argued for elections. They still argue for free elections. Such is the stuff from which empires are born.

Unlike Vietnam, the initial and overriding U.S. interest in Latin America has been clearly economic: $9 billion of U.S.-owned direct investment plus markets and raw materials have consistently proved persuasive in the formulation of official policy. Nonetheless, the Alliance for Progress has produced a Vietnam-like increase in the day-to-day administrative involvement in Latin America. The Food for Peace program has given the United States control of vast sums of local currencies, and the forthcoming War on Hunger promises a direct involvement in agriculture. AID has brought U.S. government and university personnel into advisory and administrative posts in local housing programs, agricultural programs, labor departments, industrial investment and trade union activities, education, communications, transportation, health and sanitation, community development, social welfare, and police training programs. The Department of Agriculture, the Housing and Home Financing

Agency, the Social Security Administration, the Internal Revenue Service, and literally hundreds of other government agencies engage in training programs for Latin Americans here in the United States and in long- and short-term on-the-spot advisory capacities within the Latin American bureaucracies. The government also cooperates closely with the work of private agencies such as the National Catholic Welfare Conference, the National Council of Churches (Division of Foreign Missions), the Evangelical Foreign Ministers Association, the National Council of Jewish Women, the Cooperative League of the United States of America, the Carnegie Corporations, the Ford Foundation, and the Rockefeller Foundation.

As in the case of Vietnam, most of these activities are undertaken with an ostensible concern for the political and economic development of Latin America. At their best, however, they bolster North American influence and control over the every-day decision-making of the Latin Republics, render policy-making literally irresponsible to the majority of Latin Americans (even where there are elections), perpetuate a colonial mentality among Latin Americans, and impose North American models of development where they are probably not relevant. At their worst, which is all too often the case, these programs directly serve the priorities of North American corporations and military counter-insurgency programs. And, regardless of their day-to-day impact within Latin America, the public commitment to economic development has rationalized increased economic intervention (e.g. the Hicklenlooper Amendment, the Investment Guarantee Treaties, etc.) and increased support for military imposed stability.

From the perspective of Vietnam, this new pattern of "Welfare Imperialism" implies that the escalation of U.S. involvement in Latin America will not always be as sudden and clear as in the Dominican Republic, but rather as a slow series of new programs, often in the name of liberal-supported foreign aid. It is these programs that radicals must oppose.

In Chapter 4 we will examine the role of social scientists and universities in carrying out the policies of government and business abroad. But it might be pertinent at this point to quote one statement that indicates what the radicals feel they must oppose. This quotation comes from a publication of an independent research organization that is closely tied to the military and that utilizes (and pays well for) the talents of academic social scientists: the American Institutes for Research.

The struggle between an established government and subversive or insurgent forces involves three different types of operations. The first is to make inputs into the social system that will gain the active support of an ever-increasing proportion of the local population. Threats, promises, ideological appeals, and tangible benefits are the kinds of inputs that are most frequently used. The second is to reduce or interdict the flow of competing inputs being made by the opposing side by installing anti-infiltration devices, cutting communication lines, *assassinating key spokesmen,* strengthening retaliatory mechanisms, and similar preventive measures. The third is to counteract or neutralize the political successes already achieved by groups committed to the "wrong" side. This typically involves direct military confrontation. *The social scientist can make significant contributions to the design of all three types of operations.*[3]

The phrase "welfare imperialism" connotes unmistakable (and presumably intended) disapproval of the liberal stance toward the welfare state in the United States. In fact, one pamphlet of the New Left is entitled "Domestic Imperialism," and it regards the black and the poor in our own society as subject to the same exploitative forces as the underdeveloped nations. This is why the New Left is so dubious about such programs as black capitalism; the blacks will be inevitably controlled by the white business framework in which they operate, just as the Latin American businessmen are.

But what about investments? Even if the infrastructure is controlled by United States business interests, as Weissman and Gerassi argue, the United States does provide capital for the development of Latin American countries, and in addition it risks having its investments nationalized. Surely this demonstrates our generosity. Not so, say Weissman and Gerassi: Latin America is saddled with debts while our businessmen make huge profits.

1968

from THE VIETNAMIZATION
OF LATIN AMERICA[4]

Steve Weissman and John Gerassi

The [Latin American] continent as a whole must use from 30 to 40 percent of its foreign earnings to pay off interest and service charges, *not the principal,* on loans to the industrialized world, mostly the United States. The Alliance for

---

3 American Institutes for Research, *Counter-Insurgency in Thailand,* December 1967, p. 1, quoted by Joseph Jorgensen and Eric Wolf in "Anthropology on the Warpath: An Exchange," *New York Review of Books,* 16:6 (April 8, 1971), p. 45. Emphasis added by Jorgensen and Wolf.
4 Weissman and Gerassi, *op. cit.,* pp. 264–66.

Progress claims that it is helping Latin America industrialize on a social progress basis. Now more than six years old, it has chalked up remarkable successes: right-wing coups in Argentina, Brazil, Honduras, Guatemala, Ecuador, the Dominican Republic, and Salvador. In exchange, U.S. businessmen have remitted to the U.S. $5 billion of profits while investing less than $2 billion. And the Alliance itself, which is supposed to lend money for strictly social progress projects, has kept 86 percent of its outlay to credits for U.S.-made goods, credits which are guaranteed by Latin American governments and are repayable in dollars.

Interventionist and imperialist policies of the United States in Latin America are now successfully in the third stage. Not only does the United States control Latin America's sources of raw material, not only does it control its markets for American manufactured goods, but it also controls the internal money economy altogether. Karl Marx had once warned that the first revolutionary wave in an imperialized country will come about as the result of frustration by the national bourgeoisie, which will have reached a development stage where it will have accumulated enough capital to want to become competitive to the imperializing corporations. This was not allowed to happen in Latin America.

As American corporations became acutely plagued by surplus goods, they realized that they must expand their markets in underdeveloped countries. To do so, however, they would have to help develop a national bourgeoisie which could purchase these goods. This "national" bourgeoisie, as all such classes in colonialized countries, had to be created by the service industries, yet somehow limited so that it did not become economically independent. The solution was simple. The American corporations, having set up assembly plants in São Paulo or Buenos Aires, which they called Brazilian or Argentinian corporations, decided to actually help create the subsidiary industries—with local money—themselves

Take GM, for example. First, it brought down its cars in various pieces called parts (thus eliminating import duties). Then it assembled them in São Paulo and called them Brazil-made. Next it shopped around for local entrepreneurs to launch the subsidiary industries—seat covers, spark plugs, etc. Normally, the landed oligarchy and entrepreneurs in the area would do its own investing in those subsidiary industries, and having successfully amassed large amounts of capital, would bind together to create their own car industry. It was this step that had to be avoided. Thus General Motors first offered these local entrepreneurs contracts by which it helped finance the servicing industries. Then it brought the entrepreneurs' capital into huge holding corporations which, in turn, it rigidly controlled. The holding corporations became very successful, making the entrepreneurs happy, and everyone forgot about a local, competitive car industry, making GM happy.

This procedure is best employed by IBEC, Rockefeller's mammoth investing corporation in Latin America. IBEC claims to be locally owned by Latin Americans since it does not hold controlling interest. But the 25 to 45 percent held by Standard Oil (it varies from Colombia to Venezuela to Peru) is not offset by the thousands of individual Latin investors, who, to set policy, would all have to agree among themselves and then vote in a bloc. When one corporation owns 45 percent while thousands of individual investors split the other 55 percent, the corporation sets policy—in the U.S. as well as abroad. Besides, IBEC is so successful that the local entrepreneurs "think American" even before IBEC does. In any case, the result of these holding corporations is that the national bourgeoisie in Latin America has been eliminated. It is an American bourgeoisie.

IBEC and other holding corporations use their combined local-U.S. capital to invest in all sorts of profitable ventures, from supermarkets to assembly plants. Naturally, these new corporations are set up where they can bring the most return. IBEC is not going to build a supermarket in the Venezuelan province of Falcón, where the population lives outside the money economy altogether and hence could not buy goods at the supermarket anyway. Nor would IBEC build a supermarket in Falcón because there are no roads leading there. The creation of IBEC subsidiaries in no way helps develop the infrastructure of the country.

Since such holding corporations as IBEC have their tentacles in every region of the economy, they control the money market as well (which is why U.S. corporations backed, indeed pushed, the formation of a Latin American common market at the 1967 Punta del Este Conference. Such a common market would eliminate duties on American goods assembled in Latin America and being exported from one Latin American country to another). Hence no new American investment needs to be brought down even for the 45 percent of the holding corporations. A new American investment in Latin America today is a paper investment. The new corporation is set up with local funds, which only drains the local capital reserves. And the result is an industry benefiting only those sectors which purchase American surplus goods.

Having so tied up the local economic elites, the U.S. rarely needs to intervene with marines to guarantee friendly governments. The local military, bought by the American-national interests, guarantees friendly regimes— with the approval of the local press, the local legal political parties, the local cultural centers, all of which the local money controls. And the local money is now tightly linked to American interests.

As one might expect, the economic aspects of imperialism are complicated. The following selection on Brazil deals with them in more detail. The subject does not lend itself to easy exposition, so the article is not particularly graceful, but it presents the kind of material that makes the charge of imperialism so easy for the radicals to make.

1964

ON THE MECHANISMS OF IMPERIALISM:
THE CASE OF BRAZIL[5]

Andrew Gunder Frank

The flow of capital from Brazil to the United States

It is widely believed that the United States and other developed capitalist countries contribute more capital to the underdeveloped countries than they receive from them. Nonetheless, all available statistics, including those compiled by the official agencies of the developed countries themselves, show precisely the opposite. Between 1947 and 1960, the flow of investment funds on private capital account from the United States to Brazil was $1,814 million while the capital flow of amortization, profits, royalties, interest and other transfers from Brazil to the United States totaled $3,481 million. For the seven largest Latin American countries (Argentina, Brazil, Chile, Peru, Venezuela, Colombia, Mexico), the United States Department of Commerce's conservatively calculated figures for the years 1950 to 1961 indicate $2,962 million of investment flows on private account out of the United States and remittances of profits and interest of $6,875 million; adding in American public loans and their Latin American servicing between the same years still leaves a conservatively calculated net capital flow of $2,081 million *to* the United States.

My present purpose, however, is not to dwell further on the amount of this capital transfer from Brazil and other countries to the United States. Instead it is proposed to inquire into some of the reasons for and sources of this, for Brazil and others, so prejudicial capital flow. When the facts finally force American business, political, and unfortunately also academic, spokesmen for American capital to admit the existence of this capital flow from the poor underdeveloped countries to the rich developed ones, they often try to defend it in the following terms: Either it is said that the direction of the flow is the result of the accidental or deliberate choice of a year or set of years in which the return flow on past investment happens to be greater than the outflow of new investment; or it is said instead (and sometimes in addition) that this

5 Andrew Gunder Frank, "On the Mechanisms of Imperialism: The Case of Brazil," *Monthly Review*, September 1964, pp. 285–97. Reprinted by permission of Monthly Review Press. Copyright © 1964 by Monthly Review, Inc.

drainage of capital from the poor underdeveloped countries really helps them to develop and that it is normal and logical that the capital flow into the investing and lending country—in this case into the United States—should be greater than the capital flow out of it because, after all, profits and interest legitimately earned abroad must be added to the amortization and repayment of the original investment.

The facts of economic life completely vitiate this American logic. If the disparity between capital inflow from and outflow to Brazil is as normal and legitimate as its defenders claim, then why is it that according to the late President John F. Kennedy the capital inflow to the United States from the underdeveloped countries in 1960 was $1,300 million and the capital outflow from the United States to the same countries $200 million, while in respect to the advanced countries of Western Europe the outflow from the United States ($1,500 million) exceeded the inflow ($1,000 million) by a wide margin? (Cited in *O Estado de São Paulo*, April 12, 1963.) Why does *U.S. News & World Report* (December 25, 1961), using Department of Commerce data, find the same pattern to obtain for the five-year period 1956–1961, that is, a ratio of inflow to the United States to outflow from the United States of 147 percent for Latin America, 164 percent for the underdeveloped world as a whole, and 43 percent for Western Europe? To eliminate still further the possibility that this disparity may be due to accidentally comparing years of low current outflow and high return flow of previous outflows, we may add up (as the Department of Commerce never does) the officially registered capital flows into and out of the United States for each year from 1950 to 1961 as reported in the *Survey of Current Business* and find that the total capital outflow is $13,708 million and the "corresponding" inflow $23,204 million, or an inflow/outflow ratio of 177 percent.* Are we to believe that it is normal and legitimate that profits and interest earned by the United States in weak underdeveloped countries are very much greater than in the strong developed ones, the United States included?

The disparity between capital inflows and outflows is more realistically explained by examining, as I propose to do in the paragraphs following, the source and composition of these flows than by appeal to any simplistic theories. In the first place, the argument that it is only logical for capital inflows to the United States to exceed outflows because, after all, the latter must earn a profit is premised on the unstated but erroneous assumption that official capital inflows into the United States are earnings on capital the United States previously sent abroad. As a matter of fact, much of the capital on which Americans "earn" profits in Brazil is Brazilian in origin and American only in ownership, control, and earnings. The Brazilian origins of "American" capital are manifold. We here take note of only those which fall under the titles of loans, concessions, and foreign exchange privileges.†

---

* These totals can be computed from the following issues of the *Survey of Current Business:* November 1954, pp. 9, 13; August 1955, pp. 18, 20; August 1957, p. 25; August 1959, p. 31; August 1961, pp. 22, 23; August 1962, pp. 22, 23.
† The reader should note that the author thus omits entirely the largest single source, namely, the plowing back of profits by American branches and subsidiaries of a large part of the profits realized on their Brazilian operations.—The Editors [of *Monthly Review*]

Direct loans from the government's Bank of Brazil to American firms and to mixed American-Brazilian consortia are common in industry, commerce, and agriculture. The two giant American world-wide cotton merchants, SANBRA and Anderson & Clayton, in 1961 received $54 billion cruzeiros in loans from the Bank of Brazil, or 47 percent of that bank's entire agricultural and industrial loan portfolio (reported by Congressman Jacob Frantz in Congressional debate and cited in *Semanario*, May 30–June 6, 1963). By re-loaning this money (at higher interest rates of course) to wholesalers and producers of cotton whom they thereby control; by buying up harvested stocks, storing them in government-provided bins, and speculating with them later; by monopolizing important sectors of organization and distribution—these American firms use *Brazilian* capital to control much of the Brazilian domestic and export cotton market (as they also do that of many other countries) and to ship the profits therefrom home to the United States. Swift, Armour, and Wilson (recently involved in a public scandal for having partly exported and partly held back for a higher price the meat consigned to them by the government for storage and sale to the public), the A. & P.'s sudsidiary American Coffee Company, and other American monopolies similarly derive fat profits from using Brazilian capital to monopolize critical sectors of the domestic and export markets. American banks like the ubiquitous National City Bank of New York, insurance companies, and other financial institutions evidently work almost entirely with Brazilian capital, loan much of it to American non-financial firms in Brazil, and then serve as a channel to send their own and others' profits on this Brazilian capital "back" home.

In the public utility sector especially, the ownership and earnings of so-called American capital are based, not on original investment of capital, but on concessions, exorbitant use rates, and other privileges. The capital is provided by Brazil. The São Paulo Light Co. (now merged with the Rio Light, Rio Gas, Brazilian Telephone, and other companies in the Brazilian Traction Co.) in 1907 took over a concession already granted to two Brazilian individuals until 1950 and then got it extended to 1990. By engaging an ex-President as its lawyer to fight a legal battle through several courts up to the Supreme Court— still staffed by the ex-President's appointees—the company in 1923, contrary to the stipulations of its contract, obtained an extension of the concession for its telephone subsidiary. Later the concession of the gas subsidiary was also extended. For its starting capital the São Paulo Light issued bonds for $6 million. It then took over the already existing streetcars and associated properties. Following the usual procedure, the various light companies financed expansion of service to new areas by assessments on, and more recently by loans from, the communities to be served, while equipment was purchased out of earnings from exorbitant public utility rates. Even so, as any user can testify, service always lags far behind demand (electricity rationing is now normal in Rio and sometimes reaches blackouts of five hours daily). Through political influence and bribery, the company managed to delay the construction of competing facilities for 15 years at one site. In 1948 the company received $90 million in loans from the International Bank for which it obtained a guarantee from the Brazilian government. Part of this foreign exchange was used, of course, not to import new equipment, but to convert cruzeiro earnings into dollars for remittance to the United States. To avoid showing exorbitant profits, the company increased its registered capital base by issuing stock dividends to its owners. Between 1918 and 1947, Brazilian Traction made profits of $550 million of which $165 million were sent home. Now that public utilities have become unprofitable relative to other industries and that the Brazilian government wants to take them over in order to permit the expansion of needed service, the American owners bring all possible diplomatic and other pressure to bear in usually successful attempts to obtain once again the remaining equipment's value several times over through "expropriation." (Sources: Paulo F. Alves Pinto, *Antologia Nacionalista*, vol. 2, cited in Barbosa Lima Sobrinho, *Maquinas para transformar cruzeiros em dolares* and Sylvio Monteiro, *Camo Atua o imperialismo ianque?*)

Addressing the Brazilian Senate in 1953, President Vargas' Treasury Minister said, "I have to declare that foreign capital ... demands guarantees to enter the country, greater guarantees to remain in it, and still greater ones to withdraw from it. Therefore, it does not seem desirable for any country and still less for Brazil." (Quoted in Osny Duarte Perira, *Quem faz as leis no Brasil?*, p. 97.) After the establishment of a state petroleum company and threatening to do the same with electric power, the government of Vargas was, owing to foreign and domestic pressure, replaced by one which proposed the "creation of a climate favorable for the investment of foreign capital in the country." To this end the Superintendency of Money and Credit (SUMOC) issued Instruction 113 according to which, in the words of the President of the Federation of Industries of the State of São Paulo, "foreign firms can bring their entire equipment in at the free market price ... national ones, however, have to do so through exchange licenses established in import categories. In this way there was created veritable discrimination against national industry. We do not plead for preferential treatment but for equal opportunities." (Quoted in Jocelyn Brasil, *O Pao, O Feijao, e as Forcas Ocultas*, p. 185.) Moreover, foreign firms were permitted to import used equipment (often already depreciated for tax purposes at home), while Brazilians could import only new machinery. As a result, Brazilians, who on this basis were unable to compete with foreign firms and/or who were unable to get assignments of foreign exchange from the Central Bank, were forced to combine with non-Brazilians who, though they might not contribute much of any capital to the common enterprise, could contribute and capitalize on special privileges as foreigners. Ten years after Vargas, President Goulart was still forced to observe (*O Semanario*, September 26, 1963): "In fact it is incomprehensible—and much less justifiable—that in this time of renewed heavy burden for the people, innumerable superfluous or easily dispensable products which are consumed mainly by the richer classes continue to enjoy the benefits of an exchange rate of 475 cruzeiros [the market rate was then 800 cruzeiros]. The same exchange rate as for petroleum products and other basic goods is enjoyed by extract of whisky and of Coca-Cola.... The disappearance of our scarce foreign exchange resources occurs not only through imports. The concession of exchange privileges to remit foreign exchange destined for the payment of unessential services causes the same harmful effects to our balance of payments." It is worthy of note that, "fascist" or "communizing" or not, as

Presidents Vargas and Goulart respectively have been termed by the foreign press, the effective power of these Presidents was evidently insufficient to combat the forces, inside and outside their own governments, which benefit from and fight to maintain those privileges which accrue to small but powerful foreign and domestic interests at the cost of national development. There are, of course, influential Brazilian interests which willingly cooperate in this provision of Brazilian national capital to American firms so long as, in association with this powerful ally from the North, they can participate in some of the spoils.

Effects on Brazilian economic and industrial structure

Spokesmen for the supposed advantages for Brazil of American investment often claim that the distribution of American investments and loans among productive sectors in the receiving country contributes to that country's economic development, and that the resulting import substitution is converting the Brazilian economy into one capable of self-sustained overall economic growth. The facts support neither of these contentions.

We have already noted in part what kind of contribution American-owned, *but not supplied,* capital makes to Brazilian development in the trade and public utilities sectors which, according to the Department of Commerce, absorb 43 percent of the total. Of the 791 American firms in Brazil in 1960, we must certainly call into question the allegedly essential contribution to the development of its economy made by the 125 import, export, and other commercial houses; the banking, insurance, real estate, and other financial institutions, which are 64 in number; petroleum distribution (by the world-wide petroleum monopoly of notorious fame); retailing (such as Sears and Roebuck which outside the United States is a luxury chain); and publishing, advertising, hotels, cinema, and other services (including towel supply), which account for 77 more dubious contributions to a solid basis for Brazilian economic development (Barbosa Lima Sobrinho citing Editora Banas, in *Semanario,* September 26, 1963). Coca-Cola at least built or equipped a manufacturing plant.

As for the 54 percent of American capital which the Department of Commerce attributes to manufacturing, no detailed breakdown is given. In 1959, light consumer-goods industry accounted for 48 percent of foreign, including American, manufacturing in Brazil, of which approximately 20 percent was in the food and beverage sector, including 17 bottling and ice cream firms (Editora Banas, *Capital extranjero no Brasil*). Even the 40 percent of United States investment which the Department of Commerce attributes to basic industry is not telling. To serve as a base for self-sustained industrialization and growth, investment must, all will agree, produce the materials and equipment—steel, machinery, trucks, tractors—necessary for expanded production. But the bulk of this investment is in the automotive industry, and there it does not produce primarily trucks and tractors which are needed for development purposes but which are not immediately profitable; rather, it seeks maximum profits in the production of passenger cars for the high-income market.

In general, then, American enterprises in Brazil tend to produce non-essentials, and they do so largely with Brazilian capital.

But this is not all. The composition of foreign investment and its effects on the structure of the Brazilian economy are crucial to the maintenance of underdevelopment there. It is often claimed that American investment in Brazil results in import substitution which creates Brazilian capacity for autonomously directed and self-sustained economic development. Examining only American investment in the most basic sectors, we find, unfortunately, that the facts demonstrate largely the opposite. It is characteristic of American investment in Brazil and elsewhere that the giant investing corporations set up only a part of a particular productive process abroad and keep a critical, though it may be a smaller, part under their immediate control at home. The archetype of this arrangement is the Brazilian assembly plant of an American corporation which is made to depend on the import from the parent corporation of the basic equipment needed, later of its spare parts and replacements, often of critical components, especially the highly tooled ones, of critical basic materials, associated patents, technicians, transport, insurance, and above all, of the technical and organizational schema of the productive process.* Significantly, this arrangement also serves to eliminate any existing or potential Brazilian markets for inventive engineering and ties Brazilian technological development to the American economic structure; the reason is, of course, that the solutions to technical problems are already engineered into the productive process in the United States and are exported to Brazil in the form of the technological organization established there.

The Brazilian economy is tied still further to the stronger American economy when American interests "cooperate" with Brazilian capital in joint enterprises, or when American firms farm out part of the productive process to local suppliers of components. While the propaganda has it that the United States is stimulating private enterprise and economic development, the reality is that American corporations use Brazilian capital for their own purposes, transferring part of the risk and cost of demand fluctuations to the local supplier, channeling Brazilian capital into the provision of goods and services which maximize the American corporations' profits, and binding the Brazilian economy increasingly to themselves in particular and the American economy in general. Moreover, American influence thus increases not only in the Brazilian economy but also in Brazilian political life; and, interestingly, in view of the claims about import substitution, this process results in increasing American determination of the composition even of Brazilian imports. Brazilian exports, of course, have been largely in American hands. Thus, what to Americans may appear as "the natural process of import substitution" appears to Brazilians, other than those directly cooperating in the process, as what it is: the progressive domination of the Brazilian economy and the strangulation of its capacity for national development.

The problem of imports is compounded by that of exports which are not keeping pace. The United Nations Economic Commission for Latin America

---

* Much the same pattern was noted and criticized by the American observer John Gerassi (*The Great Fear*, 1963) in Latin American petroleum, mining, steel, automotive, machine building, and other industries.

(ECLA) notes that, subtracting petroleum, Latin American exports have risen only 40 percent since 1938, while world trade has doubled and the trade of the developed countries has tripled. ECLA notes further, "that the deterioration of Latin America in world trade is one of the most important points of strangulation of its economic and social development." (*Jornal do Brasil,* January 22, 1964.) Add to this the drain of capital out of Brazil and the misuses of its own resources engendered by foreign investment, and the result is Brazil's chronic balance of payments deficit. Now come the foreign loans.

These loans, we are asked to believe, are also development-producing. The fact is that to an increasing extent they are deposited in New York banks to cover the dollar needs of Americans in Brazil. As Simon Hanson has repeatedly pointed out in his *Latin American Letter* (for American businessmen) and in *Inter-American Economic Affairs* (Summer 1962), Alliance for Progress dollars are destined to serve as the source of the foreign exchange needed by Brazil to buy out American-owned (but as we saw, not supplied) capital in Brazilian public utilities, and to pay for imported equipment, materials, technicians, and service "needs" that (as we also saw above) American corporations have built into the Brazilian economy's underdeveloped structure. As these loans come with economic and political strings attached, Brazil thus loses control of critical sectors of her economy to foreign interests on foreign investment, domestic production, export, import, and loan accounts. These levers of control integrate the weaker Brazilian economy ever more into the stronger American economy, render the oligarchic Brazilian allies of American interests ever more dependent on the United States, and structure *under-development* all the more firmly into the very foundations of Brazilian society.

Beyond these considerations, some observations about recent features of American aid in Brazil may be illuminating. It is well to note that, though included in the dollar totals of aid, loans under Public Law 480, euphemistically called "Food for Peace," do not supply a single dollar but consist rather of cruzeiros derived from the sale in Brazil of American surplus wheat which, like all other "dumping," competes unfairly with and inhibits the development of Brazilian wheat production.

The major American-financed capital project in Brazil, the Volta Redonda steel mill, was, in fact, built by the United States during the Second World War to provide steel in Brazil for the United States' own wartime needs: Brazilians have been paying for the mill ever since. As for the much heralded aid for the development of the "depressed Northeast," the governor of one of its states has publicly pointed out that with a population of 25 million and one of the world's lowest standards of living, this area received $13 million from the Alliance for Progress while the state of Guanabara (including the city of Rio de Janeiro) with 4 million inhabitants and the highest per capita income among Brazil's 22 states was allocated $71 million. The governor of this latter state, it just so happens, is the presidential candidate of the ultra-right economic interests, the Brazilian Barry Goldwater, who spends his American-supplied dollars on parkways marked "works of the government of Carlos Lacerda" and on other projects such as forcing slum dwellers to move out to "John Kennedy village" located 20 miles out of town, while burning down their houses in the center of town to make room for a new tourist hotel. That's development!

Underdevelopment, industrialization, and foreign investment

Finally we may briefly broach what is undoubtedly the most difficult but the most important matter of all, the economic history of underdevelopment and development, and the role of foreign trade and investment therein. The events in this history which are critical for the understanding of the problems under discussion are universally known albeit all-too-conveniently forgotten in certain circles.

The expansion of metropolitan mercantilism and capitalism to Latin America, Africa, and Asia wrought the destruction of productive and viable agricultural and also industrial economies on these continents and most notoriously in Mexico, Peru, West and East Africa, and India. Arriving mostly by force of arms and establishing alliances in these societies (and in newly established ones such as Brazil) with old and newly created exploitative oligarchies, the metropolitan economies reduced the large bulk of the world's people to levels of abject poverty that they had never suffered at the hands of their previous own or foreign masters. In our times, it has become fashionable to call these societies "underdeveloped," as though they have always been this way. The developing metropolitan powers pillaged the peoples in these political and economic colonies of capital which they used to industrialize their own economies. By incorporating them into what is now known euphemistically as the world market, they converted these now *underdeveloping* economies into appendages of their own. As we have seen above, this process continues unabated in our day.

Lest it be thought that the United States is only a newcomer to this exploitative process which produces development for some at the expense of underdevelopment for others, it is well to remember that the initial industrial capital of the Northeastern United States was derived largely from the slave trade and from the products of Southern slavery. Though the forms have been modernized, the content and the effects of the expansion of capitalism in contemporary times remain essentially what they always have been; the level of living of the majority of the people is still *falling*. The United Nations Food and Agricultural Organization (FAO) supplies part of the evidence. Taking per capita food production in 1934–1938 as 100, in the three crop years 1959/60, 1960/61, and 1961/62, it was 99, 100, and 98 in Latin America, Africa, and Asia (excluding the socialist countries) respectively; while it was 113 for the world as a whole, and 145 for the countries universally known for the failure of their agriculture, the Soviet Union and Eastern Europe (FAO, *The World State of Agriculture and Nutrition*, 1962, p. 15 of the Spanish edition). But these figures tell only part of the story. The other part lies in the combination of low or negative economic growth rates with the increasing *inequality* of the distribution of income in countries for which estimates are available, such as Brazil, Argentina, Mexico, and India. The result is that while foreign and domestic exploiters enrich themselves, the masses of the people in the underdeveloping countries are suffering an absolute decline in their per capita incomes.

This article has been an attempt to report on a few of the mechanisms of imperialist exploitation of underdeveloped countries. It is not, and is not intended to be, a substitute for inquiry into the structure and transformation of the imperialist system. But even these structurally derived mechanisms of imperialism in action, though no doubt familiar to practicing imperialist and allied businessmen and diplomats, are all too unfamiliar to many of those who would combat imperialism. Yet an understanding of contemporary imperialism in action is essential to the theoretical base necessary for any successful struggle against the system. And there are many more such mechanisms of imperialism in action. (Hamza Alavi has recently reported on some others in his "U.S. Aid to Pakistan," *Economic Weekly*, Bombay, Special Number July, 1963, reprinted in French as "Pakistan: le fardeau de l'aide americaine" in *Revolution*, Paris.) But even where reports of economic mechanisms of imperialism exist, they are usually studies of individual firms, industries, incidents, etc. Not only do these make tedious, if necessary, reading, as those who have followed this report this far will have found out; but in the absence of more inclusive and quantitative information on such matters as real profit rates and totals, concessions, financial control, imperialist-nationalist joint ventures, etc., we can reach only a very inadequate understanding of even these mechanisms of imperialism. It is hoped, therefore, that students in the underdeveloped countries, as well as in underdeveloped regions and sectors of the industrialized nations, will increasingly report on the hard facts of imperialism.

The hard facts of imperialism are increasingly reported. The 1960's saw publication of the second edition of Marxist Paul Baran's *The Political Economy of Growth*, Harry Magdoff's *The Age of Imperialism*, and more popular expositions such as David Horowitz's *Free World Colossus* and Carl Oglesby and Richard Shaull's *Containment and Change*.[6] The New Left reads. For them, the arguments about the small financial stake the United States has in underdeveloped areas, the capital we generously export, the infrastructures we are building, our humanitarian Food for Peace

6 See Paul Baran, *The Political Economy of Growth*, 2nd ed. (New York: Monthly Review Press, Monthly Review Paperbacks, 1968); Harry Magdoff, *The Age of Imperialism* (New York: Monthly Review Press, 1969); David Horowitz, *Free World Colossus* (New York: Hill & Wang, 1965) and *Containment and Revolution* (Boston: Beacon Press, 1968); Carl Oglesby and Richard Shaull, *Containment and Change* (New York: Macmillan, 1962). See also William Appleman Williams, *The Tragedy of American Diplomacy*, rev. ed. (New York: Delta/Del, 1962), and *Roots of the Modern American Empire* (New York: Random House, 1969).

program (recently found by a Senate committee to be a cover for supplying military goods), and innovations such as the Peace Corps and the studies of land-tenure systems at major American universities are all a part of the massive misinformation propagated by corporations and government working hand in hand.

The moral justification of imperialism has a long and distinguished history. Magdoff notes that in the time of the Opium Wars, John Quincy Adams defended this effort in terms of "the moral obligation of commercial intercourse between nations." The Office of Naval Intelligence frankly titled a 1922 bulletin "The U.S. Navy as an Industrial Asset." Here are Magdoff's comments on the United States' foreign aid program.

1966

from ECONOMIC ASPECTS
OF U.S. IMPERIALISM [7]

Harry Magdoff

The interrelation between economic interests and foreign policy is seen more clearly by business-minded observers. Thus the former president and chairman of the World Bank, Eugene R. Black, informs us that "our foreign aid programs constitute a distinct benefit to American business. The three major benefits are: (1) Foreign aid provides a substantial and immediate market for U.S. goods and services. (2) Foreign aid stimulates the development of new overseas markets for U.S. companies. (3) Foreign aid orients national economies toward a free enterprise system in which U.S. firms can prosper." *

More specifically, an Assistant Secretary of Commerce for Economic Affairs explains to businessmen that "if these [military and economic] aid programs were discontinued, private investments might be a waste because it would not be safe enough for you to make them." †

---

[7] Harry Magdoff, "Economic Aspects of U.S. Imperialism," *Monthly Review*, November 1966, p. 4. The entire essay is included in Magdoff's *The Age of Imperialism* (New York: Monthly Review Press, 1969). Reprinted by permission of Monthly Review Press. Copyright © 1969 by Harry Magdoff.
* Eugene R. Black, *The Domestic Dividends of Foreign Aid* in *Columbia Journal of World Business*, Vol. 1, Fall 1965, p. 23.
† Address by Assistant Commerce Secretary Andrew F. Brimmer at a meeting of the Tax Foundation, Inc., as reported in the *New York Times*, December 5, 1965.

On a much more elevated plane, we are told by a specialist on international business practice, a teacher at MIT and Harvard: "It would seem that there is a horrible urgency in making Western economic concepts internationally viable if man's dignity is to be preserved—and incidentally, a profitable private business." *

And as an indication of how in fact some influential members of the business community see the "one-ness" of economic, political, and security interests, listen to the view expressed in 1965 by the Vice-president of Chase Manhattan Bank who supervises Far Eastern operations:

> In the past, foreign investors have been somewhat wary of the over-all political prospect for the [Southeast Asia] region. I must say, though, that the U.S. actions in Vietnam this year—which have demonstrated that the U.S. will continue to give effective protection to the free nations of the region—have considerably reassured both Asian and Western investors. In fact, I see some reason for hope that the same sort of economic growth may take place in the free economies of Asia that took place in Europe after the Truman Doctrine and after NATO provided a protective shield. The same thing also took place in Japan after the U.S. intervention in Korea removed investor doubts.†

Investor doubts have rarely been grave, except in occasional specific cases. Overseas investments are concerned with "moveable goods"—agricultural products, mining products, manufactures, and freight receipts. Magdoff arrives at a "conservative estimate," based on official figures, that the foreign market for locally owned and U.S.-owned foreign firms, rather than being a drop in the bucket compared to the output of American farms, factories, and mines, is actually equal to 40 percent of that output. (Furthermore, this figure understates the amount because it ignores the sales abroad of foreign firms operating under copyright and patent agreements arranged by American firms.) Exports may constitute only 6 percent of our GNP, but when we look closer at the foreign market for United States businesses in the area of moveable goods, we can see that we are talking about extensive economic interests with serious domestic consequences.

In 1964 foreign sources of earnings accounted for about 22 percent of domestic nonfinancial corporate profits (up from 10 percent in 1950). For various reasons, these figures are understated to a considerable extent. More important, these figures represent all nonfinancial corporations, not just those that operate abroad. Even so, the figure is quite substantial. Marxists and businessmen alike consider the steady growth of foreign investment and sales to be the result of the increasing relative saturation of the domestic market. Of course, the poor in the United States are not

* Richard D. Robinson, *International Business Policy*, New York, Holt, Rinehart and Winston, 1966, p. 220.
† *Economic Considerations in Foreign Relations—An Interview with Alfred Wentworth* in *Political*, Vol. 1, No. 1, July 1965, pp. 45–6.

saturated, but it is easier to expand sales to the affluent abroad, whether they live in Europe or Brazil, than to revise income distribution in the United States. Foreign sales by American-owned corporations have been increasing at twice the rate of domestic sales for well over a decade. Magdoff quotes the treasurer of General Electric, who was commenting on "the need that American business has to keep expanding its foreign operations":

> In this respect, I think business has reached a point in the road from which there is no turning back. American industry's marvelous technology and abundant capital resources have enabled us to produce the most remarkable run of peacetime prosperity in the nation's history. To keep this going, we have for several years sought additional outlets for these sources in foreign markets. For many companies, including General Electric, these offshore markets offer the most promising opportunities for expansion that we can see.[8]

The "additional outlets" for our "marvelous technology and abundant capital resources" have not been simply foreign markets. The favorable terms of trade we are used to need protection, and a strong military posture ensures that they will get it. Military sales are another outlet for business. This interdependence is seen most dramatically in the capital-goods industries. Magdoff used the input-output analysis of the U.S. economy for 1958 to measure the impact. For industries producing nonresidential investment goods, he calculated the proportion of output going into exports and the proportion going into purchases by the federal government, purchases that are almost entirely for military needs. In only one industry, that of farm machinery and equipment, did the combination of export and military demand come to less than 20 percent of the total output. At the other extreme, the military-oriented industries of ordnance and aircraft, the proportions were 88 and 93 percent, as might be expected. The striking finding, however, was that for the other twenty-one industries, the proportions were between 20 and 50 percent. This was the impact of export and military sales on the crucial capital-goods sector of the economy. For the radical, this statistic is one more estimate of the importance of imperialism in the United States business system. The figures for foreign investment and profits will undoubtedly turn out much higher during the 1960's, with the Vietnam War going on and the dependence on foreign markets rapidly increasing.

Here are Magdoff's conclusions.

---

8 Quoted in Magdoff, *op. cit.*, p. 12.

1966

from ECONOMIC ASPECTS OF U.S. IMPERIALISM[9]

Harry Magdoff

... (1) there are sound business reasons why investments flow in the direction they do and not in such ways as to meet the potential needs of this country—for example, to eliminate poverty, to provide the industry which would create equal opportunity to Negroes, to develop the underdeveloped regions of the United States, or to create adequate housing. More important, business cannot invest to accomplish these ends and at the same time meet its necessary standards of profit, growth, and security for invested capital. Exports of capital goods and military demand flowing to the capital-goods producers, on the other hand, are uniquely advantageous in that they strengthen and make more profitable the established investment structure; they also contribute to an expansion of the industries that are most harmonious with and most profitable for the existing composition of capital.

(2) The support given by foreign economic involvement—both military and civilian commodities—makes a singular contribution by acting as a bulwark against the slippage of minor recessions into major depressions. It has accomplished this by shoring up one of the strategic balance wheels of the economy, the production of investment-type equipment—by supplying, as we have seen, from 20 to 50 percent of the market for these goods.

(3) We need also to take into account that it is *monopolistic* industry which dominates the volume and flow of investment and that such monopolistic businesses characteristically gear their investment policies to the "sure thing," where good profits and safety of investment are reliably assured. Here the tie-in of government action and foreign policy is of paramount interest. The military-goods market usually has the decided advantage of supplying long-term contracts, often accompanied by enough guarantees to reduce and even eliminate any risk in building additional plant equipment, plant and equipment which may also be used for civilian purposes. In addition, military contracts pay for related research and development expenses, again removing risky aspects of normal investment programs. As for the foreign countries, the United States military presence, its foreign policy, and its national security commitments provide a valuable protective apparatus for the investments made in foreign markets. These foreign investments, together with the demand created by governmental foreign aid, contribute importantly to the demand

9 *Ibid.*, pp. 17–18.

for the exports of the capital-goods and other manufacturing industries. The confidence in the consistency of government foreign policy and its complementary military policy can, and surely must, act as a valuable frame of reference for the domestic as well as foreign investment practices of monopolistic business.

(4) The extra 20 to 50 percent of business provided by exports plus military demand ... provides a much greater percentage of the total profits of these firms.

In addition to its sheer profits (apparently made at the expense of local capital in the underdeveloped country), its search for new markets in both underdeveloped and developed countries, and its desire to even out domestic fluctuations, American business is vitally concerned with raw materials. In Latin America, Asia, and Africa, the majority of investment is in the extractive industries; some of these are concerned with vital materials without which the industrial engine would quickly falter and stop. According to the *Minerals Yearbook,* in 1963 the United States imported 94 percent of its manganese, 98 percent of its cobalt, 100 percent of its chromite, 86 percent of its nickel (which represented 35 percent of the world production), and 8 percent of its bauxite (31 percent of the world production). Heather Dean discusses this crucial need for raw materials as an explanation for United States imperialism.

1966

from SCARCE RESOURCES: THE DYNAMICS OF AMERICAN IMPERIALISM[10]

Heather Dean

US materials policy studies, 1950–1960

"Has the United States of America the material means to sustain its civilization?"

In 1952, the US President's Materials Policy Commission opened its report

10 Heather Dean, *Scarce Resources: The Dynamics of American Imperialism* (Detroit: The Radical Education Project, 1966), pp. 2–3, 5–9.

with this question. Its answer shattered forever the myth of Cornucopian natural resources on the North American continent, and introduced a new alarm into the consciousness of policy makers: the US depended on foreign sources for every significant industrial resource except molybdenum and magnesium.

The Commission, headed by William S. Paley,* hired a phalanx of experts to predict US demand for natural resources for the next 25 years, and to advise the President on legislation necessary to ensure that these resources would be available.

Its report is far from a dry compilation of statistics; its principal author seems to see himself as something of a philosopher-poet. In the introduction he reflects on the wry workings of fate, which makes materials a key factor in the struggle between the Spirit of Man and the Forces of Materialism. The report concluded that the materials would not be lacking. However, it found domestic reserves adequate to meet only a small and shrinking fraction of American needs.

The Third World is expected to supply the bulk of the raw materials used by US industry. In another burst of lyricism the Report details the mutual benefits to arise from this Free World division of labor. Each nation has its appointed role: that of the underdeveloped countries is to produce, that of the US is to consume. (It's highly reminiscent of the speeches on peaceful co-existence that the Russians keep delivering to the Chinese.) By selling to US markets, Third World nations will accumulate the capital necessary to finance their own industrialization. But this eventuality appears only in the rhetoric of the report. Their statistical projections do not allow for a significant increase in consumption of industrial raw materials in the underdeveloped countries.

In response to the Paley Report, defense stockpiling was undertaken on a massive scale to safeguard against such supply shortages as had occurred during the Korean War. Government subsidies (since largely discontinued) encouraged exploitation of inferior domestic ores in hopes of making technological breakthroughs. Government commissions were set up to give early warning of financial or political threats to foreign sources of defense materials.

Most important, and probably most successful, an organization was established with Ford Foundation money to refine and expand the work of the Paley Commission. "Resources for the Future" (RFF) was incorporated to do research, publish, and make policy recommendations. Paley was joined in its administration by such pillars of the American Establishment as George P. Brown,† Frank Pace,‡ and Laurance Rockefeller.§

The major publication of RFF is "Resources in America's Future." It is a massive collection of statistics and extrapolations that attempts to predict patterns of American consumption to the year 2000, allowing for substitutions, probable technological innovations, etc. In tone its publications seem to be

---

* Chairman of CBS and life trustee of Columbia University.
† United Shoe Machinery, Boston Herald-Traveller Corp., First National Bank of Boston, New England Tel & Tel, Old Colony Trust Co.
‡ Time, Inc., Colgate-Palmolive, Continental Oil, Banker's Trust, Eurofund, etc.
§ President, Rockefeller Brothers Fund, Rockefeller Brothers, Inc., etc.

one-half of a debate with Rachel Carson. One feels the presence of an unseen Conservationist Lobby proposing crimps in the style of the barons of the extractive industries, many of them on the board of RFF. This report, too, concludes that the raw materials America needs will be available. But for those of us to whom "America's interests" are not the whole spectrum of concern, the means by which this conclusion was reached are ominous. The introduction warns:

It should be pointed out clearly, however, that our conclusion that there is no general resource shortage problem for the balance of the century applies specifically to the United States; it cannot be extended automatically to other countries. In many less developed countries, especially in Asia, Africa and Latin America, population presses hard on available natural resources; for them a sustained increase in living levels can by no means be guaranteed with the assurance it can be for the United States and other more advanced industrial countries.

In plainer words, the surpluses of industrial raw materials which America expects to import from Asia, Africa, and Latin America are illusory. They would vanish from world markets if the intolerable stagnation of Third World economies were ended. To ensure their continued availability will require complete political and economic control of Third World countries—a control exercised against the most elemental interests of their populations.

. . .

Is there enough to go around?

With approximately 8% of the NCW [noncommunist world] population, the United States is presently planning to reserve for her own industries and her own consumption between 50% and 100% of the world's mineral resources. Her assurance that these resources will be available to her use is hard to explain. Even using the figures given for NCW demand, there would appear to be a bitter competition for resources imminent. And those figures are predicated upon continuing desperate poverty for one-half of the world.

NCW demand was calculated by assuming a growth rate of consumption of industrial raw materials of between 3% and 6%, most of it to come from Europe. To see these figures in proper perspective, consider the past history of developing nations.

United States. Between 1867 and 1905, steel production increased an average of 25% per annum. This average reflects even higher rates of increase in boom times, followed by severe depressions. After a period of stagnation, World War I sparked another surge in production of 15–20% per annum.

Japan. In arming for World War II, Japan increased her steel production from 2.5 million tons in 1932 to 8 million tons in 1943. Due to deliberate occupation policy, her steel-making capacity was reduced to 3 million tons until 1949. In 1964 she produced 40 million tons—an average rate of growth over 15 years of more than 10%.

. . .

What surpluses of raw materials would be available to the US if the UN undertook a development program designed to bring the Third World to the consumption level of a poor European country by the year 2000? (By which time the US GNP will have quadrupled.) The obvious pattern consumption would follow, from the examples above, would be far from a stately 3% of nothing increase per annum. For the first few years, reflecting the smallness of the base, production and consumption would increase by 50% to 300% per annum, and then settle to a steady 10% growth rate.

What will the year 2000 find in fact? Surely not the world predicted in the US studies, where half the world is swept with plagues and famines as they trudge out to the mines to dig up raw materials for an American affluence of science fiction proportions! The rate of development I have hypothesized is possible. The Third World knows it. They know that the much-vaunted roads, railways, and telegraphs that American money has gifted them with lead from the mines to the ports. If they refuse to accept the division of labor on American terms, there will be far too little to go around.

The US represents approximately 8% of the "non-communist world" population. Europe and Canada are approximately twice that. But they need the greater part of all known reserves to maintain their current level of consumption; in some cases they need more than all known reserves, as with copper and tungsten. Is the enemy the US confronts really communism— or is it in fact industrialization?

Implications for US policy

It must be a conscious and primary aim of American foreign policy to ensure that the flow of raw materials from the Third World is never interrupted.

Imagine a situation in which pro-Peking Community Parties controlled all overseas sources of raw materials for America's steel industry. They could cripple the US as an economic and military power.

But America runs the risk of political opposition from many strains of political opinion besides the Maoist. And the important conclusion to be drawn from the first part of this paper is that there are economic reasons for any honest and independent government—communist, socialist, liberal democratic or even revolutionary-right—to stop selling raw materials to the United States. An examination of all the possible contingencies that could motivate a government to cut off American supplies makes it quite clear that American dependency on foreign suppliers makes it necessary for her to maintain regimes in power that are under her total control.

First, and most vital, a country may wish to conserve its resource base for its own industrial development. It will not be impressed by arguments that the necessity of containing communism requires economic sacrifices from the underdeveloped countries.

Second, there will be competition for what surpluses they may wish to sell, and they will have no reason to hand America a monopoly of their exports. America will have to compete with capitalist and socialist Europe, and with other Third World countries. Since her competitive position will not be strong, she will probably lose open competitions. Primary producers will sell raw materials in those markets from which they can purchase back finished goods at the lowest prices. This is much more likely to be Japan, for instance, than it is the United States.

Third, there will inevitably be anti-American sentiments associated with any independence Movement, and that may provide a political motive for giving preference to non-American buyers, as a symbol of independence or an expression of a legacy of bitterness.

Fourth, there might be sanctions in protest against American foreign policy in other Third World nations. For example, an independent Asian government such as Sihanouk's Cambodia would be unlikely to sell war material to the United States while it was engaged in a counter-insurgency war such as in Vietnam.

A military consideration makes it equally imperative, from the American viewpoint, to maintain American puppets in Asia. Any number of Asian countries are located along the shipping routes by which the US obtains strategic materials. If any one of them were to collaborate with a country (guess who) with whom America was engaged in a protracted land war, it could seriously interfere with American war industry.

. . .

Hot spots, or, God save Africa

If you make a list of troubled areas around the world—South Korea, Indonesia, Brazil, Congo, Rhodesia, Chile, Ghana, British Guiana, Philippines—you have also made a list of sources of critical raw materials.

At the moment we seem to be trading Africa for Asia, which is cruel for the Africans, but may move us one step from the brink. Africa is particularly valuable, not only for the vast reserves of copper, chromium, manganese, and cobalt, but also for power. The Volta project, whose future has just been taken from Kwame Nkrumah's hands, will generate enough power to take aluminum production out of the hands of the northern hemisphere.

We may expect to see Africa and Asia firmly in the hands of "responsible" leadership, who will stress traditional agriculture and fiscal stability over industrialization. Or else.

The Cornucopians

Some economists, known to the Conservationists as "the Cornucopians," see in each exploited raw material not the use of an irreplaceable resource, but the forging of a key to even greater resources. They point to past history and current trends to show that technological innovations have made possible substitutions or mining of inferior ores at lower costs than earlier exploitation of high-grade ores.

In considering the impact of scarce resources on American foreign policy, two questions arise. How far can technology deliver us from the Law of Diminishing Returns? and How many of US policy makers are Cornucopians abroad as well as at home?

Theoretically, the whole earth is exploitable as a source of industrial minerals; the barriers are cost in dollars, and cost in time, training, and machines. If the US were presented with a *fait accompli;* if all her colonies were denied her and she were thrown back on her own and Canada's reserves, she could probably find ways of surviving as an advanced civilization. She has the knowledge, the training centers, the tax base, the power, the tools.

But short of that, will she do it, or will she continue to loot the poor countries of the earth?

At least three times in man's history, great civilizations have grown stagnant and been destroyed because they lacked the social forms that would realize the potential of their sciences. Steam powered the doors of temples while slaves rowed ships.

The capacity of American technology to solve the resource problem is not in question. It is in the selection of priorities, not the capacity for research, that our civilization is failing.

The space race is everybody's prime example of misallocation of our human and technical resources. Throughout the '50s, reformers cried, "In some countries in the Far East and Africa, 50% of the population is blind! Forget the moon, and find a cure for trachoma." Immunization against the trachoma virus was finally developed through a breakthrough in virological research comparable to the development of the Salk vaccine—by the Chinese.

The system as it is presently structured will not lead to creative alternatives to imperialism as solutions to the resource problem. So long as ownership and control lie in the hands of the great international cartels, and so long as research priorities are determined by market mechanisms, looting will remain the logical solution to a problem with such initial components.

Although the human race as a whole is going to have to find means of using the less accessible and less easily reduced ores, at any given point, a strong competitive advantage will accrue to whomever has the cheapest raw materials. It is technically feasible for the United States to find ways of mining manganese from the ocean bottom, but as long as Indian coolies are scratching 50% ore out of the ground with wooden spades, it is economically ridiculous to produce it at 20 times the cost. The Russians and the Chinese both possess substantial deposits of most of the minerals America and Europe

lack. As long as their low-cost ores are on the market, Americans will purchase on world markets, and keep secondary sources in Asia, Africa, and
Latin America "on ice." But since the status quo in these countries is a
standard of living below subsistence and declining, the status quo can only
be maintained by force.

Vested interests

(*No, I am not now, nor have I ever been . . .*)

What this phrase means is simply demonstrated. The East India Company
made enormous profits out of the maintenance of India as a British colony.
It did not make as much in profits, however, as it cost to hold India by means
of a vast administrative system, an overseas army and a Pacific fleet. So for
Britain as a whole, it was not profitable to hold India, at least by force. *But*,
the people who made the profits were not the same people who paid the price.
And the people who made the profits, and had a vested interest in maintaining
the status quo, controlled the foreign policy of Britain against the interests
of its people.

The situation may now exist where enclaves of power depend for their power
on a productive system that has become obsolete for the nation as a whole.
More concretely, it will be possible to substitute agricultural fuels (alcohol)
for mineral fuels. So it is no longer in the interests of the American people to
support a war for oil, but it may well be in the interests of the Rockefellers.

A parallel and more perplexing problem is the phenomenon of vested
psychological interests. If we know enough to make competition for the
earth's resources a closed chapter in the evolution of human culture, will the
legislators of the great powers undergo the shift in consciousness that will
make fear of shortages obsolete in fact as a determinant of policy?

If some of these flying saucers would stop to offer some other-worldly
benevolent guidance, they would probably suggest a world-wide program of
search, research, and development. The needs are obvious; how to get there
from here is not.

We need an exhaustive geophysical survey, under UN auspices, of Canada,
Africa, Latin America, and all areas where reserves are suspected but not
proved. With an expanded and scattered reserve base the risks of losing
political control over any one country would be minimal.

"Do I understand, Senator, that you are prepared to take those risks with
the security of the United States and the Free World?"

The UN should also provide development capital, so that owner countries
will not run into a credit squeeze in the international capital market, and be
forced to sell to the controllers of international credit, who just happen to
include the same people who currently own most of the earth's resources
(Morgan, Rockefeller, Rothschild).

International aid should be reallocated from currency stabilization to industrial development.

With Russia and China both self-sufficient, and probably able to produce for export, there is probably enough to go around, at least potentially. But we are considering the motivations and probable decisions of groups of men committed to the security, and the competitive advantage, of a particular political and economic system that they wish to preserve unchanged. However great an abundance of raw materials are discovered in this century, the political considerations remain critical as long as one government has political control over the resources necessary to another government. It means that the resource-poor country must control the producing country, or be in some degree dependent on its good will.

A supranational body in control of prices and allocation of scarce resources might lessen the political tensions involved, but there would still be risk, still insecurity, for the developed countries. And a fair allocation would involve surrender of economic advantages that the United States is currently securing by military and paramilitary means.

"Do I understand, Senator, that you are suggesting placing the security of the United States and the Free World in the hands of the one-worlders, Black Africans, communists, and assorted riff-raff who inhabit the United Nations?"

Unfortunately, the economic motives for enforced poverty and economic stagnation in the Third World are easily elided into the "Great Black Blot" theory of communist expansion which US congressmen seem to find so compelling. They overthrow governments to defend freedom, not our inflated levels of consumption. Political unrest in an area of strategic importance is easily rationalized into a military tactic by which the international communist conspiracy is attempting to cut our supply lines. (There's a marshal's baton in every attaché case.) "Our interests" and "our commitments" are logically identical, but psychologically polar opposites.

It is past time that we made the leap in moral imagination that would let us understand that we are rich because they are poor. Guerrilla movements are swelling throughout the Third World, and the lines are becoming clearly drawn. We must commit ourselves to the creation of a system of international distribution that will permit the industrialization of the Third World, or visit more Vietnams on the poor of the earth.

Heather Dean's thesis hardly seems adequate to explain all of America's foreign policy and the actions of our international and multinational firms. A materials policy is crucial; indeed, it may account for a good part of our foreign involvement, but it alone hardly accounts for the billions poured into the war in Vietnam,[11] and the fact that we are not fighting wars in

---

11 A materials policy may go a part of the way toward accounting for United States intervention in Vietnam. The Pentagon Papers indicate that in 1949, according to a National Security Council report, the U.S. government was quite concerned that the Kremlin was trying to gain control of the resources of Southeast Asia in order to "deny them to us." The Domino Theory meant, as a 1952 NSC paper put it, that "The loss of any single country would probably lead to relatively swift submission to or an alignment with communism by the remaining countries of this group. . . ." Vietnam, of course, is one of the single countries. The same paper continues, "Southeast Asia is the principal world source of natural rubber and tin, and a producer of petroleum and other strategically important commodities. . . ." The source here was NSC 124–4. See Richard E. Ward, "Pentagon Papers Don't Tell All," *The Guardian*, August 4, 1971, p. 11.

mineral-rich African countries that are more under communist or Third World influence than the influence of the West.

For most radicals, however, an all-encompassing, internally consistent theory of imperialism is perhaps not as important as the kind of evidence presented so far in this chapter. The New Left radical is probably more willing than were doctrinaire socialists and Marxists to admit that the system is not that perfect. Mistakes are made (perhaps Vietnam eventually became one), opportunities are lost (the United States should have financed the Aswan Dam in Egypt in order to penetrate that country further, but Secretary of State John Foster Dulles made many mistakes in pursuing his rigid views on international politics), our interests are often not very clear-cut (as in some civil wars in Africa), and capitalists in Europe and Japan have muddied the water considerably. All these considerations can be admitted without refuting the imperialist argument. Imperialism can help sustain capitalist production without accounting for all events. There is substantial agreement among business leaders that the Free World must remain open to American business interests. Given the conditions in much of that world and the profitability of United States business, with its appetite for irreplaceable raw materials, the radical needs no more.

Harry Magdoff finds that the issue of raw materials fits comfortably with his economic interpretation of imperialism. Focusing not on strategic minerals in short supply, such as tungsten, but on the general picture of all raw materials, he refers to the conclusions of the Materials Policy Commission that Dean also cited.

1966

from ECONOMIC ASPECTS OF U.S. IMPERIALISM [12]

Harry Magdoff

...*Resources for Freedom* (Washington, D.C., 1952) graphically summarized the dramatic change in the following comparison for all raw materials other than food and gold: at the turn of the century, the U.S. produced on the

---

[12] Magdoff, *op. cit.*, pp. 24–26. See also Magdoff's reply to S. M. Miller, Roy Bennett, and Cyril Alapatl's "Does the U.S. Economy Require Imperialism?" *Social Policy*, 1:3 (September–October 1970), 20–29.

whole some 15 percent more of these raw materials than was domestically consumed; this surplus had by 1950 turned into a deficit, with U.S. industry consuming 10 percent more than domestic production; extending the trends to 1975 showed that by then the overall deficit of raw materials for industry will be about 20 percent.

Perhaps the awareness of this development was a contributing factor to President Eisenhower's alerting the nation to the unity of political and economic interests in his first inaugural address (January 20, 1953):

> We know . . . that we are linked to all free peoples not merely by a noble idea but by a simple need. No free people can for long cling to any privilege or enjoy any safety in economic solitude. For all our own material might, even we need markets in the world for the surpluses of our farms and our factories. Equally, we need for these same farms and factories vital materials and products of distant lands. This basic law of interdependence, so manifest in the commerce of peace, applies with thousand-fold intensity in the event of war.

As is so often the case, economic interests harmonize comfortably with political and security goals, since so many of the basic raw materials are considered essential to effective war preparedness. Quite understandably the government makes its contribution to the security of the nation as well as to the security of business via diplomatic maneuvers, maintenance of convenient military bases in various parts of the world, military aid to help maintain stable governments, and last but not least a foreign aid program which is a fine blend of declared humanitarian aims about industrialization and a realistic appreciation that such progress should not interfere with the ability of supplying countries to maintain a proper flow of raw materials. To do a real job of assuring an adequate supply of raw materials in the light of possible exhaustion of already exploited deposits, and in view of possible needs for missiles and space programs, the government can make its greatest contribution by keeping as much of the world as possible "free" and safe for mineral development. Clarence B. Randall, president of Inland Steel Co. and adviser on foreign aid in Washington, comments on the fortunate availability of uranium deposits in the Belgian Congo as the atom bomb was developed:

> What a break it was for us that the mother country was on our side! And who can possibly foresee today which of the vast unexplored areas of the world may likewise possess some unique deposit of a rare raw material which in the fullness of time our industry or our defense program may most urgently need? *

The integration of less developed capitalisms into the world market is reliable and continuous suppliers of their natural resources results, with rare exceptions, in a continuous dependency on the centers of monopoly control that is sanctified and cemented by the market structure which evolves from this very dependency. Integration into world capitalist markets has almost

---

* Clarence B. Randall, *The Communist Challenge to American Business*, Little, Brown & Co., Boston, 1959, p. 36.

uniform effects on the supplying countries: (1) they depart from, or never enter, the paths of development that require independence and self-reliance; (2) they lose their economic self-sufficiency and become dependent on exports for their economic viability; (3) their industrial structure becomes adapted to the needs of supplying specialized exports at prices acceptable to the buyers, reducing thereby such flexibility of productive resources as is needed for a diversified and growing economic productivity. The familiar symptom of this process is still seen in Latin America, where, despite industrialization efforts and the stimulus of two world wars, well over 90 percent of most countries' total exports consists of the export of agricultural and mineral products.* The extreme dependence on exports, and on a severely restricted number of export products at that, keeps such economies off balance in their international economic relations and creates frequent need for borrowing. Debt engenders increasing debt, for the servicing of the debt adds additional balance of payments difficulties. And in all such relations of borrowing and lending, the channels of international finance are in the hands of the foreign investors, their business associates, and their government agencies.

The chains of dependence may be manipulated by the political, financial, and military arms of the centers of empire, with the help of the Marines, military bases, bribery, CIA operations, financial maneuvers, and the like. But the material basis of this dependence is an industrial and financial structure which through the so-called normal operations of the marketplace reproduces the conditions of economic dependence.

A critical element of the market patterns which helps perpetuate the underdeveloped countries as dependable suppliers of raw materials is the financial tribute to the foreign owners who extract not only natural resources but handsome profits as well. . . .

In the underdeveloped regions almost three times as much money was taken out as was put in. And note well that besides drawing out almost three times as much as they put in, investors were able to increase the value of the assets owned in these regions manifold: in Latin America, direct investments owned by United States business during this period increased from $4.5 to $10.3 billion; in Asia and Africa, from $1.3 to $4.7 billion.

These are indeed tidy sums. They are hardly a basis for celebrating "American generosity," however.

SUMMARY

These selections have presented the imperialist argument in bits and pieces. The major elements, most of which are drawn from Marxist and socialist thought that predated the New Left, are worth summarizing. In crude terms, the argument runs like this:

* Joseph Grunwald, "Resource Aspects of Latin American Development," in Marion Clawson, ed., *National Resources and International Development*, Johns Hopkins Press, Baltimore, 1964, p. 315.

The basic problem for capitalism is that with technological improvements (better factory organization, better machines and techniques), more goods are produced than can be consumed in the domestic market as it is now structured. The lower classes cannot afford to buy more, and the middle and upper classes are increasingly glutted. Raising the income of the lower classes so that they could consume more would reduce profits, and it would also reduce their tractability. The capitalist engine produces more profit if there is plenty of cheap labor and a "plantation economy" that allows business to lay off workers during dips in the business cycle with minimal costs to the employer and to reabsorb them when they are needed again. Experiencing economic insecurity, workers are unlikely to challenge the power of the ruling class.

Consumption by the middle and upper classes can be increased to some degree by production for *waste,* rather than for use or for real needs. When basic needs are satisfied, plastic baubles and goods to satisfy artificially stimulated tastes are created, along with space circuses. The enormous advertising industry is directed toward this end.

In the long run, however, the population unfortunately keeps increasing, creating a demand for more jobs. But productivity also increases, proportionally reducing the need for new jobs. Massive, long-term unemployment, combined with a realization of the true nature of the system, could create a revolutionary situation. Therefore the system must prevent massive unemployment. But the private sector cannot prevent unemployment; that sector cannot generate the necessary jobs without a dramatic restructuring of the social order and production for use rather than waste.

In 1965 Harry Magdoff calculated that between 1957 and 1963, while total nonfarm employment increased by 4.3 million, the full-time jobs generated by private demand amounted to a mere 300,000. The rest of the jobs came from an increase in government employment, from nonprofit institutions such as schools and hospitals, and from jobs created by government purchases from business, largely in the military and in the aerospace industry.[13] To keep unemployment at "tolerable" levels—considered to be from 4 to 6 percent of the work force—the United States must create huge government bureaucracies and military expenditures. The funds for this waste of manpower come from a somewhat regressive tax structure. The working class is disproportionately taxed to take up the slack in employment created by the business system.

The system reaps huge profits from this state of affairs. But under the present structure, neither all the goods that the system produces nor all the profits that it generates can find an outlet within the nation. Profits are thus used to expand markets for the excess goods abroad and to create pro-

[13] Harry Magdoff, "Problems of U.S. Capitalism," *Socialist Register 1965* (New York: Monthly Review Press, 1965), pp. 62–79. The difference between Magdoff's calculations and those generally cited is that he includes jobs created by government purchases from business.

ductive units generating more profits abroad. Most of this export of capital and goods goes to Canada and to Europe (increasing their dependency on the United States, which is almost complete in the case of Canada). But the same saturation of demand and the rise of unemployment are likely to occur there in time, especially because they are doing their own capitalist thing. Thus other markets are needed.

The threat of communism or socialism is not primarily an ideological one, then, but a threat that markets and investment opportunities either will be closed to American business interests or will be open only on unacceptable terms. American business is quite prepared to export goods to Russia and has tried to establish investments there. For example, the Ford Motor Company bid on a huge truck factory in Russia (but the error of Dulles in the case of the Aswan Dam was repeated: the State Department forced the company to withdraw). America has quite favorable trading terms with socialist Yugoslavia. Vast markets in China may be opened up to American business; General Electric will presumably sell all the light bulbs it can to Communist China, if the terms are favorable. The threat of Latin American countries going socialist, as in the case of Chile, is not an ideological threat. What is at stake there are the very favorable terms of penetration—the development of an infrastructure appropriate to American interests, the appropriation of local capital, the remittance to the United States of large profits. Economic independence, rather than political ideologies, is the crux of the matter.

Finally, most of the scarce resources needed to keep the capitalist engine running are in the underdeveloped nations. This country cannot be cut off from the extraction of these resources for its own use, nor are alternative sources likely to be feasible. Manganese mined from the ocean floor is enormously more expensive than that mined by exploited natives.

Therefore, if the peaceful penetration of a country fails or if a country is threatened with a revolution, the United States conveniently has a huge military and political apparatus ready to secure its interests. Iran, Guatemala, Brazil, the Dominican Republic, Korea, Vietnam, and many other smaller operations have required the United States to make commitments to more than forty-three nations, demonstrated by the existence of 375 major and 3,000 minor American bases around the world, and to maintain a huge domestic military apparatus geared to fast deployment and limited-war capabilities. It was the genius of John F. Kennedy and Robert S. McNamara to upgrade American facilities in this respect as trouble began to break out all over the globe.

This military posture not only protects our access to other countries and our present investments, it also has convenient secondary benefits at home. As long as there appears to be a threat of international communism, internal surveillance and control of disruptive elements in our society are justified. Where once the government suppressed suspected communists at home, it has since moved on to fellow-travelers, then to antibomb groups, and now to peace marchers. All these groups threaten the imperial ventures of capitalism. Furthermore, the military absorbs surplus manpower and surplus productivity, which it finances from general tax revenues. Finally, the communist threat is a circus meant to entertain the nation and to divert the lower class from realizing the degree to which it is exploited.

(Some hold that a basic weakening of the capitalist system at this advanced stage of "contradiction," where productivity has increased so much and internal markets have become so mature, is that a new generation is growing up that is unconvinced of the reality of the communist threat. Its lack of fear would weaken the justification for intervention in the internal affairs of underdeveloped countries and expose the true nature of our worldwide activities.)

If this is the logic, then the fact that the United States has few private investments in Vietnam is irrelevant. What is at stake there is the access to the raw materials and eventual markets of all of Southeast Asia. The United States may, in fact, have succeeded in Vietnam in these terms. It has penetrated the economies of numerous countries in the area. By normalizing relations with the People's Republic of China, the United States may ensure continued access to South Vietnam even if the Viet Cong takes over the government of South Vietnam after United States forces leave. No doubt Vietnam cost the United States more than it intended to spend, but as Weissman and Gerassi argued in the first selection, it all began with foreign aid programs, and each step was a logical development.

For the sophisticated radical, even if American intervention in Vietnam proves to be a failure for American capitalism in the long run, there is nothing in the radical position that says that capitalism is all-powerful. More polemical tracts suggest that it is (although, paradoxically, it is ready to be brought down by an aroused working class and the exploited peoples of the world). Preoccupied with Europe and disgusted with Chiang Kai-shek, the United States did not prevent China from falling to the communists. America's leaders were unsure about intervening in Africa during civil wars, and with the political menace of Russia declining at the same time its military might increased, they were unwilling to support the rebels in Hungary. The invasion of Cuba was a failure, but the Korean War, while costly, "removed investor doubts" regarding Japan and Korea, as the man from Chase Manhattan put it. The United States succeeded in Guatemala and the Dominican Republic, but if the socialist regime in Chile survives, it may prove to cost us more than some expropriations of American investments.

These setbacks and missed opportunities, and the growing understanding of the nature of corporate capitalism and its imperialistic appetites, may stem the advance of economic imperialism. If so, according to Marxist theory, a crisis of overproduction and underconsumption awaits the business system unless the structure of corporate capitalism, and thus of the United

States itself, changes. Of course, the crisis might be no greater for capitalism than that of the worldwide depression of the 1930's. It may also produce no greater restructuring of our society than occurred then, which was little enough. The New Left, however, counts on a growing awareness of both the nature of the system and the failure of liberal reforms to create a movement toward a new society and toward nonexploitative interdependencies with other nations. They offer few realistic scripts either for our system or for a global system; much remains to be done in the way of analysis and awareness before specific proposals could ever emerge.

But let us return to shallower water, to the analysis of corporate capitalism in America today. If capitalism is *the* American system, it does not exist in isolation from other institutional complexes in our society; every significant institution must support it, including the universities.

CHAPTER 4

University complicity

The United States came out of the Second World War with a number of advantages: an intact economy and production facilities unmatched anywhere; proportionally fewer manpower losses through casualties than any other major nation; a dominant political role in many countries; surplus arms to sell; a chance to gain an economic foothold in Europe; goods and food for sale abroad; and, most important for the content of this chapter, a keen appreciation of the role of science in military and industrial affairs. The atomic bomb, the proximity fuse, and the refinement of radar were only the most spectacular successes of science during the war. While the military machine was being rapidly dismantled—not completely, by any means, but so substantially that the proportion of the federal budget for the military could be cut from more than 80 percent in 1944 to close to 30 percent by 1948 —the funding for science and engineering experienced no such drastic cutback. Wartime scientific laboratories kept their personnel and equipment, and new centers of scientific research were started. While a desultory debate went on within the scientific community and in Congress over the wisdom of establishing a National Science Foundation, the Navy poured millions of dollars into science. President Truman vetoed the first NSF bill on the grounds that it gave private citizens—scientists—unprecedented public resources with no public control. But the sciences hardly needed a government foundation as yet. The Navy, appreciating its dependence on technology, set up the Office of Naval Research and toured the country selling university presidents and university scientists on the pleasures of continued financial support from the taxpayer with few strings attached. The ONR kept science from dropping back to the penury that had characterized its prewar state and, indeed, swathed it in money on the grounds that science and technology were crucial for the nation's military and economic supremacy in the world.[1]

Work on the Bomb continued at Los Alamos, New Mexico, and while Russia managed to construct a hydrogen weapon first, the United States was not far behind. Research on chemical warfare leaped ahead. Delivery systems for bombs became increasingly sophisticated. The scientists, in one of several efforts directed toward peace that stand out from an otherwise self-serving posture, lobbied effectively to establish civilian control over atomic research and to turn some of that research toward peaceful uses. Thus in 1946 the Atomic Energy Commission was established with civilian control. But after the Eisenhower administration came in and Admiral Lewis Strauss became chairman of the Atomic Energy Commission, that effort was more or less nullified. The commission became a captive of the military. The *Bulletin of Atomic Scientists* held out the promise of social and political concern among scientists, but the billions poured into high-energy physics, the squabbles over where to build the next multimillion dollar cyclotron or accelerator, and the fiasco over Mohole suggest that scientists were subject to at least the normal degree of human frailty. The vanity, greed, chicanery, deception, and witch-hunting of scientists are documented chapters of this history.

In all this, science willingly accepted the priorities and premises of the national political leaders and the military, and served them dutifully and well. By extension (in the view of the New Left), they also served capitalism. Science took its place in Washington alongside the industrial trade associations, the unions, the medical lobby, and the right-wing and the liberal lobbies to peddle its influence and to seek more. It is still there. The United States has become a nation that thrives on science and technology developed for industry and the military, and, until recently, few scientists have thought to question their public duty to advise business and the federal government. Even Robert Oppenheimer, the tragic figure who was disgraced in a security trial in the 1950's, rarely questioned the role of science. He could question the aims of the government, perhaps even his own paramount and selfless role in building the atomic bomb, but not the relationship of the independent scientist to the federal government.[2]

1 For supporting data for this and the following paragraph, see the lively account by Daniel S. Greenberg, *The Politics of Pure Science* (New York: World, 1967). See also H. L. Nieburg, *In the Name of Science*, rev. ed. (Chicago: Quadrangle Books, 1970), first published in 1966.
2 For a fascinating account of the Oppenheimer case, see Neul Pharr Davis, *Lawrence and Oppenheimer* (New York: Simon & Schuster, 1968).

The scientists were trained at, and most of them still worked in, the universities. What was the impact of military support for research and development on these institutions? What should have been their role in the postwar years, when research with no conceivable practical benefit (such as particle physics) swallowed millions of dollars annually while so much poverty went unnoticed by the academic community? No one asked. The reason is not hard for the New Left to find. The universities are the hand-maidens of the system; they do the research and the training for government and industry. Neither business nor the government has been disposed to reallocate profits or tax monies from prestigious engineering monuments to human needs. For years, this was not even an issue.

By and large, the universities do their research and training at public expense. Private colleges and universities are supported by fees and donations, but they are also tax-exempt. This exemption means that the taxes on their land and property are forgone, so the federal and local government must raise that money elsewhere. Gifts and endowments also represent a disposition of property that evades taxes. Public institutions of higher learning also participate in these tax-forgone devices, as well as receiving partial support directly from tax revenues. The working class pays proportionately more of its income in state and local taxes than the middle and upper classes do, but children of working-class families have a very poor chance of getting into the colleges and universities their taxes support.[3] Thus the business system benefits from higher education by getting trained manpower and research partly at public expense.

Presumably the nation as a whole needs manpower and knowledge, and thus the factory worker benefits from the uses to which his tax dollars are put. But what kind of knowledge is being produced, and what kind of manpower? Is it that which might most benefit the nation and improve the quality of life for all? Not at all, says the New Left. Despite the reputation for radicalism, and despite some genuine independence in the arts and the humanities, the bulk of the resources in these "knowledge factories" is given over to the processing of technocrats who will fill the slots of an increasingly sophisticated business system. There are, of course, the business administration students, the engineers, and the lawyers. They work in the center of the system. Beyond that, the universities train social workers who are taught to pick up the pieces that the capitalist engine rejects, as well as to expand the classification of deviation in order to narrow the orthodoxy of normality. There are the scientists who calculate trajectories, develop weapons, locate minerals, improve manufacturing techniques, adulterate foods, and develop pesticides. The medical schools acquiesce in restricting the supply of doctors, encourage esoteric specialization and re-

3 W. L. Hansen and B. A. Weisbrod, "The Distribution of Costs and Direct Benefits of Public Higher Education—The Case of California," *Journal of Human Resources*, Vol. 4 (1969), 176.

search, and socialize students to private, middle-class practice. The education schools practice and preach conformity and mediocrity. The social scientists, although overwhelmingly liberal in political values, find themselves seeking ways to make workers more content, to increase the efficiency of managers, to develop tools for economic forecasting so that the system can be more finely tuned, to memorialize the anachronisms of politicians in an age of increasing centralization of power, and to discover how the child learns the values and manners preferred in a corporate society.

Occasionally, the relationship between the university and its client, the corporate elite, is stated with refreshing candor. For example, after the Santa Barbara oil spill in 1969, the Chief Deputy Attorney General of the State of California telephoned some professors of petroleum engineering at various campuses of the University of California. These professors are literally working for the state, and the Chief Deputy wished to find one who would testify that the huge pools of oil washing ashore were of the kind that could have come from ruptured oil wells. It was a simple legal matter. He was frustrated, however, because the professors would not make the examination and testify. One told him, according to a report in the press, that he could not testify "because my work depends on good relations with the petroleum industry. My interest is serving the petroleum industry. I view my obligation to the community as supplying it with well-trained petroleum engineers. We train the industry's engineers and they help us." [4]

One comes to expect this sort of thing, and it hardly needs comment on the part of the New Left. This is what the sciences, the business schools, the education schools and so on are set up to do—service the economy. The New Left has been far more vocal about the conditions of its major constituency—students. The power of professors has been heavily attacked; one popular article, "The Student as Nigger," portrays the college student as treated by the faculty no better than a slave in the South. Also under attack have been the triviality of courses, the emphasis on grades, the bureaucratic machinery (recall the famous slogan, "I am a student. Do not fold, bend, or staple"), the *in loco parentis* mentality, the exploitation of graduate students as teaching assistants, and so on.

This chapter will focus on more direct challenges to the business system than the exploitation of students and on less obvious concerns than the trade-school mentality of the science, engineering, and business curricula. We will look at the interlocking relationships of university leaders and the business community and at the ways in which business defines what shall be the important and legitimate interests of the scholarly community. How does business control the university, other than the obvious ways of offering good jobs to those who pursue degrees in chemistry or engineering?

4 Quoted in Harvey Molotch, "Santa Barbara: Oil in the Velvet Playground," in *Eco-Catastrophe*, by the editors of *Ramparts* (New York: Harper & Row, 1970), p. 96.

BERKELEY AND BUSINESS

The following article on agriculture briefly makes many of the salient points about the relationship of business and higher education. Conducting agricultural research, organizing the growers, and helping them with marketing and other business problems have been central concerns of the University of California. The conditions of workers have been of very little concern. The efforts of the agricultural industry are financed in part by state taxes (which are regressive). Economy drives do not touch the agricultural services significantly. The dominant men in agriculture are well represented on the Board of Regents. Business reaches into the university not only through the regents but also through foundations, which have the power to censor unfavorable reports. Although the growth of agriculture benefits the state in general, the direction of that growth and the distribution of its benefits are in private hands, which leads to the exploitation of labor and to the sale of adulterated and even poisoned foods. In all these activities, the University of California has played a willing role.

1970

from BANKERS RUN CALIFORNIA AGRIBUSINESS[5]

Bruce Severy

No class of people or type of worker has been more ruthlessly exploited by American corporate power than California's three-quarter million farm workers. Agribusiness—the profitable combination of Bank of America, the University of California and a handful of powerful corporations—makes up the bulk of California's business, far ahead of the aerospace industry.

California leads the nation in total cash farm income, last year over $4 billion. But by the time 200-odd commercial crops are harvested, transported, processed and packaged, their actual market value is upwards of $16 billion. California agriculture is responsible for producing 40% of the nation's

5 Bruce Severy, "Bankers Run California Agribusiness," *The Guardian*, November 28, 1970, p. 6.

vegetables, fruits and nut crops. It produces the overwhelming bulk of 15 vital crops, including 92% of the nation's grapes.

One out of three jobs in California is dependent on agriculture or its related industries. Capital gains for agribusiness are steady at $100 million a year. Yet, the average farm laborer earns hardly enough to subsist. Even former Gov. Edmund G. Brown complained about farm workers' sub-human housing, high accident rates, lack of sanitary facilities and working conditions that involved dangerous pesticides.

Ownership of farm land in California continues to coalesce into the hands of fewer and fewer people. The number of farms is decreasing by 3000 a year. The average California farm is nearly 460 acres and valued at $216,000, much higher than the national average. Some 6.1% of the farms take up 78.6% of available land.

The key to ownership of farm land in California is held rather selectively by Bank of America, the world's largest bank. Bank founder A. P. Giannini started out in the produce business around the San Francisco Bay area at the turn of the century. He inherited a seat on a local bank but left soon after to open his own Bank of Italy in 1904. He made money on the reconstruction of San Francisco after its disastrous earthquakes. But Bank of Italy became what it is today because of the Depression.

Agriculture in California had been in decline since the end of World War I. Giannini's agents would loan money to any farmer and would foreclose on anyone's mortgage with equal ease. Foreclosing on 1321 farms between 1926 and 1930 alone made the Bank of Italy the state's largest private landowner in agriculture. Through its California lands company, the bank continued to grow and to create the objective conditions for Steinbeck's "Grapes of Wrath" and Carey McWilliams' "Factories in the Field," while it changed its name to Bank of America and some of its activities to sponsor F. D. Roosevelt for President (an investment which was to pay off very well later).

Bank of America reaped huge benefits from the Roosevelt administrations. New laws allowing an extension of their branch banking plans, guaranteed riskless home mortgage loans and sole financing of the many pork-barrel projects granted to Giannini's friend Henry Kaiser mark Bank of America's growth.

As its ties to big government were strengthened, Bank of America sought to strengthen its friends—the California corporations centered around a reviving agricultural business. Bank of America sold much of its property in farmland to select corporations, in return for interlocking directorships, seats on controlling boards and key stocks. What has come about is Kern County Lands, Hunt Foods, Foremost Dairies, California Packing, DiGiorgio, Libby, Safeway Stores, S & H Sugar and several others, all intricately connected to Bank of America. Rudolph Peterson, the bank's president, estimates conservatively that the bank's capital commitment alone is beyond $3 billion.

Closely related to the creation, maintenance and growth of California agribusiness is the University of California. Taking advantage of the Morrill Act of 1862, the university was founded around a program of agricultural extension projects and farm experiment stations. Agents from the university extension programs were involved in founding the first Farm Bureaus in the

1920s. In 1919, the director of the agriculture extension service was responsible for the founding of the California Farm Bureau Federation, what now comprises the powerful agribusiness lobby in this state. Its main office still operates out of UC Berkeley. In 1934, this growing organization created the Associated Farmers of California, a vigilante-type group that proved instrumental in smashing strikes by farm workers during the 1930s.

In 1928, Bank of America's Giannini financed with $1.5 million the Giannini Foundation of Agricultural Economics at Berkeley. W. B. Camp, a former high executive of Bank of America, left to organize the Associated Farmers and was instrumental in breaking up farm worker strikes in 1934, 1936, 1937 and the 1939 strike against DiGiorgio pear orchards. Bank of America, though it denied any involvement, financed part of the terrorist attacks on workers. More importantly, Bank of America always extended to any limit credit to growers suffering through strikes.

At Berkeley, the Agricultural Sciences continued to grow until today it is not only the largest department of the university, but commands its own university vice president. Through its octopus-like growth, the agricultural extension service spread throughout the UC system, revealing itself in a myriad of research projects of direct benefit to agribusiness. Research was proving to be a major force not only in research development, but in areas of corporate organization, creating new marketable products and programming the means of distributing them as well.

The overwhelming percentage of research done by the University of California is made available to agribusiness free of charge. The federal government pays for some of it through grants and other aid. Agricultural research funds usually come out of the general UC budget—i.e., money collected in high property taxes charged the residents of the state of California. When Gov. Ronald Reagan made his $3 million slash in the UC budget of $33 million for research, agricultural research—accounting for over 60% of total research—was cut by only 4%. The Industrial Relations Institute at UCLA, an organization dealing with 7 million workers in the state, was cut by 25%. The agricultural lobby had been hard at work.

Key men benefit

Efforts at setting up similar research programs to benefit workers and labor movements in general have either been cut to the bone or severely crippled by finances or memos coming down from the offices of the regents of the UC. Part of the agribusiness story involves these men. While the regents control and direct the activities of the University of California, they also tend their own corporate and land interests: Bank of America, two oil corporations, three aircraft companies, two shipping lines, two airlines, a trucking line, chain stores, two publishing empires and more than half the food-packing industry. This is on top of huge farm land holdings; e.g., regent Edward Carter, who owns 20% of Orange County in Southern California.

A classic example of how key men control an integrated corporate-university setup is to be found in Roger Heyns, chancellor of UC Berkeley and member of the board of Norton Simon, Inc. (Simon is a regent of UC), one of whose sub-corporations is Hunt Foods, largest of agribusiness' processing facilities. A similar example is Franklin Murphy, ex-chancellor of UCLA, who at the same time helped staff the board of Los Angeles Times-Mirror Co. (owned by another regent).

Government complicity with agribusiness was most evident in the Bracero Program. This was initiated in 1951 as Public Law 78, purportedly to compensate for Korean war labor shortages. Over 100,000 Mexican nationals were allowed under this law to be brought into the abundant California fields. The program offered many good points as far as the growers were concerned: no one had to worry about the braceros' health, the abysmally low wages, or the complaints usually to be found among any of the native field workers. If a bracero grumbled, he was instantly deported. Mexicans were used until 1964 for keeping down the wages of local workers, for threatening the local workers if they complained about wages or working conditions and for breaking up strikes as a ready scab force.

While UCLA's Institute of Industrial Relations had done a study in 1964 showing that there were enough domestic laborers able and willing to work, the university's Giannini Foundation mutilated the report, deleting 17 pages under the direction of Eric Thor, foundation director.

Agribusiness continues to deny its domestic labor force an equal share in the wealth it helps create. It would rather use old or obscure laws to keep importing foreign labor and continue to use its powerful lobby to block legislation that would help the poor, starving and ill farm workers; to block legislation giving farm workers a minimum wage, sanitary facilities in the fields, health and unemployment insurance and other conventional benefits.

In the second part of this article, which is not reprinted here, the author notes:

According to the California State Dept. of Labor, 700,000 farm workers have an average life span of 49 years, have 50 to 60 deaths and 200 to 300 on-the-job injuries a year, have an income of $2050 per year (males), have housing three-fourths of which is "unfit for human habitation" and have an infant mortality rate 125% higher than the national average.[6]

Presumably the University of California and the Giannini Foundation of Agricultural Research are paying as little attention to these aspects of agriculture today as they have over the past decades. From the enormous profits of large-scale agriculture in California, it would appear that growers

6 *Ibid.*, December 5, 1970, p. 6.

could raise the standard of living of some 700,000 farm workers substantially and still pay respectable dividends and attract new capital from the Bank of America.

STANFORD AND IMPERIALISM

The academic year 1968–69 was perhaps the high point of New Left insurgency on the campuses of the nation. Cries of "End military research" and "The university has always been in politics" went up all over the country. Dramatic sit-ins against programs funded by the Department of Defense, against Reserve Officer Training Corps programs, and against the complicity of the social sciences with the Vietnam War occurred on many campuses. The protests at Stanford University in Palo Alto, California, were not the most dramatic, although buildings were seized, but they produced one of the New Left's most interesting and dramatic documents dealing with university complicity: the minority report of two students appended to the final report of the Stanford-SRI Study Committee.

SRI stands for the Stanford Research Institute, a large operation attached to the university that lives off contract research for the military and business and that used the university's good name and some of its good professors.

Student concern about the activities of the SRI first surfaced in 1965 with the disclosure by a peace group of chemical and biological warfare (CBW) contracts held by the institute. More detailed studies of SRI war research came in 1967, and a small group marched on the SRI facilities. More extensive reports of counterinsurgency work by the SRI in Southeast Asia and Latin America came early in 1968, and they were widely publicized in an SDS "radical guide to Stanford" in the fall. The issue rapidly escalated and involved most of the university community. Forums, disruptions, and finally a sit-in resulted. Meanwhile, the administration formed a twelve-member committee to report on present and possible future relationships between Stanford and SRI. Its report was finished in April 1969. Attached to it was the minority statement of the two student members.

The minority report is an excellent example of the kind of detailed research and cool exposition of which the New Left is capable. The contrast between the students' detailed history of SRI and the bland, official view of the majority report is dramatic. The student report nicely weaves in many of the themes of this book, indicating in yet another way that the attack on the system is of a piece because students see the system as a piece. Business, government, foundations, and university leaders are all *dramatis personae.* The interdependencies and interrelations are evidenced not only in this report but also in the reappearance in the rest of this chapter of the same key names and organizations time and time again. The proposals of the students were, of course, not acted upon. SRI was separated from Stanford University and allowed to develop its own means of serving business and government, free from the objections of noisy students. This was a defeat for the students, who wanted SRI to come under close control by the university community, but it was hardly a victory for SRI and Stanford. That the issue could even have arisen testifies to the temper of the times and to the resourcefulness of the New Left.

1969

from STUDENT MINORITY REPORT ON THE STANFORD RESEARCH INSTITUTE [7]

Ann C. Bauer and Harry M. Cleaver

Introduction

Prefacing a report on AID and the University, Stanford trustee John Gardner remarked: "There isn't one American in a hundred, perhaps a thousand, who has a clear grasp of the unique partnership that is evolving between public and private instrumentalities in this country." SRI, along with a handful of not-for-profit research institutes elsewhere, is best viewed as a new component in this evolving partnership and a key coordinator of the joint efforts of competing corporations, of corporations with government, of government and industry with the university.

· · ·

On October 10, 1968, two days after SDS formally demanded that "Stanford Get Out of Southeast Asia," Acting President Robert Glaser announced the formation of a twelve-member committee to report on present and possible future relationships between Stanford and SRI. For over six months the authors of this dissenting report tried to work within the framework of that committee. Although we recognized that the formation of the committee was just putting off the inevitable confrontation, we had hoped that the committee could help place new information before the community in the course of its deliberations and that its report could clarify some of the important issues.

[7] Ann C. Bauer and Harry M. Cleaver, "Minority Report," *Campus Report Supplement* (Stanford University Relations Office), No. 5 (April 14, 1969), 37–50, 51–52.

We had hoped that the committee could help illuminate the core of the Stanford–SRI relationship—the personal influences of the David Packards and Ernest Arbuckles; the market power of big business, big government, and the big foundations; the ideological impact of elite values and top-down methodologies widely shared in both institutions.

But we soon discovered a fixation of the majority of the committee members on legal and formal SRI–University connections. They preferred to dwell on the technical aspects of alternative future actions. Unwilling to cause radical division within the committee, which we feared would impede its data gathering function, we found ourselves avoiding frequent conflict when expressions of our own concerns met with no sympathetic response in the committee.

Inexorably the drive of the committee became one towards consensus on "feasible alternatives" and rigorously detailing them. Having expected the division of community opinion between divestment of SRI and closer ties, we thought ourselves ready to deal with this. But we slowly were taken in by the endless hours of haggling over fine details of imaginary formulations, until our objections to the overall direction of the committee were lost in a forest of words. We, too, began to think that some "neutral," "objective" view of the alternatives could issue from the interplay in the committee.

To this end we thought we could amend *our* interpretation of the situation and therein draw our own conclusions as a minority statement. Indeed, only a week before termination of the report we had an eighteen-page draft of such a statement.

It was then that we began to understand dimly what had happened. For three days we struggled with the contradiction between our draft and the "objective" and "neutral" cost-benefit approach to which we were appending it. In this struggle we came to recognize the impact such an approach had upon the ideas and facts we emphasized. The very functioning of the committee had insured that the most vital issues be excluded. The cost-benefit approach was couched in a set of premises which assume away any basic conflict of interest between students and faculty and their business men trustees. Once we recognized this we were forced to disassociate from that which we had helped construct. We were faced with the necessity of expanding our draft sufficiently to create a new report which would speak to the issues we feel to be critical—one which would do so within the context of the very real political struggle swirling around us.

We had to do this in a very short time period. We regret the unpolished form of this report. We take responsibility for any of our research inaccuracies or factual errors. However, we hope that our efforts will be of use to the Stanford community in coming to grips with its present problems.

Part I. From little acorns

SRI's origins, in retrospect, seem quite modest. The West Coast economy emerged from World War II greatly strengthened, but with today's aerospace and electronics riches still only a gleam in the eye of a few visionaries like Stanford's Frederick Terman. By and large the economy rested on the pre-war chemical, petroleum, and food industries. In a post-war world where knowledge would become power in new and profitable ways, Western universities had fallen well behind Harvard, Johns Hopkins, MIT, and the other Eastern schools then swimming in the spill-over from wartime research. Terman found Stanford "an under-privileged institution" largely left out of "the exciting engineering and scientific activity associated with the war." The pioneer not-for-profit research institutes—Mellon, Batelle, Armour—or even profit-making researchers like Boston's Arthur D. Little Company had no counterparts in the West. At the same time, regional leaders in the Midwest, South, and Southwest were busily laying plans for institutes of their own.

But Western businessmen and educators were quite responsive to the region's research gap. In fact present antagonists of SRI can lodge paternity suits against at least three different groups. The first centered around three Stanford men—Robert E. Swain, professor of chemistry and for a time acting president of Stanford; Stanford chemist Philip A. Leighton, decorated at the end of WW II for his part at Stanford in the creation of firebombs and later a researcher in the meteorological aspects of Chemical-Biological Warfare (CBW); and alumnus Dudley Swim, later board chairman of National Airlines. Self-christened "The Three Musketeers," the group had discussed the idea of a Stanford-based research institute as early as 1939, at an encampment of San Francisco's exclusive Bohemian Club. They revived the idea after the war, gaining the support of University President Donald B. Tresidder.

Also at the close of the war, three members of the wartime staff of Lockheed Aircraft Corporation actually set up a Pacific Research Foundation in Los Angeles. This group eventually joined in the formative talks about SRI, folding up their own shop when the Stanford-based institute became a reality.

But the most important of the founding fathers was Atholl McBean, a prominent San Francisco industrialist and director of Standard Oil of California. With the cooperation of Stanford Vice President Alvin C. Eurich, McBean invited recommendations for a Pacific Coast research center from Clyde Williams, president of Batelle Memorial Institute, and Henry T. Heald, president of the Illinois Institute of Technology and the Armour Research Foundation, and later of the Ford Foundation. Heald presented his recommendations on January 24, 1946, to a gathering of San Francisco business executives. In his short three-page statement, he called for a high quality industrial research institute to serve individual companies, groups of companies in association, and agencies of government—federal, state, and local.

Trustees keep power

All three of the founding groups favored a strong link between industry and education. Heald called for university affiliation, specifically with Stanford. A month later, responding to the enthusiasm generated by the McBean-Heald report and to McBean's pledge of $100,000, the Stanford Board of Trustees agreed in principle on the creation of the Stanford Research Institute. Then, in December, sitting as the general members of SRI, the Stanford trustees approved a set of by-laws and elected a slate of directors to govern the new institute. They retained for themselves the power to elect directors annually and to dissolve the corporation at their discretion. They also assumed some measure of financial responsibility, which resulted in a $600,000 loan in 1948 and 1951, offered access to some of the university's library and laboratory resources, provided consultants (53 by 1968) and teaching positions to SRI staff (14 in 1968), and lent the prestige of Stanford, which aided in attracting staff.

In the words of the university public relations office, SRI became a "wholly owned subsidiary of the university."

The real ties of power over SRI, however, were never as neat as the legal niceties. The first SRI Board of Directors, which met for the first time on January 8, 1947, was divided between members of the university board and West Coast leaders who were not Stanford trustees. From the Stanford Board came President Tresidder (Chairman), Vice President Eurich, investment banker Charles Blyth, John E. Cushing of Matson Navigation, and industrialist W. P. Fuller, Jr., father of the present Stanford trustee. The other directors, not Stanford trustees, were McBean, Paul McKee (president of Pacific Power and Light), D. J. Russell (vice president of Southern Pacific), William L. Stewart, Jr. (executive vice president of Union Oil), and James D. Zellerbach (president of Crown-Zellerbach). This combination of industrial interests provided a group even more powerful and somewhat broader than the Stanford Board of Trustees.

These men dedicated SRI chiefly to the industrial development of the Western states. They sought financial support largely from industry rather than government, and they were themselves chief among the initial SRI Associates, corporations and individuals who paid $15,000 each to help support the new venture.

Of the early SRI industrial research some 74 per cent went to petroleum and natural gas people, 11 per cent to food products firms, and 10 per cent to chemical firms. Among the early associates were Humble, Richfield, Shell, Standard Oil of California, and Union Oil. "The institute plans to do the kind of research that industry itself might do if each company could set up its own comprehensive research organization, supported by the resources of a great university," SRI publicists wrote.

The new Institute also moved in 1949 and 1950 to provide some leadership as well as research capability to West Coast business, joining with the San Francisco Chamber of Commerce, the University of California, and Stanford to organize business conferences on the industrial importance of research.

During the same year that the "Applied Research Center for the West" was building its partnership with industry, it was also serving government (though to a far lesser degree). At its founding SRI postulated "an important obligation to the government of the United States to assist with scientific research needed for the national defense and welfare, and to keep our facilities open for a national emergency." By 1950 SRI had yielded even more of its basic emphasis on industrial research, possibly hoping that defense department dollars for electrical equipment studies and research on "explosion phenomena" might help fill the Institute's $450,000 deficit. Still, about three-fourths of SRI's $2 million research budget came from private clients.

Korean War

Then, in mid-1950, the Korean War erupted, and SRI's hot and cold war partnership with the Pentagon began in earnest. Doubling the portion of its government research from 23 per cent in January to 45 per cent in December, the Institute undertook work in advanced engineering design, strategy planning, projects for the Atomic Energy Commission, and studies of government research facilities. On the basis of such work, much of it classified, SRI continued to gain a larger and larger percentage of its revenue from government contracts through 1965.

But in this shift, SRI did more than simply produce *for* the new military demand. It also helped *produce* the demand itself.

SRI did this in several ways. Its earliest military studies, for example, helped prepare a climate of opinion favorable to the expansion of armaments and, not incidentally, of the particular armaments firm growing to maturity in the West Coast economy. Studying the time it would take to build the giant fleet of aircraft in 1948, if war should break out, SRI scientists posed two alternatives: mobilization with a year (1949) and mobilization with three years (1951). This multi-disciplinary M-Day approach did in fact aid the eventual mobilization. But its self-fulfilling assumptions, later applied to electronic equipment and aircraft engine production, also heightened the likelihood that mobilization would come. Other studies over the years of how to maintain U.S. production in full scale air war, development of civil defense and preparedness programs, and the like helped shape the cold war climate of the fifties, in which Americans could all too easily think the unthinkable.

SRI executives also sponsored "the world struggle against Communism" and the garrison state partnership in less academic fashion. "Even now," wrote 1950 director Jesse Hobson, "the united research endeavors of industry, government, private individuals, and research organizations present an imposing bulwark for the safety of this nation." "Research," he urged, "is a sword that is sharpened by use."

At meetings of SRI Associates, speakers such as Donald D. Quarles, the Assistant Secretary of Defense for Research and Development in 1963, urged the associates "to help us create public confidence that we are in fact making wise disposition of our defense resources." And, in enlarging the Board, SRI leaders brought in leading aerospace industrialists like Donald W. Douglas, vice president of Douglas Aircraft in 1949, and in 1951, industrialist John A. McCone, the Deputy Secretary of Defense in 1948, Undersecretary of the Air Force in 1950, and later director of the Atomic Energy Commission and the Central Intelligence Agency. Then setting new policy in 1954, after Korea, the Board moved to strengthen defense orientation.

ABM recoups losses

To be fair, SRI leadership in this process was really overshadowed by the work of the University itself. Where SRI's directions placed its initial faith in private industry, the real architect of the Peninsula defense economy, Stanford's Frederick E. Terman, then dean of engineering, looked much more hopefully to military financing of research-oriented industry.

Consequently, he built up a "steeple of excellence" with key university departments, opened university labs to industry, helped spin-off firms like Varian and Granger Associates, and led in the creation of the Stanford Industrial Park in 1951. These efforts, and of course the federal financing, actually made aerospace and electronics the big guns of California industry. During the first eighteen months of the Korean War, for example, California employment in the electronics industry rose 117 per cent.

Faced with an entirely new economy, SRI's course was clear. Merely to maintain its partnership with industry, it would have to integrate the new industrialists, both from the Peninsula and from Southern California, and further tie itself to the Pentagon.

The process of integration was dramatic. In 1955 Terman joined the SRI board as vice chairman of the newly formed executive committee. Then, in 1956 came Arnold Beckman of Beckman Instruments in the Industrial Park, followed by industrialist Edgar Kaiser in 1957, David Packard in 1958. Tom Jones, president of Northrup Aircraft, joined in 1961, along with General William A. Draper and Thomas P. Pike, both of whom had occupied high administrative positions in the Department of Defense during the Eisenhower administration. The number of new defense industries among SRI Associates was equally impressive.

Under the leadership of these men and corporations, SRI established a Naval Warfare Research Center, a Strategic Studies Center, and a Tactical Operations Program to search for more effective weapons systems and the concepts for their use, along with millions of dollars of research in space and missile science.

But the real clincher is SRI's leadership in an increasingly unpopular field of missile defense. By 1963, research on the ABM had become important to SRI and to associated industries. Facing a downturn in the California defense economy, SRI executive vice president Weldon Gibson spoke publicly about "possible existence of agreements between the United States and the Soviet Union leading toward arms limitation" and "the fact that more and more leaders are supporting the judgment that the arsenal of missiles and warheads has reached a point of diminishing returns."

By 1964, however, at the bottom of the pre-Vietnam economic lull, he saw "indications that short-term losses over the next few years may be recouped later in the decade with new developments in anti-missile missiles or a new generation of strategic weapons."

Vietnam pulled Gibson and the California economy out of that particular crisis, but now that the very escalation in Vietnam has started to hurt economically, especially in those industries dependent on subsidized research, the ABM is once again with us ... and with SRI.

According to the government's 1968 Technical Abstract Bulletin, among SRI reports are the following [identification numbers of the reports are omitted— C. P.]: A Methodology For National Deployment of Local Ballistic Missile Defense Batteries; National Effectiveness Evaluation Methods for BMD. In addition the Institute is studying a series of civil defense projects related to missile defense, as follows: A Metholodology for Estimating Fallout Casualties; Light Attack Shelter Requirements and Defense Avoidance Fallout Tactics; Civil Defense Interactions with BMD in a Direct Attack; Computer Implementation of the Miller Fallout Model; Civil Defense Interactions with Ballistic Missile Defense.

Part II. Around the world

Coordination

Though tempting, it would be misleading to focus too heavily on SRI's leadership in the "military-industrial-academic complex." The SRI board was interested in more than simple defense industries, and the Institute itself has appetites far beyond the fluctuating expenditures of the military. Expansionists, rather than merely defenders of what they already have, the SRI people have best expressed their particular genius by providing strategic leadership and technical manpower for the international expansion of West Coast corporations.

SRI's first big foreign push came in 1957, a natural internationalization of the earlier emphasis on regional development through private industry. Weldon Gibson, the man who has headed SRI's international program since its beginning in 1949, has stated that SRI is dedicated to two objectives:

economic progress, and the strengthening of private business on an international scale. These are good and noble causes and we are proud to stand with international companies the world over in pursuit of the fundamentals involved. Our objective is to do everything within our power to develop the private sector as the basic factor in economic strength and progress. (SRI-International, No. 11–1969, *The Lima Report.*)

The Institute also had a solid base of experience in piecemeal research and special projects. These experiences were as diverse as development studies on Cuba, Pakistan, India, Peru, Venezuela, Bolivia, Chile, Argentina, and Brazil, the establishment of a technical information service for American firms in Europe and an office in Zurich, liaison with research institutes abroad, and management trips abroad. But the main thrust, naturally enough, was in the Pacific area. In 1949 Secretary of State George C. Marshall and Harold Stassen invited SRI staff-member Eugene Staley to Washington to "help revise the American policy on China" and to study the "problem of halting the advance of Communism in the rest of the Far East." SRI was at the time studying the decline of Oriental commerce along the West Coast, and later undertook a study for Matson Navigation Co. on the feasibility of re-establishing passenger service in the Pacific. (On Matson's board sat Stanford trustee and SRI director Charles R. Blyth, president of Blyth & Co., Inc.) SRI also cooperated with the

Asia Foundation, which has been known as a CIA conduit, in an exploration of private investment possibilities and potentials in Pakistan, Ceylon, Burma, Thailand, Indonesia, Japan, and the Philippines.

The landmark in the development of SRI's internationalism and in the supra-national union of private enterprise it represented was the International Industrial Development Conference (IIDC) of 1957. Co-sponsored with Time-Life International, the conference brought 500 "key business executives" from 62 nations together—something of a first in the post-war period. Their common dedication was "to the role of private enterprise in stimulating economic and industrial development in the free world. The major objective of the meeting is to pool the experience of banking and industrial leaders in an examination of problems and proposals effecting industrial development throughout the world." (*Research for Industry*, Vol. 9, No. 7.) Among others addressing the conference, two names stand out: Henry Luce of Time-Life and Alfried Krupp von Bohlen, proprietor of a well-known German family business.

With the conference, SRI moved even farther from its origins as a department store for corporation research and closer to its present task of reducing international competition. Through inter-business communication and "a dynamic partnership and philosophy among those who guide much of the economic destiny of the free world," a movement toward the reduction of competition among individual firms seems to be at hand. By focusing on "relationships in newly developing areas between government development programs and private enterprise" and "techniques for investor-government collaboration under private management," it sought to reduce the anachronistic competition between private enterprise and public bodies.

Institutionally, the conference led to the formation of SRI's International Industrial Development Center, and a going concern with research problems such as "Private U.S. Venture Capital for Investment in Newly Developed Countries" and "Brazil: Factors Affecting Foreign Investment." (SRI Annual Report, 1957, SRI Press Release 10/3/58.)

SRI's premise was that corporate investment capital and Third World investment "opportunities" had to be more efficiently brought together and that SRI should do the job.

Since 1957, SRI's role as a coordinator of overseas corporate strategy has grown. In 1966 the international programs that had increased through the years, often under the supervision of Staley or Weldon "Hoot" Gibson, were brought together in a new managerial entity, SRI-International, with Gibson as head. The Institute announced that this reflected "a basic policy decision by the . . . Board of Directors and management to expand research operations in the international field."

"Major emphasis will be placed on research projects for business and industry, economic development projects for government and international institutes, and projects involving major programs in the security of the United States," SRI announced. Corporate investment planning, government-sponsored "development" programs in the Third World, and counterinsurgency research thus came solidly under one roof at SRI.

The one area where these activities have been thus merged more efficiently than in any other has been the Pacific. There international cooperation has reached an advanced stage in what American industrialists are calling the "Pacific Basin strategy," something SRI-International's Weldon Gibson denied innocently in a letter to the October 11 [*Stanford*] *Daily:* "We have no Pacific Basin strategy," he said, "other than a program of research and public service aimed at accelerating economic and industrial development in all the Pacific nations."

Bank of America president Rudolph Peterson, a member of the SRI-International advisory committee, has been somewhat more candid: "There is no more vast or rich area for resource development or trade growth in the world today," he said in a Chamber of Commerce publication. "Were we California businessmen to play a more dynamic role in helping trade developments in the Pacific Rim, we would have giant, hungry new markets for our products and vast new profit potentials for our firms."

The idea of a Pacific Basin strategy is total rationalization and control by business interests of the overall Pacific economy, using government funds, agencies, and military might when necessary. "Pacific Trade," an SRI pamphlet that prepared the way for the SRI-sponsored Pacific Industrial Conference in April of 1967, outlined an idea for a Pacific Basin Organization for Economic Cooperation, through which the corporations of advanced industrial countries would cooperate rather than compete—seemingly a sort of giant price-fixing, resource-sharing, pie-slicing organization which would decide on "specialization between countries to take advantage of the potentially huge economies of scale in ... production," develop a "systematic exchange of technical information," encourage "frequent consultation among business groups," and "joint assistance and cooperation in the further development of less-industrialized areas of the Pacific basin."

The organization would be "confined at the outset to the more industrialized nations" and would be "primarily under private auspices."

SRI's Pacific Industrial Conference in Sydney, Australia, in April of last year, attended by 125 "senior executives" from 22 nations, was opened with a speech from SRI chairman and Stanford dean of business Ernest Arbuckle, no stranger to Australia, where Utah Construction has extensive iron and coal interests.

Arbuckle said that Stanford professor Eliot Mears' pre-WW II description of the Pacific Basin as "an economic community of the future" articulated a basic view "that remains today in principle and practice within both Stanford University and Stanford Research Institute."

Gibson told the businessmen that their meeting was noteworthy because "it is an act of leadership by private enterprise in the interests of free nations throughout the Pacific" and "it is organized entirely under private auspices with an emphasis on the growth of private enterprises." President Johnson sent a telegram hailing "a sense of common economic destiny ... growing among peoples in the Pacific Basin."

The Sydney meeting was the first of a plethora of such gatherings under SRI auspices. It led to the SRI-led August invasion of Indonesia by about 200 "senior executives" who arrived to "acquaint" themselves with "current conditions" and stayed to arrange corporate investments. Indonesia "contains extensive natural resources," SRI explained. The meeting "created a new and highly effective relationship between business and the government in Indonesia," Gibson said later. (Manila Agenda, p. 2.)

The Djakarta meeting in turn led to an SRI-Singapore Meeting last summer at which 170 "leaders of private enterprise" were moved to "strongly endorse the concept of regional economic development in Southeast Asia."

Southeast Asia, in fact, has been the focus of much of SRI-International's recent attention. The SRI-Singapore meeting was followed by an SRI-Manila meeting "devoted to Business in Southeast Asia," in March of this year. Opening the meeting, Gibson explained: "This part of the globe will surely be at the center of world attention during the next decade or more," he said. "This will be especially so in the economic field once military strife in the region is abated." Unfazed by the agitation among students at Stanford, Gibson eulogized "private business" as "the greatest social invention of modern times" and pledged SRI's "continuing assistance" to the development of "private enterprise" in Southeast Asia, particularly Indonesia, Malaysia, the Philippines, Singapore, and Thailand.

Other SRI-International business conferences have included the North Atlantic Industrial Conference (October, 1967, in Seville, Spain), last November's Conference on East-West Trade (Vienna), and this January's SRI-Lima Meeting in Peru, a country in which the entire Stanford complex is deeply involved. After the Peruvian meeting, Gibson wrote that all of the meetings in the series —Sydney, Djakarta, Singapore, Seville, Vienna, and Lima—"were dedicated to the advancement of economic development and to the growth of private enterprise—especially international business."

COIN

For the underdeveloped nations, the bite in the SRI-style coordination and control of investment flows is the direct tie-in with counterinsurgency efforts. Coordination of investments which benefit many of the Stanford and SRI associated corporations creates a natural interest in the economic and social "stability"—the maintenance of a proper "investment climate."

In 1957, Henry Robison, SRI senior economist, began his speech to a Stanford Alumni Association Conference on "America's Stake in World Economic Stability" with: "since World War II, the United States has been thrust upon the world's stage in a position of power and influence probably undreamed of even by those statesmen of a past generation who were imbued with a spirit of manifest destiny." Discussing "the economic factors which underlie the political relationships" between America and the Third World, he asserted that the countries of Southeast Asia "are more important for their geographic position than for their economic potential." Robison argued that "at last freed of the Western political domination of the past century," it is essential for the Third World "that their progress be made under Western guidance and Western concepts of individual freedom rather than under the heavy hand of

Communist slavery." He concluded that "The free world must not lose South-east Asia . . . as it has already lost China."

The fear of "losing" Southeast Asia is presumably just the reason that SRI did a study that same year titled "Environmental Conditions in Selected Areas of Potential Limited Warfare," which was prepared for McDonnell Aircraft Corporation and which described in detail the application of "limited" warfare techniques to certain peripheral areas of Asia, including Vietnam.

By 1961 SRI senior economist Eugene Staley was in Vietnam performing what has become a second job for SRI "developmentalists"—advising the U.S. government of methods for bringing "stability" to its subordinate dictator-ships. Staley headed President John Kennedy's special financial group to the Diem government-in-trouble in Vietnam. The group's purpose was to develop a plan of "coordinated financial action which would be in support of counter-guerrilla activities." His recommendations to JFK were for an increase in aid for military measures and for "economic and social development," including "resettlement" where it was necessary to "remove the population from Viet Cong pressures." The program was expected to "restore security within 18 months." It didn't.

In 1966, SRI took a second stab at this special kind of social reform, this time sending senior economist William Bredo to the Saigon government on the formulation and implementation of a program of land tenure reform. "In view of the critical situation in South Vietnam," began the unsolicited SRI project proposal to AID, "the proposal emphasis is on political objectives rather than economic goals."

"It is considered most important at this time to stress a program of land tenure reform which emphasizes social justice, which produces a more favor-able rearrangement of the rural power structure, and which will tend to pro-duce political results that will contribute to winning the war," the proposal said.

Maintaining a proper investment climate, land reform, financial counseling—none of these programs sound anything like as sinister as "counterinsurgency." But this subtlety is in the very nature of COIN [counterinsurgency] activities, especially as developed under the Kennedy government, and it's the reason so many COIN programs pass for charity. For, according to the Dictionary of United States Military Terms for Joint Usage, issued February 1, 1964, by the Joint Chiefs of Staff, counterinsurgency is "those military, paramilitary, po-litical, economic, psychological, and civic actions taken by a government to defeat the subversive insurgency."

Faced with so coordinated and global a strategy, the question of encouraging or prohibiting counterinsurgency depends less on the niceties of particular programs than on one's attitude toward outside intervention or on a choice between a given regime and its "subversive insurgents." At the very least, in-telligent men should come to expect that military intervention of one kind or another will often follow on the heels of SRI-style economic expansion.

As proof we need merely list those explicitly labeled counterinsurgency contracts which SRI coordinates with its programs of "economic develop-ment." After all, approximately a third of SRI's international project revenue last year was spent for South and Southeast Asian projects, mostly paid for by the Pentagon. [There follows a list of thirteen reports with such titles as "Investigation of Counterguerrilla Surveillance Processes" and "Operational Testing of Wireless Seismic Ambush Aids."—C. P.]

Part III. SRI's goodies

Even SRI's enemies are quick to point out what appear to be its obviously constructive activities in the physical and social sciences. But, as with other SRI activities, they are not always what they seem.

No one needs be told air pollution is of serious concern in California, particularly in the Bay Area, which is cursed with the third most critical air pollution problem in the U.S. SRI began research on air pollution almost immediately after its inception, but SRI's smog research differs from its defense work only in degree: instead of conducting research aimed at protecting people from air pollution, SRI gathers information which helps polluting industries escape public condemnation and more stringent regulations.

In 1949 and 1952, SRI joined the California Institute of Technology, UCLA, and USC in sponsoring two symposiums on air pollution at which scientists, industrial representatives, and government leaders were treated to lectures dealing with smog analysis and detection methods. But SRI smog research at the time was primarily funded by business organizations from industries among the prime pollutors, such as the Western Oil and Gas Association.

The November, 1948, issue of SRI's news bulletin, *Research for Industry*, cites a survey of people in Los Angeles, the greater number of whom attributed smog to industry. But an investigation at that time under the direction of SRI's supervisor of air pollution research dealt only with the impact of the Los Angeles climate on smog.

More recently, when pollution from the Pacific Gas and Electric (PG&E) plant at Moss Landing aroused a furor among citizens in Monterey County, PG&E brought in the head of SRI's Environmental Research Department, Elmer Robinson, as one expert witness. PG&E's president, Shermer Sibley, sits on the board of SRI, as do four other past or present directors of PG&E or its subsidiaries. Robinson is a member and past chairman of the Bay Area Air Pollution Control District (BAAPCD) advisory council, an agency which, by failing to enforce existing pollution regulations, often seems to be working more for the pollutor than the consumer. Much of Robinson's research at SRI is sponsored directly by the very industries the BAAPCD is expected to control.

Robinson's testimony concerning PG&E's Moss Landing plant exonerated the company and contradicted that of biologists from Stanford's Hopkins Marine Station in Pacific Grove and scientists from UC Santa Cruz and Monterey Peninsula College.

According to Ed Munson, Air Pollution Control Officer for Monterey County, the PG&E plant dumps more nitrogen dioxide into the air than all the power plants in Los Angeles county. He says PG&E is responsible for 90 per cent of the nitrogen dioxide pollution in the Monterey region, which harms crops and causes emphysema.

Smog and gas

A research project Robinson carried out with Robert Robbins is reported in the December, 1968, issue of the SRI *Journal*. Sponsored by the American Petroleum Institute, it exonerates industrial polluters by emphasizing natural sources of pollution, such as swamp gas, decaying organic matter, and vegetation. Robinson overlooks the hydrocarbons and sulfur dioxide which are chief factors in air pollution and products of oil refineries.

At both the University and SRI, those who do smog research are often the same men who work on Chemical and Biological Warfare (CBW). Robinson worked with SRI's CBW-men, William C. Thuman and Richard D. Cadle, on building an important piece of equipment for their work, the SRI aerosol camera. In a 1954 article in the *Biological Photography Association Journal*, he described its importance: "The armed forces may use aerosols defensively as in smoke screens or offensively in chemical or biological warfare."

SRI's social science contributions are also often thought to be beneficial. These began with a 1952 conference bringing the SRI Associates together to discuss application of social science to industrial problems. Dean Ernest C. Arbuckle of the Stanford Graduate School of Business explained that "in the near future, it is possible that private business may take over from government the task of guarding the humane aspects of our industrial civilization."

What this turns out to be is guarding the boss from his employees. SRI publications document frequent calls for psychological research on worker morale, methods of screening job applicants, of increasing worker efficiency, perfecting on the job training, and the like. Social science at SRI does not generally provide models for effective labor organizing, police control boards, or self-determination by students.

In fact, SRI's education research frequently appears to channel, rather than free, students. Dr. Howard Vollmer of the SRI research staff wrote in the [*Stanford*] *Daily* last fall that "the shift to social problems has taken place in the Institute in matters like educational, urban, and minority problems"—problems, by the way, which industry and government-funded researchers are most likely to see as counterinsurgency affairs. "Funds from the Defense Department," Vollmer said, "are concentrated around behavioral and social areas and primarily concerned with improving efficiency and job satisfaction."

BART men

SRI development of designs for urban mass transit, too, seems more likely to serve the interests of the industrialists on the board than the people on trolleys. SRI did some of the feasibility surveys which preceded the creation of the

Bay Area Rapid Transit system (BART). The push for BART began in the early fifties when a group of SF businessmen connected to the Blyth-Zellerbach Committee initiated the studies. The committee, a corporate group supporting urban renewal, was formed by Charles Blyth and J. D. Zellerbach, both founding directors of SRI. Blyth was also a Stanford trustee.

As a part of the development of a downtown San Francisco business center, BART was to enable suburbanites to commute to work; but besides providing inadequate service to city dwellers (it avoids Hunters Point and bypasses the Oakland ghettoes), BART financing will be a burden to those least able to pay by increasing the tax burden and by raising property values along the route.

These studies, and others regarding plans for school desegregation, protection of business investments in the city, "reverse commuter" facilities, and the development of Oakland, raise much the same questions as other SRI research: do we approach the problems from the standpoint of business or from that of those the research ultimately affects?

What we mean by constructive research is not research framed by one self-seeking interest group, which happens to have the money to fund it. The inference can be drawn that all too frequently the SRI researcher, under pressure to sell a product, has approached a problem uncritically and unable to separate himself from the view of his contractor. Unfortunately this is characteristic of most SRI activities. The quality of work at the Institute, particularly in the social sciences, declines as it aims at preserving the status quo rather than meeting people's needs.

We have discussed some research touching upon the critical problems of cities but which has not been chosen by the people of those cities. Such work is at the least irrelevant and at the most detrimental to the needs of people. Guiding Institute research policy both to encourage self-sponsored research rather than work responding to a fluctuating market and to increase the "relevance" of such work to all people is important in redirecting policy of the future Institute.

While redirecting policy is more difficult than restricting research, we must take steps in that direction. Obviously those people affected should be asked about the needs. To ensure that SRI meet the changing social needs, we must institute continuous review and reinterpretation of policy. Only this way can we guarantee the future "benefits" of research, and a critical approach to solutions.

The rest of the student minority report suggests guidelines and mechanisms for ensuring control of SRI by the university community and some means whereby those affected by its research can have some voice in what research is carried out. The report suggests that in view of widespread community protests, all research related to the war in Southeast Asia be stopped, as well as all research dealing with chemical, biological, and radiological warfare. The authors do not argue that all military research should be forbidden, but they explicitly "reject the contention that any research the U.S. government desires to fund is acceptable, and that questions of mortality and political responsibility must be directed toward the government policy guiding the uses to which the research will be put." [8]

UNIVERSITY NEUTRALITY

For many liberals, the recommendations of Bauer and Cleaver mean the politicization of the university, and that, in turn, means the end of academic freedom. Only if the university stays clear of politics and maintains its distance from the various communities that seek to influence it can independent, value-free scholarship be guaranteed. When the New Left cast politics into the university process, it meant that the Governor Reagans, the right-wing groups, the state legislators, and local municipal agencies could rush in too. The result, according to the middle-class liberals, has been disastrous attacks on the university and the conversion of the university into a wayward instrument of varying political pressures.

For the New Left, the answer is simple: the university has always been political; it has just not been exposed as such. The university's role became clear when faculty members and students were penalized for open dissent from government policies and when research on the role of the university in national affairs was disseminated.

In the process of disseminating this research, through confrontations and other means, some people were hurt. One minor but revealing incident was reported in a story in *Look* magazine. At a meeting regarding SRI, a young physicist heard the president of SRI argue that no researcher was forced to undertake any project he found morally objectionable. The physicist contradicted him, saying that he had been pressured into doing chemical-warfare research. The physicist was fired. As the executive vice president of SRI put it, according to the magazine article, "People like that have a decision to make—do they want to support the organization or not?" [9] This would be the price of "neutrality."

It would be hard, in any case, to believe that the top thirty or so universities, with two-thirds of their regents and trustees drawn from the commercial, industrial, and financial empires of the country, could be neutral about the issues the Left was raising. One answer to the Left's charge might be to admit that the universities are not neutral in the sense that they seek to turn out the engineers, scientists, and teachers needed to man the system and inculcate the ideals of capitalism and democracy into the young. Society needs these personnel. At the same time, however, the universities foster the humanities and the social sciences, and the members of these

8 *Ibid.*, p. 48.
9 Charles W. Bailey and Frank Wright, "American Militarism: The University Arsenal," *Look*, 33:17 (August 26, 1969), 34.

disciplines are overwhelmingly more liberal in their politics than the trustees, more critical of the business system and the values it imposes, and obviously free to dissent from the prevailing ethos. These disciplines have always been centers of dissent. Thus the corporate state does not and cannot control the university in this respect. Furthermore, the trustees are intelligent men and they see the need for some degree of academic freedom and criticism; otherwise they would have begun long ago to choose which textbooks to use, which professors to hire, and what the goals of research should be. A book such as this one could not be put together if the universities had not produced the research that the New Left feeds on, paid the salaries of some contributors, and generated a market among undergraduates that would encourage a publisher to publish the book.

To this defense the New Left, in its less hyperbolic moments, would respond as follows. Stringent controls are expensive and difficult, and they are probably not worth the cost and effort. The system, until very recently, has not been seriously attacked by social scientists and humanists, so there was no need to invest much effort in attempts to control their activities. The situation may be changing now, with state legislators demanding to see reading lists in selected social science courses (New York State), cancelling recommended raises for tenured professors who have spoken out against the war (University of Wisconsin), and countless subtle and not-so-subtle political tests in hiring and promotions throughout the country.[10]

The success of the New Left may in fact put the liberal theory to a strong test, but in any case, one gathers the system is not that perfect. In addition to the costs of control, internal contradictions exist, errors are made, opportunities are lost, and a remnant of values remains in American society that makes it difficult to stamp out dissent and criticism. Given these aspects, control might be achieved through more subtle means, and the control might be selective, concerned with what the business system needs at any particular point in time. If this is the way the system does in fact operate, the next article will illustrate it. That article, "Sinews of Empire," shows how the social sciences are co-opted.

It also illustrates a more general point. The Stanford Research Institute story is not an isolated example. Universities in general are not simply passive and impartial suppliers of manpower and research for corporations. A simple supply–demand function is operating in one sense: people need jobs; some of these are good jobs, requiring high skills and offering high pay; and some mechanism must be found to train people for them. But much more is true of universities. They are a kind of active corporation in

---

10 According to a brief note in an issue of *The Guardian* in the fall of 1970, the precise date of which I cannot locate, a special sociology course entitled "The Critical Spirit" at the University of Oregon had an enrollment of more than two hundred undergraduates. University officials turned the list of students over to the FBI. For a description of repression in the California State college system, see Bruce Severy, "Purge in California Education," *The Guardian*, February 6, 1971, p. 71.

their own right, seeking out profits for business (and thus growth for themselves), interlocking with business (and government and the military) at higher levels, planning business strategies in the office of the university president or a convenient, nearby foundation, and so on. The universities thus act as power centers for the business system, as well as resource bases.

FOUNDATIONS: THE PENETRATING WEDGE

The co-optation of the social sciences takes place through the medium of foundations. Foundations, such as the Ford Foundation, the Carnegie Foundation, the Rockefeller Foundation, and the Mellon Institute hardly need to be linked to business—their ties are as obvious as their names. People often think of foundations as disinterested, independent creatures, spun off by their namesakes for humanitarian purposes. After all, the reasoning goes, they sponsor all kinds of research, they do not appear to make political checks on the recipients of their largesse, and they could even be said to sponsor activities and research occasionally that are not in the interest of business and industry.

The argument of the New Left is that such foundations represent the liberal wing of business, that is, corporate liberalism, which is designed to bring along the reactionary and conservative members of the business community a bit faster. Monopoly capitalism is a dynamic system, and it creates all sorts of social problems as it moves through history. These must be ameliorated or, first, there will be the possibility of a revolution or, second, national purchasing power will fall so low that it will invite ruinous depressions. To prevent these disasters, corporate liberalism endorses insurance programs for industrial accidents and unemployment, Social Security, and some system of medical care for the poor. None of these programs really redistributes income in the population—the distribution does not appear to have changed appreciably over the last seventy years— or measurably reduces the power of the capitalists. Although their power of gross exploitation is limited, they are still left in power. These programs are largely the result of foundation activity. The foundations finance study groups, centers, conferences, and so on to work out basic programs and then sell the results to business and governmental groups. G. William Domhoff presents the most extensive analysis of these activities in his recent book, *The Higher Circles*.[11]

These policy-forming groups naturally draw on social scientists, but this

---

[11] G. William Domhoff, *The Higher Circles: The Governing Class in America* (New York: Random House, 1970). See especially Chapter 5, "How the Power Elite Makes Foreign Policy," and Chapter 6, "How the Power Elite Shapes Social Legislation."

is only the tip of the iceberg. If corporate liberalism needs the more extensive, prolonged, and active involvement of social scientists, then it must penetrate the universities themselves. This it has done. The following selection by David Horowitz nicely illustrates how, in the face of growing "worldwide responsibilities" following the Second World War, the business system created the manpower and the research necessary to carry through these new and growing responsibilities. The end of the war saw the United States not only with unprecedented economic and political advantages in the world, and a deep appreciation for the economic and military fruits of physical science research and development, but also with a chance to bring the social sciences into the corporate fold.

1969

SINEWS OF EMPIRE [12]

David Horowitz

Following the student seizure of Harvard's University Hall last spring, Time Magazine reported that Harvard Dean Franklin L. Ford "emphasized that continued rifling of University files could have compromised virtually the entire faculty." This mind-boggling admission (offered in defense of the swift unleashing of police) is but one measure of how far academia has fallen from the ideal of open, critical, independent scholarship.

The universities were once thought to constitute a vital, independent, countervailing estate, but the modern university has been converted into an Office of External Research for the State Department, the Pentagon and the international corporations. The postwar takeover of the university was accomplished with less finesse and reserve than a corporate conglomerate customarily shows a newly acquired subsidiary, and it is symbolic that the new management team that was to reorganize the university from "within" was drawn largely from the unlikely and forbidding ranks of the crack American World War II intelligence arm, the OSS (Office of Strategic Services).

The university is proverbially the most conservative of institutions—tradition-bound, unable to respond and adapt to changing times. But under the postwar tutelage of its powerful outside mentors, entirely new academic fields of social and political science have been created, which cut effortlessly across tra-

12 David Horowitz, "Sinews of Empire," *Ramparts*, Vol. 8 (October 1969), 32–42. Copyright Ramparts Magazine, Inc., 1968. Reprinted by permission of the editors.

ditional academic lines and prerogatives that have so hampered innovations in, for example, black studies. These new international policy disciplines and "area studies" (e.g., Asian Studies) were provided with an avalanche of facilities—buildings, libraries, computer technology. Staffs and faculties were assembled, granted unprecedented autonomy and exalted in one jump to a kind of penthouse status in the academic hierarchy. They were provided freedom and leverage by abundant outside financing. With all of this backing, they quickly became the most powerful influence on the old horse-and-buggy departments, whose disciplines and concepts of scholarship began to follow the winning model set before them.

Thus the experts in international affairs, the new Adams of academe, were created. They were housed in the new language and area studies institutes and centers which multiplied from a handful before the war to 191 by 1968. Their power within the universities has grown apace. At Berkeley, for instance, a political science professor estimates that one-third of his department's faculty depend on institutes for part of their income.

The academic Genesis of the new professionalism is significant not only for what it reveals about the university, but for what it shows about the institutional Creators. The details of this history provide a unique insight into the operations of these institutions of power and their personnel, interests and requirements. For here they were knitting the sinews of empire—the research, the civil servants, the technicians, the ideology, the whole fabric which binds together the imperial whole and reveals the structure of empire itself.

The Second World War, and in its aftermath the collapse of the French, Dutch, German and Japanese empires, opened the way for a new global American imperium which required a vast new "service-" and policy-oriented intellectual infrastructure—the kind for which England was famous, but which America lacked. Organizations like the foundation-financed Council on Foreign Relations, a key ruling class policy organization which had come into prominence during the war (see *Ramparts*, April 1968), served as the long-range planning bodies for foreign policy. What was needed now was a reservoir of information and talent at the intermediate levels: the technicians and middle management of empire.

During the war itself, intellectuals could be mobilized directly into government. Academia naturally put itself at the service of Washington, most dramatically in the Manhattan Project, but in some ways more significantly through the OSS, the seed of the fantastic postwar symbiosis which developed between the military, the state, international business and the university. After the war the same academic energies were mobilized indirectly, based in the university yet acting as a junior partner in U.S. foreign policy. The academic vehicle for all this was the new discipline of International Studies. It was a bit like moving offices.

This transition from extraordinary war mobilization to permanent academic function was engineered not by the military or the scholars, however, but by the foundations, as is made clear in a U.S. Office of Education report on Language and Area Centers (the subdivisions of International Studies). After reviewing the immense sums spent on establishing the programs by the Rockefeller, Carnegie and other Foundations ($34 million between 1945 and 1948 alone), the report declares:

It must be noted that the significance of the money granted is out of all proportion to the amounts involved since *most universities would have no center program had they not been subsidized. Our individual inventories indicate clearly the lack of enthusiasm as well as of cash on the part of most college administrations for such programs.* (Emphasis added.)

The significance of foundation grants today, 25 years after the launching of the first programs, is as great as ever. In 11 of the 12 top universities with institutes of international studies, a single foundation, Ford, is the principal source of funds. Affiliated with the institutes at Columbia, Chicago, Berkeley, UCLA, Cornell, Harvard, Indiana, MIT, Michigan State, Stanford and Wisconsin are 95 individual centers. Ford is a sole or major source of funds for 83 of these, Carnegie for five, AID for two, the Government of Liberia for one, and assorted government contracts, foundations and endowments for four.

To be sure, there were always scholars willing to play a role in the development of the international studies programs. And there was no compulsion— a professor is always free to undertake any project that somebody is willing to pay for. There are excellent scholars of all stripes and persuasions, capable of forming all kinds of programs. Only some get to do so. And it certainly helps if the big foundations happen to share your interests—or you theirs. In the control of scholarship by wealth, it is neither necessary nor desirable that professors hold a certain orientation because they receive a grant. The important thing is that they receive the grant because they hold the orientation. (Exceptions in the case of isolated radical individuals, of course, do nothing to counter the momentum and direction imparted by vast funding programs to a whole profession or discipline.)

Viewed in the abstract, the academic objections which were raised against the "area studies" concept (i.e., the integration of several disciplines to illuminate a particular geographical area) would seem insuperable (at least as insuperable as the objections to autonomous black studies programs, and in many ways parallel). The area program would override the academic departments. It would, it was maintained, produce not scholars, but dilettantes. Who would be qualified to run such programs, to set and maintain standards? Area research would become the refuge of the incapable and incompetent.

Beyond that were the hard political objections. Perpetual competition for students, courses, influence and money already existed within the university. A new overlapping department would be a formidable competitor and would therefore naturally be resisted by the existing departments. All these arguments and forces did come into play when the international studies programs were first being sponsored by the foundations, but all of them amounted to the merest whiffle of wind. In effect, academia's most sacred sanctuaries were invaded, its most honored shibboleths forsworn, its most rigid bureaucratic rules and "professional" standards circumvented and contravened without a finger of opposition being lifted. All it took was money, prestige, access to strategic personnel and collusion with those in the highest reaches of the academic administrations. As for the professors, they went along like sheep.

Newton thought that the planets were originally thrown into their orbits by the arm of God, but continued in them perpetually due to inertia. Such also is the principle of foundation intercession in the affairs of men. In the development of any complex and dispersed social institution, the initiating stages, the prototypes, are the key to the future evolution of the whole. The initiators naturally become the experts in the field. They are called upon to advise in the setting up of the offspring organizations, and they are the teachers and superiors of the personnel who staff them. This logic of innovation is particularly marked in academic institutions, which, like guilds, are structured as self-perpetuating hierarchies of experience. Most academics are oriented toward their own increasingly mobile careers rather than toward the local institution, whose direction they tend to accept as a given, beyond their power or understanding.

The first major international studies center was Columbia's School of International Affairs, set up in 1946 as an outgrowth of Columbia's wartime Naval School of Military Government and Administration. The head of the Naval School, Professor Schuyler Wallace (later an executive of the Ford Foundation), also became the first director of the School of International Affairs and remained in that post until 1960. According to the official history of the offspring school, the Naval School "provided a broad basis of experience for the formation of the School of International Affairs." The history also states: "Of paramount importance [in the new School] was the task of training students for technical and managerial posts in those agencies of the government which maintained a foreign service...."

In 1960, the School issued a pamphlet entitled *Employment Opportunities for Students Trained in International Affairs.* The first such opportunity described was the Central Intelligence Agency, the second the State Department, the third AID, the fourth the U.S. Information Agency, the fifth the National Security Agency, and then corporations such as the Bank of America, the Chase Manhattan Bank, the First National City Bank, Mobil Oil, Standard Oil of New Jersey and so forth. Finally, the U.N. and other civic, cultural and international agencies were mentioned. It was no surprise, then, when in 1968 the director of the School, Andrew Cordier (a consultant to the State Department and Ford Foundation), revealed that 40 per cent of the School's graduates go directly into government service and 20–30 per cent into "international banking and business."

Since its inception, the real substance of the School has been in its new affiliated area institutes, the first of which was the Russian Institute. Discussions about the Institute had been initiated by Geroid T. Robinson, the head of the OSS Research and Analysis Branch, USSR Division, who was to become the Russian Institute's first director. In 1945 the Rockefeller Foundation made a five-year starter grant of $1,250,000. Joseph Willits, the Rockefeller Foundation's director of Social Sciences who disbursed the funds was, like Geroid Robinson and Schuyler Wallace, a member of the Council on Foreign Relations (CFR), as were of course David, Nelson and John D. Rockefeller themselves.

With financing assured, the Institute's staff was appointed. Most important was Philip E. Mosely, who succeeded Robinson as director in 1951. Also a member of the CFR (he later became its director of studies), Mosely was a former State Department officer. Of the entire five-man steering staff of the Russian Institute, only Geroid Robinson had had any prior connection with Columbia University, but four had been associated with the OSS or the State Department, three were in the CFR, and three were members of the upper-class Century Club (as were Schuyler Wallace and Allen Dulles, the OSS veteran who went on to head the CIA). Such are the basic credentials of the new academic discipline.

The foundations not only provided funds for the staff salaries, libraries and physical facilities of these centers and institutes, but financed the students and trainees as well. Thus in 1947 the Rockefeller Foundation chipped in $75,000 worth of postgraduate fellowships for the Russian Institute. This was followed by $100,000 from the Carnegie Corporation for less advanced students. From 1947 through 1953, 140 Carnegie grants were made to 116 students of the Institute who were also eligible for regular Columbia grants. To financial privilege was added bureaucratic forbearance: the Ph.D. requirement (which, thanks to the old Carnegie Foundation, acted as a vise on the creativity and freedom of every academician) was waived for Senior Fellows at the Russian Institute, and an opening made for "mature men of unusual ability," such as former members of government agencies and political emigré figures.

Prime importance was given to the influential propagation of ideas—in short, publication. "It appeared to the staff urgently necessary," the official history reports, "that the most valuable of the Institute's research results be guaranteed publication in spite of soaring costs and of shrinking markets for high-priced scholarly books." How many scholars have wished likewise! But the Institute had the angels on its side, and thanks to the Rockefeller Foundation it was able to set up a "revolving publication fund" to subsidize Institute books, ensuring their publication and widespread academic distribution.

Similarly, Institute academics had easy access to such prestigious ruling-class publications as the Council on Foreign Relations' influential magazine, *Foreign Affairs*. They had funds for their own scholarly journals, which quickly became leaders and opinion makers in what was an open field. They had access to the leading publications of the various older disciplines, which were usually controlled by academic politicians of the Social Science Research Council (SSRC) or the other foundation-financed academic "steering committees." Thus the successive Russian Institute heads, Geroid Robinson and Philip Mosely, both served on the original World Areas Research Committee of the SSRC. Mosely was also chairman of the Joint Committee on Slavic Studies of the SSRC and the American Council of Learned Societies. Finally, they had access to the university presses, which, like the other instruments of organized influence in the university community, are controlled by the administrative foundation-oriented elite. So, for example, Schuyler Wallace was not only director of Columbia's School of International Affairs from 1946 to 1960, as well as of several of its institutes, but was also director of the Social Science Research Council (1952–1958), an associate of the Ford Foundation (1952–1960), and director of the Columbia University Press (1955–1962).

All this served to create an intellectual juggernaut of unrivaled power in its field. In 1964, the current director of the Russian Institute boasted that its 500 alumni constituted the majority of all American experts in the Soviet field. By force of its example, by the direct influence of its personnel and by the enabling support of the CFR-foundation power elite, the Institute was able to dominate the field of Russian affairs both in the academic world and in the sphere of government policy.

The Russian Institute was the most important of the many influential institutes in Columbia's School of International Affairs, but it was in all respects typical—both in genesis and direction. "Late in 1947," recounts the official history, "the creation of an East Asian Institute ... was placed before the Rockefeller Foundation. With the aid of a grant from that body, the Institute was formally established in 1948." Like the Russian Institute, it was the first of its kind in America and was guided by former State Department and foreign service officers. In September 1949, a Carnegie grant produced the European Institute, which was initially headed by Grayson Kirk, Columbia professor, Carnegie Corporation trustee, CFR member and Mobil Oil director. When Kirk resigned the following year to take on the Columbia provostship, he was succeeded as Institute director by Schuyler Wallace. The present director is Philip Mosely. Like the Hapsburg Royalty, they like to keep the family small and intimate.

As the American empire and its problems expanded, so the School of International Affairs broadened to include centers on the Middle East, Africa, Latin America and Southeast Asia. Its funding also shifted from the Carnegie and Rockefeller pilot fish to the great Ford Whale itself. Thus by 1968, there were 15 affiliated institutes and centers, nine funded exclusively by the Ford Foundation, four by Ford and one or two other foundations, and one by Ford and the federal government. All operated beyond any regular academic authority, responsible only to the provost of the university and its president, presently the venerable Grayson Kirk.

A remarkable team spirit prevails among the administrations of the School, the foundations and the government. This was neatly illustrated in a letter liberated during the Spring 1968 Columbia student rebellion. The letter, from Columbia's Grayson Kirk to Gerald Freund of the Rockefeller Foundation, concerned a former Indonesian official whose politics were attractive to the State Department, but whom the Department presumably did not wish to discredit with direct support. Wrote Kirk on February 22, 1966:

Dean Cordier reports to me that he has discussed with you the possible financial support from the Rockefeller Foundation for a research project to be undertaken by Mr. Biar Tie Khonw, a former high official in the Indonesian government. We have been informed by knowledgeable people in the Department of State, by Mr. Slater of the Ford Foundation, and others, that Mr. Khonw is very well qualified to contribute to the restoration of economic order and stability in Indonesia in such time as it becomes politically possible.... The grant is to include travel expenses to the Netherlands and several trips to Washington.... Mr. Khonw would be attached to the faculty of international affairs as a visiting scholar.

Yes. But can he teach?

As in the university system generally, the "lead system" played a central role in the creation of the international studies centers. The centers were concentrated for maximum effectiveness at a few "leading" universities from which their influence would radiate to others. Of the 191 centers listed by the State Department, more than half cluster around 12 institutions. Clearly Harvard, the Pentagon of America's academic legions, would have to be a keystone in the structure. And indeed the creation of the Russian Research Center there in 1947, and of the inclusive Center for International Affairs a decade later, reveals even more graphically than the prototypical case of Columbia the nexus of power in the field.

The initiative for Harvard's Russian Research Center came from John W. Gardner, then a recent OSS graduate, later Secretary of HEW, and now head of the Urban Coalition. But Gardner himself had been set in motion by a Wall Street lawyer named Devereux Josephs. Reputed by one whimsical but perspicacious observer to be one of the four men who run America (the other three being bankers Robert A. Lovett, John J. McCloy and Douglas Dillon), Devereux Josephs is a Groton and Harvard alumnus, a Century club member, a director of such nerve centers of finance as the New York Life Insurance Company and Rockefeller Center, Inc., and such globally oriented industrials as the American Smelting and Refining Co.—and he was president of the Carnegie Corporation. It was presumably in this last role, as educator one might say, that Josephs found he had, in the words of *Fortune* Magazine, "a specific field in mind for Gardner. Josephs was convinced that American universities would have to widen the curriculum of international studies, then long on history and language but short on contemporary information."

So in the spring of 1947, Gardner and the Carnegie staff became actively concerned with the development of a Russian studies program. At first they were thinking of an inter-university organization, with Clyde Kluckhohn of Harvard (formerly of the OSS) as a possible chairman. Subsequently, they decided that it would be more practical to plant the program in a single institution. They chose Harvard.

During the early autumn of 1947, informal discussions were undertaken between Gardner and select members of the Harvard faculty. Then in October, two meetings were held between Gardner, the selected faculty members, the provost of Harvard and Charles Dollard of the Carnegie Corporation. The provost then consulted with the president, and "Harvard" agreed to accept the Carnegie invitation to organize its program. In mid-October, Kluckhohn was indeed asked to serve as director and the Center was underway, powered by a Carnegie Corporation munificence of $750,000 to be doled out at a rate of $150,000 per year—a five-year plan which was renewed in 1953. (Eventually this financing was taken over by the Ford Foundation.)

Despite all this largesse, the staff quickly learned new ways to make a living. In 1949, they began a project on the Soviet Social System, known more familiarly as the Refugee Interview Project, which involved intensive interviewing of Soviet refugees and was financed by the intriguingly named Human Resources Research Institute of the U.S. Air Force. In one stroke it quadrupled the Center's 1950 income, while providing a grateful Defense Department with information that it would normally expect from the CIA.

The Center itself is prevented, by Harvard decorum, from accepting contracts involving classified materials, but individual staff members are not (a nice distinction—for once very academic). In addition to frequenting lectures at the National Army, Navy, Air and Industrial War Colleges, staff members also serve as consultants to classified projects within the following agencies: the Army, the Navy, the Air Force, the RAND Corporation, the Research and Development Board, the Department of State and the Central Intelligence Agency. Ivory tower indeed!

In this manner the Center studied (as the original Gardner memo defined its scope) "fields which lie peculiarly within the professional competence of social psychologists, sociologists and cultural anthropologists." These disciplines were so rewarding that within a year a new Center for International Studies was being formed as a sister project on the MIT campus, with Harvard and MIT faculty (and others) participating.

A liberated document from Harvard titled "The Nature and Objectives of the Center for International Studies" describes the initial impetus: "In the summer of 1950, MIT which has been engaged for some years in research on behalf of the U.S. military establishment was asked by the civilian wing of the government to put together a team of the best research minds available to work intensively for three or four months on how to penetrate the Iron Curtain with ideas." Out of this scholarly initiative developed a permanent Center at MIT which rapidly grew in prestige.

MIT's Advisory Board on Soviet Bloc Studies, for example, was composed of these four academic luminaries: Charles Bohlen of the State Department, Allen Dulles of the CIA, Philip E. Mosely of Columbia's Russian Institute and Leslie G. Stevens, a retired vice admiral of the U.S. Navy.

If the MIT Center seemed to carry to their logical conclusion the on-campus extension programs of the State Department and the CIA, that was perhaps because it was set up directly with CIA funds under the guiding hand of Professor W. W. Rostow, former OSS officer and later director of the State Department's Policy Planning Staff under Kennedy and Johnson. The Center's first director, Max Millikan, was appointed in 1952 after a stint as assistant director of the CIA. Carnegie and Rockefeller joined in the funding, which by now, as in so many other cases, has passed on to Ford.

It wasn't until 1957 that Harvard got its own full-fledged Center for International Affairs. According to liberated documents, the Center was conceived as "an extension and development" of the Defense Studies Seminar whose objective was "to provide training for civilians who might later be involved in the formation of defense policy" and which was funded by the Ford Foundation, and then Carnegie.

The Harvard Center is probably unmatched in its tight interlacing of the knots of power. Among the key individuals who were involved in the creation of the Center were: Robert R. Bowie, its first director and head of the State Department Policy Planning Staff under John Foster Dulles (the dean of Harvard's Graduate School of Public Administration, which gave Bowie his legitimizing "university appointment"); Henry A. Kissinger, who became associate director; Dean Rusk of the Rockefeller Foundation, who followed J. F. Dulles first at the Foundation and then in the State Department; James

A. Perkins of the Carnegie Corporation, who went on to become president of Cornell and a director of the Chase Manhattan Bank; Don K. Price, vice president of the Ford Foundation, formerly of the staff of Harvard's School of Public Administration, who later returned to become dean after his stint at Ford.

McGeorge Bundy, who originally organized the Center, went on to become the overseer of JFK's national security policy. Bundy later left the White House to become head of the Ford Foundation, his key White House post being filled by the MIT Center's Rostow. When the Nixon team took over, there at the head of foreign policy planning was Henry A. Kissinger, fresh out of Harvard's Center for International Affairs. The circle was not accidental and was more than symbolic.

In university service to the empire, the grimier field work is often left to unprestigious social climbers like Michigan State University. MSU's now notorious (see *Ramparts*, April 1966) CIA cover operation in South Viet-Nam— writing Diem's constitution, training his police, supplying him with arms— was merely part of the school's long globe-trotting pursuit of plush, parvenu academic prominence for itself and for its guiding genius, president John A. Hannah.

Hannah began his career in what might aptly be termed obscurity—as a specialist in poultry husbandry. After rising rapidly to the position of managing agent of the Federal Hatcheries Coordinating Committee in Kansas City, he became secretary to the MSU trustee—whence, loyal and trustworthy, he was elevated to the MSU presidency. In 1949 came his formative experience: serving under Nelson Rockefeller on a Presidential Commission to map out Truman's new Point IV Cold War foreign aid program.

Seeing the wave of the future, Hannah made Michigan State "one of the largest operators of service and educational programs overseas." The rise of MSU was paralleled by the rise of Hannah, who became an Assistant Secretary of Defense, board chairman of the Chicago Federal Reserve Bank, a director of Michigan Bell Telephone and eventually chairman of the foundation-financed American Council on Education (perhaps scholardom's most important lobby in Washington).*

MSU makes it clear that a university's external liaisons are not merely peripheral, isolated affairs. Hannah himself proclaims: "...we are trying to create a general environment and an international dimension which will permeate all relevant segments of the university over the years ahead." A 1965 report from Education and World Affairs concurs: "MSU's international involvement is widespread, taking in [sic] almost every college and department: it has stimulated new areas of concern for the faculty, changed the nature of the faculty over the years, and altered the education of their primary charges, the students."

Meanwhile MSU, having learned the ropes in Viet-Nam, has moved on to

---

* [In a speech in September 1961, Hannah anticipated his Defense Department role: "Our colleges and universities must be regarded as bastions of our defense, as essential to the preservation of our country and our way of life as supersonic bombers, nuclear-powered submarines, and international ballistic missiles."—C. P.]

other areas. They have, for example, set out under an AID contract to plan a comprehensive education program for Thailand. The Ford Foundation is currently pitching in on this effort, which no doubt is satisfying to David Bell, the director of AID when the MSU contract was awarded and now the Foundation's vice president in charge of international programs. Fittingly, President Nixon has now appointed MSU chief John Hannah to replace Bell as the head of AID.

No one finds university independence a more pleasant joke than the director of the CIA himself, Admiral William Raborn:

> ...in actual numbers we could easily staff the faculty of a university with our experts. In a way we do. Many of those who leave us join the faculties of universities and colleges. Some of our personnel take a leave of absence to teach and renew their contacts in the academic world. I suppose this is only fair; our energetic recruiting effort not only looks for the best young graduate students we can find, but also picks up a few professors from time to time.

It should be noted in passing that the congeniality of foundation-dominated scholarship to the CIA reflects the harmony of interest between the upper-class captains of the CIA and the upper-class trustees of the great foundations. The interconnections are too extensive to be recounted here, but the Bundy brothers (William, CIA; McGeorge, Ford) and Chadbourne Gilpatric, OSS and CIA from 1943 to 1949, Rockefeller Foundation from 1949 on, can be taken as illustrative. Richard Bissell, the genius of the Bay of Pigs (and brother-in-law of Philip Mosely of Columbia's Russian Institute), reversed the usual sequence, going from Ford to the CIA. (Characters in our story, so far, who belonged to a single upper-class club—the Cosmos—include Millikan, Rostow, Mosely, Gardner, Price, Perkins, Kissinger and Hannah.)

Of course turning professors into CIA agents is not the most common way in which scholarship is made to serve the international status quo. It is not a matter of giving professors secret instructions to falsify research results in the dead of night, but simply of determining what questions they will study. That is where the Ford Foundation comes in. So, for example, with part of the $2 million Ford grant that launched the Institute of International Studies at Berkeley as a major center, a Comparative Political Elites Archive Program was established there in 1965. In practice, the political elites studied turned out to be the ruling elites in communist countries and the potential revolutionary elites in countries within the U.S.'s imperial orbit; the power structure of the American overseas system itself was naturally not a subject of interest. Not surprisingly, the Defense Department and the RAND Corporation were also participants in the Archive Program, which until recently was developing a kind of computerized international mug file.

Occasionally there is an impotent attempt to impart integrity to these institutes, such as the "guidelines" established in response to student protests at Berkeley. "No project," the key point warned, "can be regarded as acceptable either for Institute or extramural funds if an outside agency designs the basic character of the research without the full participation and agreement of a faculty member." This important code would defend a faculty member from being forced by an outside agency (his wife and children being held hostage, perhaps, in a Pentagon dungeon) into research without his agreement. Other than that, little is ruled out; it was really a plea for decorous subtlety. (And if a professor undertook a research project financed by the NLF, one wonders if the only question raised would concern the procedure of its design.)

The inescapable reality is that so long as discretion over the vast majority of research funds and all innovative financing remains outside the university community, it is fatuous to speak of disinterested scholarship or anything remotely resembling what is commonly understood as an academic enterprise. This implication is seldom realized, because the monopoly is so complete that the very possibility of any alternative orientation is not permitted to arise for serious consideration. To appreciate the limits placed on institutionalized efforts to establish an alternative perspective in international studies in the academic world, one must turn to the one independent, critical center that managed to sustain itself in the postwar period, only to be crushed by a power so potent and ubiquitous in the structure of higher learning as to be virtually invisible to academic eyes.

One of the oldest programs of inter-American studies in the U.S. was the Institute of Hispanic American and Luso-Brazilian Studies, established at Stanford University in 1944 by Professor Ronald Hilton, a tough-minded liberal scholar. In 1948 the Institute began publishing a monthly, the *Hispanic American Report*, which until its demise was the sole journal providing scholarly reports and analyses of developments in Spanish- and Portuguese-speaking countries. Over the years it established an international reputation and was, in the words of Gregory Rabassa, professor of Spanish and Portuguese at Columbia, "without a doubt the finest compendium of news from the whole Hispanic world." Yet because Hilton was neither a servant of power nor one of its sycophants, in all their years, neither the *Report* nor the Institute received a penny of foundation support, although small contributions were forthcoming from personal friends of Hilton. For its own part, Stanford was benefited not only by the distinguished specialists and earnest young scholars who gravitated to the Institute, but by the prestige of the journal. Yet Hilton received no payment beyond his professional salary, for which he taught a full load in addition to hours put in on the Institute. His researchers and colleagues also went uncompensated for their Institute work.

In 1960, the *Report* dramatically demonstrated its value—and independence —by revealing that the CIA was training Cuban exiles in Guatemala for an invasion of Cuba. Needless to say, Hilton's continuing dissent from U.S. policy on Cuba did not endear him to officials in Washington or to the representatives of international corporations among the Stanford trustees.

The following year, the Ford Foundation offered $25 million to Stanford, if they could match it with $75 million in other gifts. The chairman of the "major gifts" committee was David Packard, who had made a personal fortune of $300 million as a military-industrialist and has since gone on to become Deputy Secretary of Defense in the current Administration. Packard an. inced at the end of the fund-raising campaign that more than two-thirds of the $75 million which had been raised to match the Ford grant was in gifts of $100,000 or more from 150 individuals, corporations and foundations. And among these major benefactors, more than one expressed misgivings about the Hilton Institute. According to Hilton, who had been attacked by the Standard Oil Company of California and the Stanford provost among others,

It was suggested [by university officials] that I avoid offending powerful fund raisers; a key member of the administration demanded that, even in editorials bearing my signature, I cease expressing controversial opinions ... and that, while no attention was paid to the Institute's two advisory boards who gave me every support, the administration proposed to appoint two secret committees to keep an eye on the *Report*.

At precisely the time when the financial patrons of learning were expressing their misgivings about Hilton, the question of obtaining funds for an international studies program at Stanford, including Latin American studies, came up. Beginning in 1959, the Ford Foundation had embarked on a $42 million program to support international studies at select universities. At Stanford the task of drawing up a prospectus was given to a committee headed by Dean Carl Spaeth. Academically speaking, Spaeth, a law professor, was not spectacularly qualified for the job. But to preside over yet another extension of the foundation/State Department hegemony, his credentials were impeccable. He had been Nelson Rockefeller's assistant in the State Department and the Ford Foundation's director of the Division of Overseas Activities. Who could be better equipped to induce the God at Ford to breathe life into Stanford's international studies efforts?

Accordingly, in 1962 Ford made a major grant to support international studies at Stanford. The grant stipulated that all of the funds would be allocated to Spaeth's committee. It also excluded Latin American studies, pending further studies of how best to strengthen the field. Shortly thereafter, Spaeth called a conference of Latin Americanists at the modern ranch house quarters which the Ford Foundation had built in the Palo Alto hills for its Center for the Study of Behavioral Sciences. Professor Hilton was not invited.

A year of "studies" ensued, during which the problem was allowed to simmer. Then, at the direction of the dean of Graduate Students, all Ph.D. candidates were removed from the Hispanic Institute, and Professor Hilton was informed that the Institute would henceforth concentrate on practical instruction at the M.A. level. There had been no discussion with Hilton, a senior faculty member, and no explanations were offered. When he asked how the administration could do such a thing without consulting the responsible faculty member, he was told: "The administration can do anything it pleases." Hilton resigned from the Institute and from his post as editor of the *Report*, hoping it would compel the administration to take a stand. But the administration accepted his resignation without discussion and suspended publication of the *Report*. Within two weeks the Ford Foundation granted Stanford $550,000 for Latin American studies.

One of the more revealing ironies of the destruction of the Hilton program was the general agreement that Latin American studies was the least developed of any area in the field. Just months before Hilton's resignation, a conference on Social Science Research on Latin America had been held at Stanford. The results were summed up: "Little capital (funds, talent, or organizational experience) has been invested in political studies of Latin America.... Personnel with adequate training and appropriate technical competence have been in scarce supply ... and the level of productivity has been low." A survey revealed that there was not one senior professor of Latin American politics at any one of the ten major departments across the country.

The loss of the Institute and the *Report*, representing a lifetime effort, was a personal tragedy for Hilton, but for the profession it was an acid test. In fact, the destruction of one of the only independent and therefore intellectually respectable institutes of substance in the academic world produced only a ripple of protest. Hilton was unable to obtain financing to revive the Institute and the *Report*. The organized profession took no interest. Nor is this so mysterious when it is considered that Ford's $550,000 had gone to those Stanford Latinists who didn't make an issue of the Institute, and that this largesse was repeated on every campus where significant efforts on Latin America were taking place. In May 1966, the Latinists formed a guild, the Latin American Studies Association, which also ignored the Hilton affair. That is not surprising either. It was set up with Ford funds and its first president was Professor Kalman Silvert, who is now program advisor on Latin America for the Ford Foundation.

In its "objective" account of the Hilton affair, the Ford-funded organization, Education and World Affairs, acknowledges as a major source of conflicts the *Report*'s treatment of "Castro's takeover," which "made the Stanford administration uneasy." The issue, they explained, was that Hilton "was responsible to no one for [the *Report*'s] contents or comments; it was not beholden to Stanford—and yet it carried the Stanford reputation behind it."

The concern for "Stanford" is touching. As we have seen (and the cases we have taken are wholly representative; there are no exceptions), the international institutes and centers are responsible to *no* universities, if "university" means a community of students and scholars. At most they are responsible to the president, provost or chancellor of the university, and occasionally to a select committee; but even then, if a conflict arises, the institute is free to take its manpower, prestige and munificence wherever its money sources will follow (or lead) it. Early in the history of the institutes, the Yale Center of International Studies, as a result of a policy difference between its director, Frederick S. Dunn, and the Yale administration, moved lock, stock and barrel to Princeton. Significantly, only the director, Dunn—a member, naturally, of the Council on Foreign Relations—and the associate director Klaus Knorr received appointments to the Princeton faculty. Yet although clearly "unbeholden" to Princeton "standards," the Center enjoys the prestige of association with Princeton, teaches courses in Princeton's Woodrow Wilson School where it is housed, and uses Princeton facilities and faculty members.

Financial support came from the Ford Foundation and Carnegie Corporation, as well as the Rockefeller-associated Milbank Memorial Fund. Thus a director who had the confidence of the foundations was able to find a new university shell for his operation.

Stanford itself houses a rather extreme (but only because so blatant) example of institute independence in the form of the Hoover Institution on War, Revolution and Peace. Originally an archive, the Institution's character was changed in 1960 by fiat of its benefactor, Herbert Hoover, who eased out its liberal director and replaced him with a conservative economist, Wesley Glenn Campbell (formerly of the Defense Department, the U.S. Chamber of Commerce and the right-wing American Enterprise Institute). Hoover also laid down the scholarly lines that his institute would be required to follow:

> The purpose of this Institution must be, by its research and publications, to demonstrate the evils of the doctrines of Karl Marx —whether Communism, Socialism, economic materialism, or atheism —thus to protect the American way of life from such ideologies, their conspiracies, and to reaffirm the validity of the American system.

Stanford, which pays at least $334,000 a year to support the Hoover Institution, was perfectly satisfied with these academic strictures.

To prevent his man from becoming a mere figurehead and his statement of purpose mere paper, Hoover also offered a resolution, which the Stanford trustees genially accepted, establishing the Institution's independence within the University. Under Hoover's plan the director has complete autonomy over his staff and budget and reports only to the president of the University. Some faculty members at Stanford had the temerity to complain that Campbell was using his power to build a staff in his own conservative image (his executive assistant is a former chief aide of J. Edgar Hoover, while Campbell's wife, whose publications include attacks on social security, Medicare and welfare, is one of the few senior staff members). When asked about these faculty complaints, Campbell told *Washington Monthly* reporter Berkeley Rice: "I wish the faculty would keep their noses out of my business."

Not surprisingly, Campbell is an impressive figure to people like Ronald Reagan, who made him a regent of the University of California, perhaps on the basis of his expertise in handling faculty-administrative relations. Moreover, the Hoover Institution budget has grown from $400,000 to $2 million as a result of fund drives during Campbell's tenure. The co-chairman of the long-range fund drive until his appointment to the Pentagon was that benefactor of Stanford scholarship, David Packard. Financial support has been forthcoming from foundations, alumni and top executives from Standard Oil (New Jersey), Gulf Oil, Mobil Oil, Union Carbide and Lockheed. Like the more politic (and no less political) liberal institutes, the Hoover Institution does lucrative contract work for the government and subsidizes its "scholarly" products (through the CIA-involved Praeger publishing house). Not surprisingly, its experts have found a home in the Nixon Administration, particularly in the Defense Department's office of International Security Affairs, which coordinates U.S. military and foreign policy and where Hoover men occupy several top posts.

The Hilton and Hoover episodes are merely exceptionally graphic illustrations of a system in which the prostitution of intellect has become so pervasive and profound that all but a small minority mistake it for academic virtue. The foundations, with their practical monopoly on substantial discretionary funds, have purchased control over the fundamental direction of research and academic energies on a national scale. Even if individual researchers and ideologues are not corrupted—though plenty of them are—the *system* of academic research and ideology formation is. Most academics no more perceive the ideological basis of their work than we smell air or taste water. The politically inoffensive (not neutral) is seen as unbiased, objective, value-free science; a radical orientation stands out as prejudiced, inappropriate and, gravest of all, unprofessional.

Perhaps the most critical point of leverage in academic control is in the formation of perspectives, analytic models, agendas for research. Not all social phenomena are visible to all analytic models and methodologies, and the social scientist who shapes his tools to collect government and foundation finances will not be equipped to research or even ask questions which, though crucial to an understanding of the contemporary world, would not be looked on favorably by those agencies.

For example, the American overseas system consists of some 3000 military bases, mutual security treaties with more than 30 nations, and more than $60 billion in direct capital investments around the world. To begin to understand the workings and the impact of this system, one would need to research (1) U.S. corporate and financial interests overseas, their interest group structure, their significance in the U.S. economy, their political influence on U.S. foreign policy, on local regimes, etc.; (2) U.S. military bases, installations and alliances, their interlockings with corporate and political interests, their economic impact, etc.; (3) U.S. and U.S.-dominated international agencies, foundations, universities, their overseas operations and interlockings with the above interests and so on. Yet on the basis of the State Department's directory of foreign affairs research in American universities, it can be said with reasonable certainty that there is not one institutional attempt being made anywhere to research a single one of these questions.

In the spring of 1966, the role of the CIA at Michigan State was revealed by a courageous intellectual (now without a university base) who had been the coordinator of the MSU Viet-Nam project, Stanley K. Sheinbaum. (*Ramparts,* April 1966.) In his retrospective analysis of the operation, Sheinbaum wrote: "Looking back I am appalled how supposed intellectuals ... could have been so uncritical about what they were doing." His explanation of this default was that "we lack historical perspective. We have been conditioned by our social science training not to ask the normative question; we possess neither the inclination *nor the means* to question and judge our foreign policy. We have only the capacity to be experts and technicians to serve that policy."

What may have seemed like an isolated scandal in 1966 can now be recognized as a universal condition of organized intellect in America. The saddest part is that the academics have become such eager victims. They have internalized the limits placed upon them. They fiercely uphold a strict academic professionalism. But it is no more than expert servitude to oppressive power, to a system whose wages are poverty and blood. They do not see that what they have really embraced is the perverted professionalism of the mercenary and the hired gun.

The author wishes to acknowledge the research assistance of Rob Cunning-ham, as well as of the activists who liberated the documents and produced the booklets "How Harvard Rules" (ARG and Old Mole) and "Who Rules Columbia" (NACLA).

EVEN ANTHROPOLOGY?

Among social scientists, the tiny group of anthropologists holds a special place. Their professional standards are very high; their training is rigorous; their group is small, permitting highly developed norms and much inter-action; and their research is by nature far removed from the political gales that sweep over the economists, political scientists, sociologists, and psychologists. Anthropologists deal with the past and with small "primitive" societies. Although anthropologists have increasingly become involved in research in urban industrial settings, even here they are likely to do small studies of offbeat groups. They are not involved with issues such as stratifi-cation, political power, and economic power on a national scale. All of these facts should put them above suspicion with respect to the business system. In addition, while anthropologists do not brush the business system in their work, they appear to be quite liberal in their personal views, even for social scientists. For example, the American Anthropological Association was one of the first professional groups to take a public stand in opposition to the war in Vietnam.

Alas, the business system has need for anthropologists, too. And, alas, they too appear to have been had. In 1970, the research assistant of a prominent anthropologist "liberated" a number of documents from his office file. Photocopies were made and sent to the newly formed Ethics Committee of the American Anthropological Association and made public with a press release. A profession above suspicion became suspect. I have based the following account on an article in the *New York Review of Books* by two members of the Ethics Committee, Eric Wolf and Joseph Jorgensen. Specific citations can be found in their article.[13]

The seduction of anthropology starts with the Cross-Cultural Survey of Yale University, which was established in the early 1930's as a data bank of standardized information on primitive cultures gleaned from thousands of anthropological studies. With the worldwide involvement of the United

---

[13] Eric Wolf and Joseph Jorgensen, "Anthropology on the Warpath in Thailand," *New York Review of Books*, 15:9 (November 19, 1970), 26–35. See also the extensive exchange in the April 8, 1971, issue of the *Review*, pp. 43–46.

States during the Second World War, this data became a useful source for intelligence and military purposes by the federal government. After the war, the Carnegie Foundation, the Air Force, and the Office of Naval Research sponsored an expansion of the study. Soon the Army, the Navy, the Air Force, and the CIA were making annual contributions of $50,000 each in order to build up data banks (now renamed Human Relations Area Files) on critical world areas, according to the official history of the project. In 1954 classified as well as unclassified handbooks were produced under a contract from the Army. Classified research in an academic discipline committed to the dissemination of knowledge is a delicate subject. Eventually, the Human Relations Area File project returned to the ivory towers of Yale, no longer supported by the military. For one reason, on-the-spot, up-to-date information was needed in an increasing number of undeveloped countries in the world.

A conference in 1967, the details of which were also "liberated" from the office of the anthropologist mentioned earlier, illustrates the new pressures. The Institute of Defense Analysis, a Pentagon-sponsored "think-tank" set up in 1955 to coordinate war-related work on the nation's campuses, had set up a special Jason Division. This division was to involve scientists in the solution of military problems. The 1967 conference was to explore whether an "SS Jason," a social science branch of the Jason Division, should also be established. The possibilities of studies of Thailand and the problems of its communist movement were discussed. The IDA personnel frankly said that they wanted "tools," not dialogues or discussions. Social scientists, including anthropologists, could perform an effective counterinsurgency role, it was argued. Eventually they did, or at least the military was willing to pay for this work. The Defense Department funded social science projects, for example the Himalayan Border Project in India and Project Camelot, which was to investigate the conditions for social stability (that is, the status quo) in Latin American societies. Both projects became scandals, which is why we know so much about them. Project Camelot was abruptly terminated during the planning stages when Latin American intellectuals were shown letters describing the purpose of the project in remarkably blunt counterinsurgency terms, and many major figures in United States social science were implicated and embarrassed.[14] The Indian project, operated from the Institute of International Studies at Berkeley (which still thrives), was terminated when the Indian government found that it was funded by the Defense Department.

But most projects went quietly on, and presumably still go on. Senate hearings indicate that in November 1969 the Defense Department was financing nineteen counterinsurgency projects of its own in Thailand and was

---

[14] Irving L. Horowitz, ed., *The Rise and Fall of Project Camelot* (Cambridge, Mass.: MIT Press, 1967)

maintaining sixteen external contracts for this purpose. Eleven private research institutes and universities were involved, and presumably so were a not insignificant proportion of anthropologists competent in Southeast Asian studies. The Stanford Research Institute has conducted at least five major research projects in the small nation of Thailand since 1962 and has issued more than one hundred reports. More than thirty of these reports are by social scientists (nine of them are confidential), and all deal with counter-insurgency operations.

Even those anthropologists who go to Thailand to do research and who desire no contact with activities or agents sponsored by the Defense Department or the CIA find it difficult to maintain the purity of their work. One anthropologist, critical of the disclosures and conclusions Wolf and Jorgensen make in their article, describes at length how the "main counter-insurgency research branch in northern Thailand" (the Defense Department's Advanced Research Projects Agency) used complex stratagems to penetrate and gain access to an independent research center financed primarily by the Thai and Australian governments. As Wolf and Jorgensen disclose, however, even this independent center, penetrated by the CIA, concerned itself with the hill tribes' "vulnerability to Communist subversion," according to the official report of the Secretary-General of the Southeast Asia Treaty Organization. As this official put it, "to counteract Communist subversion it is essential to have a wide knowledge of these people." [15]

Indeed, it is essential. But is that what the anthropological community, which roundly voted a denunciation of the Camelot Project, should be concerned with? If one takes the view that anthropologists are American citizens and thus have a responsibility to support the duly elected government and its military appendages, then one has no dilemma. As a president of the American Anthropological Association noted, the Second World War provided anthropologists "with an unprecedented opportunity to play a variety of applied roles in government," and that opportunity seems to have enlarged since then. If one maintains the position that science is neutral, then counteracting communist subversion becomes less palatable. If one is a member of the New Left, it becomes anathema. The New Left maintains that all insurgent movements are not necessarily communist, although they are branded as such; communism may be just what Thailand needs, and even Peking-dominated communist movements are preferable to exploitation by the United States. But regardless of this logic, the utilization of an anthropologist is just one more piece of evidence about how the system of liberal capitalism works; it buys social scientists with research money, increased salaries, professional opportunities, prestige, and "a heady sense of engagement in a global welfare operation." [16]

15 Wolf and Jorgensen in "Anthropology on the Warpath: An Exchange," *New York Review of Books*, 16:6 (April 8, 1971), 45.
16 Wolf and Jorgensen, "Anthropology on the Warpath in Thailand," p. 33.

With this involvement, the ethics of anthropology are strained. The anthropologist, even more than the sociologist, has an obligation to the people among whom he works, for he observes them closely for long periods of time. He requires their trust; in return he assumes an obligation not to reveal material that might hurt them. But that is precisely what he can no longer assume; "data gathered by the anthropologist can serve to hurt people in ways that can be neither anticipated in advance nor compensated for after the fact," note Wolf and Jorgensen.[17] They point out that it is reasonable to anticipate that the government of the United States and the multinational corporations based there will increase their efforts to centralize power and control resources on a global scale. This will necessitate increased knowledge about deprived and oppressed peoples in the trouble spots around the globe—specific knowledge about particular tribes and individuals. "As the Thailand papers show, the government is less interested in the economic, social, or political causes of discontent than in techniques of neutralizing individual or collective protest."[18] The anthropologist, even if he eschews the role of an "SS Jason," can unwittingly serve as an informer under the guise of doing pure research.

Some social scientists are quick to cite the potential application of counterinsurgency measures utilized in powerless nations abroad to problems in the United States. It was generally believed that Project Camelot would have this spinoff; conditions in the ghettos were not that different from those in Latin America. One research and development proposal made to the Defense Department by the American Institutes for Research was frank about the applicability of their work in Southeast Asia to the problem of "reducing vulnerability to insurgent appeal" in the United States. Their research would be addressed to the methodological problems of finding out what kinds of economic, social, and political action were most effective in counterinsurgency work. "And," they note, "since it has been the same methodological problem that has most hampered social action programs in the United States, the potential spinoffs of the proposed project are also exciting."[19]

Reducing insurgency at home is not only a spinoff of imperialism, but an "exciting" one. The New Left would have universities sponsor just the opposite kind of research—finding ways to promote insurgency at home. They feel that the potential for insurgency is clearly there. Since the universities and the social scientists—even the anthropologists among them—are anything but neutral, at the least the balance needs redressing, according to the Left.

---

17 *Ibid.,* p. 34.
18 *Idem.*
19 Quoted in *ibid.,* p. 28.

CHAPTER 5

What about the workers?

THE PROBLEM FOR THE LEFT

In the dogma of revolution since Marx, it is written that no revolution can succeed without the working class. The New Left seeks to bring about a revolution, but the working class appears to reject the Left's analysis of the business system, its strategies for bringing about change, its ideology, and its very life-style. If a revolution cannot succeed without the workers, then the United States is not likely to have a revolution for some time. Moreover, this country has never had the faintest chance of a revolution based on a workers' revolt, even during the depths of the Great Depression. Is the New Left serious, then?

It is hard to say, since on this issue some segments of the Left have hardly spoken out, some segments continue to follow a dogmatic Marxist line, and still others are in the middle, searching. Thus to speak about the New Left and the worker is to ignore considerable differences within the movement.

For the Marxist wing, the working class must bring about the revolution, although the Marxists themselves will be the vanguard of the working class. They picture the worker as a heroic sufferer, in some cases misled by propaganda and the blandishments of a consumer economy, but ready to rise up if only the Left would journey to their neighborhoods and raise revolutionary consciousness. At the other end of the Left spectrum are those who feel that at least the acquiescence of the working class is needed, but that the workers need not participate in organizing and carrying through a revolution. These Leftists are content to speak about the exploitation of the worker and the power of business, but their real concern seems to be with the quality of life in America and the opportunities for new life-styles. (At the far end of this group are the cultural radicals, such as the Yippies, who have received a great deal of coverage in the media but who are ignored or viewed with disdain by much of the New Left.)

Between this certitude and neglect lies the most creative sector of the New Left, which is trying to think through the problems associated with the role of the working class in a revolutionary society.[1] Relying basically on a Marxist analysis of the role and value of labor, but cognizant of persistent strains of racism and ethnocentrism in the working class and of the elaboration of strata and skill levels within that class, this segment has tried to find its way to a strategy that will not rely primarily on middle-class students and alienated intellectuals to move the society. In addition to traditional blue-collar categories, these radicals are beginning to speak of technicians and teachers as part of the working class and as potential leaders. This attempt at analysis and strategy is relatively new and has not as yet been very successful. There is far more agreement about and concrete analysis of the role of corporations, the military, government, and the universities among the Left than of the role and character of the working class. An indication of the seriousness of the problem for the New Left can be given by recounting briefly some of the recent history of the movement.

The New Left did not start out as Marxists, or even as socialists. The Port Huron Statement called for liberal reforms, which were soon rejected because of their inadequacies, but it also began by rejecting dogmatic Marxism as well. The ideology and aims of socialism crept into the movement rather slowly during the second half of the 1960's, judging from the writings of the New Left and from some of my personal contacts. Those with Marxist persuasions, with attendant rhetoric and exploration of concrete revolutionary tactics, grew in force in the late 1960's. SDS was avowedly socialist at least by 1967, but not until 1968 and 1969 did its writings lose their impressionistic character and begin to take on the abstract, hard-edged lines of Marxist revolutionary dogma. The first major split in the *organized,* self-conscious segment of the New Left occurred in 1969, when SDS abandoned its permissive policy of allowing all groups to participate

1 See the influential *Strategy for Labor* by André Gorz (Boston: Beacon Press, 1967), first published in French in 1964. I find this to be more ideology than strategy, but Gorz has kept at the strategy end to good effect. See his "Left Wing Communism in Italy," *Liberation,* Vol. 15, No. 10 (January 1971), and also the articles by Bruce Brown, "Revolution in Western Europe?" and by Staughton Lynd, "Prospects for the New Left," in the same issue. More significant is André Gorz, "Workers Control," *Socialist Revolution,* Vol. 1, No. 6 (November–December 1970), pp. 11–16. Gorz reports on a sociological study of workers at the Vauxhall plant in England that showed they were satisfied and integrated into the system. Some militants obtained a summary of the study and distributed a few hundred copies. A few days later the militants also circulated a newspaper story reporting profits for General Motors, which owned the plant, of about £900 for each worker. Wild rioting by the workers broke out and lasted for two days. When interviewed individually, the workers had told the sociologist (Professor John Goldthorpe) that they were satisfied with their lot; but when they started to discuss things among themselves, they found common dissatisfactions and a common consciousness. Gorz gives several similar examples from Europe, but none from the United States.

and ousted the Progressive Labor party faction from membership. (This faction rejected all Third World nationalist movements and independent black movements in the United States and called for a militant, disciplined organization to bring about world communism.) This ouster was followed by the fission of the remainder of SDS into the Revolutionary Youth Movement I (RYM I), which became known as the Weatherman faction, famous for its trashing and bombing, and a more moderate RYM II.[2]

Splits and doctrinaire death-struggles are, of course, endemic to revolutionary movements. The Black Panthers, organized long after SDS, had theirs a year later, in 1970. Only mainstream, establishment groups can afford the luxury of tolerating broad ranges of opinion and ideology. Establishment groups generate enough excess resources—or organizational "fat" or "slack," as it is called—to pursue without danger a variety of goals in sequence or even simultaneously. A radical group has no such resources; its efforts must be highly disciplined and directed toward a single goal.

The problem with the organized, self-conscious radical Left groups was that while they agreed on the general analysis of the business system as the root of the problem, too many other issues kept intruding that appeared to demand a concrete, even a marbleized, stand. What about the blacks? Should they be encouraged to do their own thing, or should the radical groups (overwhelmingly white until the Panthers came along) seek to bring them in? Should the focus be on the business system in the United States, even though all agree that imperialism is the driving force and thus that the Third World countries bear the major burden? or should the New Left link up with Third World movements and direct its energies toward publicizing and supporting their revolutionary struggles? or should there be no national movements at all, but only world revolution? And what about the Women's Liberation Movement? Granted, females have been exploited throughout human history, but is this really a high-priority problem in today's world? And what about the core of the radical movement itself—the youth, and especially the college youth? Should they be the main target of propaganda? Are the colleges the place to train revolutionaries or start revolutions? Does youth have that much power? What is the true nature of the class system—is it for all practical purposes the Marxian one of the bourgeoisie and proletariat? or should the "intermediate classes," to which Marx vaguely referred, be given more attention? or is it, in this advanced state of capitalism, a four- or five- or six-class system, thoroughly confused by the manipulative, brainwashing techniques of the capitalists?

All these issues figured in the intense debate between the Progressive

2 See the discussions by Paul Glusman and by David Horowitz in *Divided We Stand,* by the editors of *Ramparts* (San Francisco: Canfield Press, 1970), pp. 170–75. The ousted Progressive Labor party has continued its Maoist line and works only fitfully with other radical groups. In February 1971, at the first major gathering of the New Left since the breakup of SDS in 1969, plans were made for massive antiwar demonstrations. The PLP agreed to help finance the May Day demonstrations, which took place in Washington, D.C., and elsewhere, but stopped payment on its check when it decided that the demonstrations were not radical enough. See *The Guardian,* June 2, 1971.

Labor party, RYM, and Weatherman factions in 1970, and the argument continues today. It is not enough to agree on the nature of imperialism and corporate capitalism; all these other issues can also divide or propel a movement. Biggest of all is the issue of the proper role of the working class. If the workers are essential, how can they be won over?

No other topic in the radical press has produced as much soul-searching and recrimination or as many confessions of ideological and tactical error as the matter of winning the workers. Should the revolutionaries cut their hair and apply for jobs at the factory? leaflet the workers at the plant gate? live in their sections of the cities? try to take over their unions? win them with displays of *machismo* (as the Weathermen tried to do during their Days of Rage in Chicago in 1969)? All radicals agree that segments of the white working class are racist, imperialistic, nationalistic, and militaristic. One analyst even distinguishes a subclass within the working class "of criminals, semi-criminals and men and women living off fellow workers." [3] Reportedly, one document put out by SDS in 1969, dealing with the effort to reach the working class on the job, said: "Don't be shocked by racist remarks of the white workers, by confused political impressions, pro-war talk, 'keeping up with the Joneses' talk. If the workers understood racism, the war, middle-class morality, capitalist manipulation, etc., things would not be the way they are." [4] But that is the way things are and the way the workers are, and the Left is paralyzed if a revolution means a revolution of the working class.

To make the workers understand the nature of the business system and all its evils, a revolution is necessary. After the revolution, the workers would not be fed a pack of lies, manipulated, narcotized by gadgets, forced to fight with blacks and other minorities for scarce jobs, or required to pay taxes to support a pitiful welfare system for those whom the capitalistic system does not need and cannot employ, and so on. But while the system is in existence, it will do its diabolical best to maintain the "false consciousness," the lack of clear class consciousness, of the workers. It is a classic bootstrap problem.

THE PROBLEM FOR BUSINESS

The Left lives on hope, however, though some might call it fantasy. There is an irritant in the system that concerns even the businessmen: the worker may be changing. The system may not be all that powerful (or, alternatively, the contradictions within the system are beginning to show). Capital is beginning to wonder aloud about its partner, labor, about the ability of

3 Les Coleman, "Notes on Class Analysis: Some Implications for the Revolutionary Youth Movement," in *Debate Within SDS—RYM II vs. Weathermen* (Detroit: Radical Education Project, 1969), p. 10.
4 Quoted in *Business Week*, May 3, 1969, p. 31.

unions to keep labor in line, about the spread of consumerism, and about the publicity given to attacks on the system.

People have been predicting the resurgence of worker militancy for generations, so these speculations of the late 1960's are not especially novel. But the frequency of press reports about forms of working-class militancy, such as wildcat strikes, deposition of long-tenured labor leaders, the startling rise in strikes by public employees (from about thirty in 1965 to more than four hundred in 1969), and the opinion polls dealing with the attitudes of noncollege youth suggest that while the phenomenon may not be new, the scope and intensity of it may be. Let us examine some of the things that buoy up the hopes of the New Left.

First, business is uptight about the organized radicals. The business press carried many stories in 1969 about a student–worker alliance. Radicals from the University of California at Berkeley had made common cause with striking oil workers in the nearby town of Richmond, and students on other campuses had also supported workers. No lasting ties seem to have come from these expedient moves, but business become worried. Businessmen also feared that radicals would carry out their plans to meet the worker at his place of work. "Will SDS Crash Plant Gate?" was the title of an article in *Business Week* on May 3, 1969. The Illinois Manufacturers Association sent out a special bulletin alerting members to an "insidious" and "well-organized" plan. One activist reports that in 1969 the National Association of Manufacturers, along with the Army and the FBI, held fourteen seminars on plant security for 4,000 businessmen from 1,500 companies, oriented toward the threat of the SDS.[5] No doubt businessmen gave a sigh of relief when radicals and construction men clashed in New York City in 1970, but even business agrees that construction workers are extreme in many respects.

Even more insidious than SDS, presumably, has been the rash of wildcat strikes that started about 1969. Most commentators agree that old-line labor leaders, now usually in their sixties, and centralized, ponderous labor unions, many of them in their late thirties, are out of touch with the rank and file, have long since made their peace with business, seek narrow bread-and-butter goals, and exercise considerable discipline over workers in behalf of the business–labor "partnership." On the other hand, workers are now better educated, are younger (because the population is), demand more, do not fear as much for their livelihood, and have been shaped by institutions that are less authoritarian today (primarily the schools, but also the churches and the home). A new spirit breathes in the working class. Workers may be furious with the college radicals, who are wasting the opportunity they never had and ruining things for their own children, but that does not mean that they love the system.

The issue is well explored in a recent *Fortune* article that attracted much

5 Editors of *Ramparts, op. cit.,* p. 175.

attention from the New Left. The subtitle of the story: "Young auto workers find job disciplines harsh and uninspiring, and they vent their feelings through absenteeism, high turnover, shoddy work, and even sabotage. It's time for a new look at who's down there on the line." [6] Despite the patronizing tone in the last sentence, the story documents the harsh, depressing character of the jobs (for example, attaching brake lines to junction blocks 348 times in an eight-hour day, or once every seventy seconds, with only two coffee breaks and a thirty-minute lunch break to punctuate the day's work, and with the anticipation of doing something like this for the next thirty years, the higher level of education ("Nobody disputes that these new workers are the brightest, best-educated labor force that ever came into the plant," notes *Fortune*), the militancy, and the ruinous absenteeism. As *Fortune* notes, overtime is compulsory, while the workers "hate to go in there" and fight to get out at quitting time. They have no chance to make a telephone call, to get a haircut, or to conduct any of a variety of personal business that characterizes our complex, bureaucratic society. One might just as well take the whole day off when one has to spend an hour at the dentist's or shop for an appliance.

While *Fortune* assiduously digs out all the humanizing efforts that are being made by the auto companies, the examples are isolated and trivial (monogrammed glasses as a reward for no absenteeism), and often quickly abandoned in favor of drastic measures such as shutting down a Friday shift after four hours because some 7 percent of the 2,700 hourly workers were absent. About 2,500 workers who were there suddenly lost half a day's pay. But the vice president for personnel at GM says "absenteeism occurs not because the jobs are dull, but because of the nation's economic abundance, and the high degree of security and the many social benefits the industry provides." He thinks, says *Fortune,* that younger workers "should show more appreciation for what they have." [7] Presumably a depression, economic insecurity, and fewer social benefits are the way to motivate today's assembly-line workers.

James M. Roche, chairman of the board of General Motors until 1971, agrees. In an appropriately timed Christmas message to employees in 1969, he attacked those workers who "reject responsibility" and who "fail to respect essential disciplines and authority." Two months later he went further in a widely reported speech. "Management and the public have lately been short-changed. We have a right to more than we have been receiving." Tools and technology mean nothing, he said, if the worker is absent from his job. "We must receive a fair day's work for which we pay the fair day's wage." [8]

---

[6] Judson Gooding, "Blue Collar Blues on the Assembly Line," *Fortune,* July 1970, pp. 69–71 ff.
[7] *Ibid.,* p. 71.
[8] *Ibid.,* p. 70.

The New Left could not have characterized the greedy capitalist better—workers should respect authority and discipline; management has a *right* to more effort; tools and technology must be manned every day, every shift, overtime or not. Because it is generally agreed that the annual model change (which GM introduced) is enormously wasteful for the public, that the rate of return on invested capital at GM is phenomenal, that the resistance of car manufacturers to auto safety is well known, and that the size and power of the automotive colossus is beyond belief, the cry that "we have a right to more than we have been receiving" rings a bit hollow to the man who attaches a hose every seventy seconds, eight hours a day. The New Left may not even need to go near the plants if the younger workers experience much of this "consciousness."

CHANGING CONSCIOUSNESS

It may be that the effectiveness of the New Left will lie not in the disciplined militancy of various sects, but in the much more open, colorful, and even humorous civil disobedience and communication strategies of the mid-1960's. How many citizens really know very much about conditions in the automobile plants or the steel mills or the railroads or the telephone companies? [9] How much do workers in these industries know about the restlessness and grievances of their fellow workers? The sparks that could set off such an awareness may already be present at this time. Given some dramatic events, it might have the effect that the civil rights movement had in the early 1960's, when it made a national issue of the conditions of life for blacks. If the conditions of workers were now a national issue also—along with the war in Vietnam, the indifference of the military and the CIA to drug traffic, investments in South Africa, the exploitation of Latin America, industrial pollution, and the consequences of concentrated economic power—the interaction of these issues might spur change in all of them.

If this supposition makes any sense, then the key task of the New Left is to expose the exploitation of the workers. The workers will be more likely

---

[9] Occasionally the establishment press points to some of the realities for blue-collar workers in general, rather than just those on the assembly line. For example, this paragraph from a *Time* magazine story of November 9, 1970 (p. 69), is instructive:

Often lacking the education to seek better jobs or the money to flee to suburbia, blue-collar workers live with nagging fears of muggings, of illness or layoffs at work, and of automation. According to a recent survey by the University of Michigan, one-half of all industrial workers worry continually about their job security, and one-quarter are concerned about their safety; 14,000 were killed in on-the-job accidents last year, more than the number of U.S. servicemen who died in Viet Nam in 1969. Fully 28% have no medical coverage, 38% no life insurance and 39% no pension beyond Social Security.

to form insurgent groups within the plants and within their unions if the general climate of opinion agrees that insurgency is permissible and conceivable. That climate of opinion might come as the more educated sections of society explore these issues. College students are one important segment of the highly educated class; they create a market to which the mass media can respond, they put pressure on their parents, and they have expectations about their first jobs. But the educational effort of the New Left will fail if it consists of mindless slogans and invectives, such as those that appear in broadsides or that characterize the debate between the radical sects of the New Left.[10]

For example, just prior to May Day, 1971, the Progressive Labor party distributed a broadside at a Long Island university campus, calling for a march and rally in New York City. One passage read as follows:

WHAT DOES SOCIALISM MEAN?

Many people ask: "How would life be different under socialism?" It's this very question which we want to discuss with as many people as possible in building for and having our May Day demonstration. The following is something of an introduction to that discussion, only a small part of the picture:

HOSPITALS: We say workers will run everything under socialism. How would that change a hospital, for example? There would be no bosses, no supervisors to push around the transportation workers, nurses' aides, kitchen workers, housekeepers. No "top" and no "bottom." Everyone would do *different* kinds of work. Some would not always get the filthiest work, while others did much easier jobs. People would take turns. Nurses' aides would be able to go to school to be doctors. Doctors would sweep the floors. Surgeons would also push around litter. In short, the division between mental and manual labor would be broken down.

All the medical workers would meet—with the patients—to figure out what should be done in the hospital and how to do it. Patients would get all the care they needed—absolutely free. They would be told, so they could understand it, just what the medical workers thought was wrong with them. Kids would be trained in medicine from an early age. Medicines would be FREE.

The broadside goes on to discuss racism (which will be eliminated); male supremacy ("housework will be socialized"); education (to be "100% different" under socialism); government (which apparently will suspend due

---

10 As evidenced in the Radical Education Project pamphlet, *Debate Within SDS*, cited in footnote 3.

process because "Any hint of graft—and off to jail"); the police ("the workers themselves will be armed and formed into local militias," which is not so remarkable after all, since it seems to be working well in Cuba); nationalism (which they are against); and internationalism (which they are for because "After the socialist revolution the PLP would fight for workers in the U.S. to give *$$$$billion* back to those that 'our' bosses have stolen it from"). It does not seem likely that workers or even college students in the United States would be willing to support these kinds of programs, in which orderlies do surgery while surgeons push the carts around, and so on; nor are they likely to respond to the rhetoric. (One interesting rhetorical blast links "rich parasites like Rockefeller and the phony revolutionaries like Abbie Hoffman and Rennie Davis.")

However, the following series of three articles on the automobile workers is representative of the best writing of the New Left, and in the long run it is more likely to make an impression.

1970

BEHIND THE AUTO WORKERS' STRIKE, PART 1[11]

Patty Lee Parmalee

The huge strike by auto workers against General Motors which began Sept. 14 is basically a defensive strike. When settled, it will determine whether U.S. production workers are going to be able to stay on the same level in an erratic economy, or whether they will have to take the ups and downs while owners' profits remain secure.

There are no radical demands on the national level and the rank and file is not mobilized to fight for any. It is nevertheless one of the most important strikes in postwar years. The United Automobile, Aerospace and Agricultural Implement Workers of America have since World War II been a pacesetter in contracts for other unions and this year they are demanding that the largest industrial corporation in the world pay back all the workers' losses due to inflation and guarantee there will be no future losses.

11 The next three selections by Patty Lee Parmalee were published in *The Guardian*, October 3, 10, and 17, 1970.

Bargaining issues

Collective bargaining in the U.S. today revolves around three kinds of issues
working conditions, fringe benefits and wages. The history of the trade union
movement has been the history of the change in emphasis from working
conditions to economic demands, as unions grew more bureaucratic and the
idea of cooperation between workers and corporation gained hegemony.

The UAW, despite its militant beginnings, has been no exception, even
though in many ways it is far more democratic and progressive than most
other unions. Ever since Walter Reuther won the union presidency over the
Communist opposition in 1946, the concept of class struggle has been waning
and amicable relations with auto companies have been growing.

This approach is reflected in the introduction to the last UAW contract with
General Motors, signed in 1967:

> The management of General Motors recognizes that it can not get
> along without labor any more than labor can get along without the
> management. Both are in the same business and the success of that
> business is vital to all concerned. This requires that both management
> and the employees work together to the end that the quality and cost
> of the product will prove increasingly satisfactory and attractive so
> that the business will be continuously successful.

Class issues

There is a fourth kind of issue that unions could include in demands, but
almost never do. These are class issues, measures to strengthen the entire
working class instead of just the members of one union. Although the UAW
under Reuther has since World War II been the most politically active large
union, its political action centers on endorsement of Democratic candidates
and rarely involves the membership. The union appears to accept the notion
that it has a vested interest in keeping U.S. auto companies' profits high so
the workers will be able to get high wages, and it has systematically dropped
its earlier, more class-conscious demands.

In 1945–46, when Reuther led a four-month strike against GM just before he
became president, he included a demand that the company raise wages without raising prices—thus protecting consumers. When GM cried that it couldn't,
he demanded the company "Open the books!" and prove it couldn't raise wages
out of existing profits. This cry, so famous at the time, has not been heard
recently.

After taking office, during the late 1940s and early 1950s, Reuther destroyed
the Communist party faction in the UAW and got a clause included in the
UAW constitution forbidding the holding of local or international office by
any communist or fascist.

In the late 1940s Reuther also conceded what are known as "management prerogatives." This concession laid the basis for the union's future failure to fight on working conditions, as well as the disappearance of any suggestion that workers should help make policy decisions about production and pricing. UAW auto contracts now contain this section as a matter of course:

The bosses' privileges

The right to hire; promote; discharge or discipline for cause; and to maintain discipline and efficiency of employes, is the sole responsibility of the Corporation except that Union members shall not be discriminated against as such. In addition, the products to be manufactured, the location of plants, the schedules of production, the methods, processes and means of manufacturing are solely and exclusively the responsibility of the Corporation.

The complement to management's right to discipline workers is the grievance procedure, a cumbersome system of appeal in which the union is supposed to act as advocate for a worker who feels wronged by the company. The worker is assumed guilty until he can prove himself innocent, and has his right to strike removed from him while the union turns the wheels of justice. Except for sabotage, stopping production is the only lever of power workers have, especially on the assembly lines where if some stop all must stop.

After the concession of management prerogatives it became clear to auto makers, who had bitterly opposed unions at first, that the unions could help increase production by preventing frequent work stoppages.

Alfred P. Sloan, Jr., who was for 30 years a top GM executive, finishes his book "My Years with General Motors" (1963) by explaining that early opposition to the union stemmed from

the persistent union attempt to invade basic management prerogatives. Our right to determine production schedules, set work standards, and to discipline workers were all suddenly called into question. Add to this the recurrent tendency of the union to inject itself into pricing policy, and it is easy to understand why it seemed, to some corporate officials, as though the union might one day be virtually in control of our operations.

"We retain all power"

But, he continues, "In the end we were fairly successful in combating these invasions of management rights.... We have moved to ... discuss workers' grievances with union representatives, and to submit for arbitration the few grievances that remain unsettled. But on the whole, we have retained all the basic powers to manage." The last paragraph of his book makes clear that if the unions give up the class struggle, they become harmless or even helpful to the companies: "The issue of unionism at General Motors is long since settled. We have achieved workable relations with all of the unions representing our employes."

In a further weakening of workers' power, the UAW has agreed to inclusion of a no-strike clause in its contracts, though unlike other unions it does allow for exceptions in the case of speedup or safety-condition violations in a plant.

The demand for a shorter work week—once an issue that unions fought on constantly just like wages—has also fallen by the wayside. In 1958 Reuther suddenly scrapped the demand for a four-day work week in favor of a "profit-sharing" scheme, and the shorter week has since then been forgotten. The implications are important: shortening work time without diminishing pay would help provide more employment and assist the whole working class; profit-sharing, on the other hand, increases class collaboration by causing workers to want higher profits for the company, even to accept speedup and increased overtime.

Barriers to class-consciousness

Lack of class-consciousness is also clear from the racism and sexism that exist even within the union, let alone from failure to include demands for blacks and women in bargaining. Racism, sexism and anticommunism are of course the three methods employers use to keep workers divided, and by failing to combat them or even encouraging them the union only weakens the class it supposedly represents.

Although it has indeed helped its members to get salaries higher than two-thirds of American workers, in order to achieve this the UAW has dampened fighting spirit and rank-and-file initiative. As one California GM assembly-line worker put it, workers think of the union like an insurance company. They pay the mandatory premium out of their checks but they wouldn't think of going to one of the tedious meetings. They are never encouraged to mobilize themselves.

In fact if workers were to act on their own initiative, there is danger that the union leadership might not be able to fulfill its side of its bargain with the companies: in exchange for a wage raise, to deliver a tractable work force. Leonard Woodcock, president of the UAW, is a brilliant negotiator, but before he can bring home a fat contract he has to convince GM that it will be able to count on the workers to help get the added costs back for the company.

Militancy sacrificed

Thus, in order to represent the workers' economic interests, the union has had to sacrifice its militancy. This is a logical result of assuming that capitalism is here to stay and therefore U.S. workers will benefit from expanding capitalist profits. It is not just the result of a desire on the part of individual union bureaucrats to hold power and manipulate workers. The collective bargaining system, if it is separated from consciousness of class struggle and the goal of transcending private ownership, must lead to bureaucracy and passivity in the unions.

The inevitable contradiction in the collective bargaining system is that unions both do and do not represent workers' interests. They are neither company union nor revolutionary organization, but caught in the tension between the two poles.

This works as long as the leaders can bring home the bacon in an expanding economy. In the recent inflation and loss of profits, however, companies are not so sure they'll be able to recoup wage increases by raising prices, and workers know their real wages are falling. Union leaders are caught in the middle.

According to the Sept. 6 *New York Times*, union members are voting down more negotiated contracts than at any time in history (one in eight), "wildcat strikes have reached almost epidemic proportions after a period of some years during which union leaders were able to enforce no-strike provisions in their contracts," and more local officials are being voted out of office than ever before.

Signs of discontent are spreading beyond the shop and union hall, and suddenly this is the year in which everyone is courting the blue-collar worker. Portions of the new left are developing a working-class perspective, though the right is beating them to it, in the classic prefascist pattern of capitalizing on worker anxiety with easy answers and scapegoats. Management, too, is trying to find ways of gaining the allegiance of alienated workers (see *Fortune* magazine for July and September) and even the government is studying token measures to return the working class to quiescence.

BEHIND THE AUTO WORKERS' STRIKE, PART 2

The UAW membership has never rejected a national settlement negotiated by its leaders. This is partly because of true skill in bargaining, partly because of skill in selling the contract to the workers and partly because the auto industry's superprofits made large settlements possible.

Now after 24 years the UAW has a new president—Leonard Woodcock—who has dared to take on GM nationally for the first time in the same number of years, who has raised worker expectations with rhetoric about bringing GM to its knees and who must prove himself at a time when company profits are down $20,000,000 (only 10%, to be sure). He can't afford to lose, but it won't be easy to win.

A "win" this year would consist of protection against inflation for the workers. This would be a victory for the whole working class, since the UAW, a strong, militant union in a strategic industry, sets a pattern for other unions. It has often introduced new concepts into negotiations—especially in the area of fringe benefits—which are then copied by other unions and industries.

The cost of winning

In order to win an economic victory, however, Woodcock may have to sacrifice some aspect of working conditions, yielding even more to "management prerogatives." This is what the company is demanding (specifically, more flexible work schedules, a crackdown by the union on absenteeism and weakening of the grievance procedure).

The Sept. 10 *Wall Street Journal* reported that in order to get GM back to the bargaining table—even before the strike—Woodcock dropped 24 non-economic demands relating to seniority, working hours and promotion and transfers. The only issues on which negotiators have reported back to the membership are economic.

The three demands on working conditions emphasized by the union are an end to in-plant pollution, improvement of the grievance procedure and voluntary overtime. The first refers mainly to vehicles driven inside the plant which produce unhealthy air. Speeding up the grievance procedure and rewriting it so a worker is innocent until proven guilty are long-standing demands. Voluntary overtime is perhaps the most significant of these demands; at present a plant manager can force workers to work whenever he wishes to catch up on his quota.

As in the army, the workers are not allowed to refuse a direct order. At Ford and Chrysler, a 24-hour warning about overtime is required, but at GM, where working conditions are in many respects worse, there is no set time. Time-and-a-half is paid, but this is cheaper for the company than hiring more workers, since no additional fringe benefits have to be paid. By forcing overtime, GM will be able to make up most of the time lost during the strike, with workers on shifts that last as long as 12 hours getting dangerously tired.

Terrible conditions

These few demands barely begin to cover the terrible conditions in a GM plant. In the body shop (with predominantly black workers) the noise is deafening and the fumes from welding are worse. The foundries and paint shop ovens are hot; heating and ventilation are erratic; and everywhere the inexorable assembly line turns men into automatons, making the same motions all day long, every day.

To an observer on a tour of the plant the work appears simple, but for a worker stuck at one point on the line attaching the same parts to a car every minute or so can be backbreaking and monotonous enough to drive him mad. And there is no respite except short, regulated breaks: the line never stops except for occasional welcome breakdowns.

On the contrary, if a foreman finds a worker has a second left over, he will find some other motion to fill that time and the line is periodically speeded up, never slowed down. All assembly workers hate their job and they soon learn not to care whether they do it well; sometimes they deliberately sabotage quality. A California worker told the *Guardian* that just before the strike cars were made especially sloppily and the Sept. 18 *Wall Street Journal* confirms this by quoting a Los Angeles dealer: "The workers really threw these together. They're in horrible shape. It looks like a deliberate thing."

Like sergeants in the army, foremen are trained to keep the workers feeling angry, frustrated and helpless. Firings are arbitrary, since "crimes" and punishments are not fixed in the contract and foremen keep workers divided by picking on some, leaving others alone. Black and Latin workers suffer from racist remarks and the women GM is now hiring for the assembly line must put up with a sexist kind of favoritism and passes.

Any act of solidarity between workers brings on harassment by the foreman with particular force, and petty power games develop between workers and foremen, preventing any focus on the company as the enemy. There is one foreman for each 20–30 workers, but only one committeeman (shop steward) for each 200–300. (Rank and file organizations are demanding a steward for each foreman.)

No protection

The grievance procedure is no protection against racism and sexism or the impersonality of the line. Workers learn to take it and vent their frustrations by doing a lousy job and thinking about their paycheck; or they get fired; or they crack up. At a Chrysler plant in Detroit last July 15, a black conveyor loader named James Johnson was suspended for insubordination after complaining about being moved to the brake shoe oven, a job done in 120 degree heat. After a long history of company harassment of himself and other workers (two had recently died due to company negligence and 14 committeemen had been fired after a wildcat), this was too much for Johnson and he came back with a .30-caliber carbine, told the workers to stand back while he searched for the foreman who suspended him and killed two foremen and a worker who tried to disarm him.

The union claims to be helpless to deal with conditions so bad, since they can only be enforced on a local level and the only real power the leadership has is a national strike. Even provisions written into the contract about working conditions are unenforceable if the workers in the plant are passive. The contract states, for instance, that the line shall not be speeded up even to make up for breakdowns unless the work force is augmented; this is blatantly violated constantly with no action taken. Neglecting working conditions in national negotiations is not exactly a "sellout," since an agreement is meaningless if it isn't enforced by a mobilized membership.

It is in the area of fringe benefits that the UAW's leadership has been most progressive. Reuther's creative demands brought auto workers total health insurance, life insurance, a good pension plan and supplemental unemployment benefits (SUB) or layoff insurance that amounts to a guaranteed annual wage. This year the union is demanding a dental plan and the company is demanding that increases in health insurance premiums after next year be paid by workers. (Note that when companies speak of rising payroll costs they include the rising cost of insurance, social security, etc., which the worker never sees.)

· · ·

Excuse for raising prices

In fact, in the past GM has always been happy to raise wages and use the increased labor costs as a publicity excuse for raising prices even more. Daniel Bell (in *Commentary*, March 1960) shows how this has worked in the "standard volume" pricing system GM has used since 1924. Prices are set such that net return on investment will be 20% even if the plant operates only 55% of the time (a conservative estimate).

This fantastic profit is achieved by inordinately high prices. All profits are distributed to stockholders or plowed back into the company, never are they passed on to the consumer as cheaper prices. These unnaturally high prices have been possible because of collusion between the auto companies, a period of expanding demand for cars (abetted by oil, steel and rubber interests, built-in obsolescence and government support for highway building) and consumer acceptance of the prices. Price increases were accepted partly because ever-increasing wages made costs look much higher. Actually, not only did GM get back by increasing productivity what it spent on wages, but each time it raised wages it raised prices far more. Reuther showed that from 1947–56 GM raised prices approximately $3.75 for each dollar of increased labor costs.

Thus profits were increased and inflation blamed on the striking worker. And furthermore, white-collar workers (who seldom strike) got tandem raises in salaries that were much larger than production workers, but the latter got all the blame. (In all industry, in 1947 salaries were one-fourth of manufacturing labor costs; one-third in 1957. During that time salaries rose 26% and wages 16%—Federal Reserve data.)

With these monopoly pricing policies GM was able from 1958 to 1968 to double its net working capital, an extraordinary achievement. During that time some one million stockholders received $10 billion in dividends. About 10% of GM stockholders hold over 200 shares; these people received at least $2 million each in those 10 years—some of them much more. (Figures from GM annual report.) And the actual work that produced that wealth was done by workers whose average wages reached $8000 by 1968, in addition to consumers who paid inflated prices for cheaply-made cars.

from BEHIND THE AUTO WORKERS' STRIKE, PART 3

The automobile industry has done for the 20th century U.S. economy what the railroads did for the 19th. With demand ever expanding and monopoly pricing possible, it has been easy for auto makers to meet workers' wage demands; in fact, they could have paid twice as much and still made higher than average profits.

The amount of money GM has made per production worker (surplus value) has approximately doubled from 1958 to 1968. Salaries and wages have also gone up two and one-half times, but workers are getting a diminishing percentage of the increase in gross profits. There is no question that those who get rich off GM could let workers have the increase they want, without going bankrupt.

But not only are we in a recession period now—a bad time for a strike— there are also signs that the American auto industry may be reaching the end of a boom. The ultimate problem for capitalist industry is finding markets and the market for U.S.-made automobiles may be diminishing. GM could still afford to pay higher wages in that case, but it certainly wouldn't want to.

HARD HATS, HIGH PAY, AND HAWKS

It is not hard for anyone to agree that the lot of the assembly-line worker is likely to be a poor one, unless one is a top official of General Motors. But what about other segments of American labor? For example, what about the construction workers, much maligned since 1969 for their fantastic pay raises? It is easy to get agreement among liberals and conservatives alike (and possibly the New Left as well) that this privileged class of workers makes very high wages, can shut down construction at the drop of a hard hat, and strenuously resists all attempts to let black workers at the honey pot. The resistance to letting black workers into the skilled and semi-skilled trades is well documented, but the issue of wage rates is another matter. Rather than being paid for working fifty-two weeks a year, the average construction worker is likely to work only about forty weeks (and the work is quite hazardous at that). According to Labor Department statistics, construction workers average only about 1,550 hours of work in a fairly good year. The January 1971 average hourly earnings of union construction workers was $6.39 per hour. If a worker were fortunate enough to be employed for 1,550 hours in a year, he would have earned about $9,900 which is below the $11,000 that the Bureau of Labor Statistics says is needed to maintain a modest standard of living for an urban working family of four at

1970 prices.[12] No wonder construction workers worry about competition from blacks.

Furthermore, the on-site labor component in home building is not a substantial factor in housing costs. According to statistics from the Bureau of Labor and from the National Association of Home Builders, the proportion of on-site labor costs for the average home in 1969 was only 18 percent, down from 33 percent in 1949. The high cost of housing is due to the rising costs of money (interest) and land; that is, to the "capitalistic" rather than to the labor aspects of the market. A 20 percent cut in the wages of construction workers would reduce the monthly occupancy cost to either a home owner or an apartment renter by about 2 percent.[13]

These figures are not part of the radical attack on business, but they do tend to challenge the counterattack of business on labor. Construction workers have been one symbol of what is wrong with labor, what causes high prices, and what prevents Americans from realizing the modest housing goals set by the federal government. (A recent *Fortune* article was titled "The Building Trades Versus the People," not "The Banks and Real-Estate Interests Versus the People." [14])

While construction workers presumably have unions with racist policies, one might doubt that either the policies of the unions or the supporting attitudes of the workers are really that important in maintaining a racist society. Just as the wealth of construction workers might be exaggerated while the profits of banks and real-estate interests might be minimized when discussing construction costs, so might the policies of the unions and the attitudes of their members be exaggerated when discussing racism. For example, the United States Commission on Civil Rights recently laid the blame squarely on government and management for failing to make even a modest dent in the housing needs of the nation and for maintaining policies of racial segregation in new construction.[15] The actions of government and business appear to have more impact than those of labor.

It is possible, however, that the New Left has overestimated the illiberal views of the working class, even as they may romanticize the possibility of a worker–student alliance. At the SDS National Council meeting in Colorado in the fall of 1968, the success of George Wallace in attracting working-class support was seen both as a threat (racism) and as a sign of hope (his appeal to the workers' sense of powerlessness). But Wallace's appeal to the working class was grossly overestimated by the New Left, as well as by almost all political pundits in the nation. His support in the South, it is true, was stronger among the working class than the middle

---

12 Data supplied from the Department of Research, AFL-CIO, courtesy of Frank Pollara.
13 See the two articles by Nat Goldfinger, "The Myth of Housing Costs" and "The Economic Squeeze on the Worker," in the AFL-CIO's *American Federationist*, December 1969 and August 1970.
14 Gilbert Burck, "The Building Trades Versus the People," *Fortune*, October 1970, pp. 77–97 ff.
15 See *The New York Times*, June 11, 1971, p. 1.

class, although much of this working-class support came from rural and small-town areas. But outside the South his support was no different by class; the percentage of the middle- and working-class votes for Wallace was almost identical.

Similarly, a careful analysis of survey research results over two decades by Richard Hamilton indicates that even on noneconomic issues (such as race, communism, hawkish war stands, dissent) there is no clear indication that the working class is more illiberal than the middle class.[16] On economic issues (government control of business, welfare, and so on) the working class is clearly more liberal, as all agree. If one removes the traditionally liberal Catholics and Jews from the middle and upper class and considers only the white Anglo-Saxon Protestants (WASPs), the lower class is substantially more liberal on both economic and social issues than WASPs are. As Hamilton points out, the New Left has tended to debunk social science and especially survey research at their peril. Once one abandons the preconceptions of establishment social science and examines the data carefully, there is more support for the fantasies of the New Left about the noble worker than for the nightmares about his racism and jingoism.

FEATHER BEDS ON THE RAILS

Another colorful symbol of working-class greed, power, and indifference to the needs of the nation is the railroad workers and the issue of featherbedding. The business press has devoted considerable space to this dramatization, as it has to the depiction of malingering, greedy construction workers. However, some alternative views do exist.

For example, while freight volume has gone up in the past twenty years, the number of employees has gone down by more than half. Rather than competing with alternative transportation means, the large railroads have invested heavily in them. The colossal financial scandal of the newly merged Penn Central Railroad had nothing to do with unions or work rules, let alone featherbedding, but with gross mismanagement by the officers of the company. (The scandal over the subsidiary firm, Executive Jet, alone is a worthy subject for a Kurt Vonnegut novel.) Also bearing heavy responsibility for the crisis were the blatantly unethical accounting practices of a prestigious auditing firm. The newly merged railroad, hit by scandals and inefficiency, promptly applied to the taxpayers for welfare payments to bail them out, while institutional bondholders threatened to block the use of any funds for new equipment or modernization that would be received from the sale of valuable New York City properties belonging to the company.

Meanwhile, the profits of a well-managed octopus such as the Southern

16 Richard Hamilton, *Class and Politics in the United States* (New York: Wiley, forthcoming).

Pacific are enormous. The railroads appear to have planned the decline in passenger service because carrying freight is so much more profitable, even though in the past the industry received huge land grants and federal funds on the assumption that it would provide passenger service. The industry has made almost no investment in research and development to improve long-range efficiency that could save the passenger and short-haul aspects of the business. Instead, the passenger business is handed over to the government, once it becomes uneconomical through neglect and concentration on the profits of freight. The steady rise in railroad accidents is a direct result of cutting corners on maintenance. Wages of workers do not compare favorably with those of other industries, despite their greater hazards and grim working conditions. Featherbedding does occur, but it is a small part of the picture and a response to fears of layoffs, which have been substantial, and thus it could be settled on rational grounds. This is the way the New Left looks at this important industry. Some of these themes are discussed, with documentation, in the following piece.

1970

BEHIND THE RAIL STRIKE, PART 1[17]

Patty Lee Parmalee

The dramatic one-day rail strike this month was solid—but Congress was more solid still.

The brief strike was broken, at least for the time being, but it had demonstrated that railroad workers are beginning to regain a little of their old militancy.

Despite rumors to the contrary, the nation's rails are absolutely crucial to the economy and workers are crucial to the rails. In the weeks before Christmas especially, the railroads are flooded with mail and products. At any time, the Vietnam war requires a steady flow of material—by rail. Trains are needed to carry 42% of all freight shipped, including 86% of pulp and paper, 78% of lumber, 76% of autos, 63% of chemicals, and 46% of meat and dairy products. Many industrial products can only be shipped by rail, including machines and parts that are programmed for immediate use in production, so that a rail

[17] Patty Lee Parmalee, "Behind the Rail Strike," *The Guardian*, December 26, 1970, and January 2, 1971.

strike would quickly close down other industries. Secretary of Labor James Hodgson told Congress that a week-long rail strike would raise unemployment to 8.4%, and an eight-week-long strike to 22.1%.

Railway workers should, then, have more economic leverage than any other workers in the country, especially since they all belong to unions. Yet the wages of skilled rail workers who served a four-year apprenticeship are lower than those of unskilled workers in other highly unionized industries; their unemployment and sickness benefits (set by law) are less than in other industries; they cannot retire until 65 (except with reduced pension at 62); they receive no extra compensation for working night shifts or erratic hours. Job security for workers without many years' seniority is very low. Members of the operating crafts, who travel with the trains, put in long irregular hours, becoming appendages to the machines and spending days away from home—and therefore suffering a very high divorce rate. Members of the non-operating crafts (clerks, maintenance-of-trains) and unskilled maintenance-of-way workers are subject to outdoor work in winter and to speedup. In an era of a shortening work week, rail workers' average weekly work has increased from 45 hours in 1957 to 47 in 1969.

Cynical toward safety

As has been the case through a century of profit-taking by American railroads, some of the companies are on the verge of bankruptcy due to mismanagement or, in the case of small companies, to competition. But others, such as California's Southern Pacific, are among the most solid corporations in the country, expanding into vast holdings and distributing large profits in stock. Yet their workers are paid the same low wages. The companies have also, since the earliest days of railroading and of the stock market, had a completely cynical attitude toward safety of workers and passengers alike. Only those safety regulations are obeyed that can be enforced by the very infrequent visits of ICC inspectors; workers are ordered to ignore safety rules such as checking the brakes on every car, which would require a larger labor force than the company is willing to hire. It is often cheaper to pay occasional accident and death claims than to pay for extra workers or repair equipment. Supervisors have orders when an ICC man does show up to distract him from seeing the conscious violation of regulations.

Working conditions are not only dangerous, they are also oppressive, due to an autocratic system of rules, big-brotherism and hierarchy. At the bottom of the hierarchy are maintenance-of-way workers (in California nearly all Chicanos, many of them Mexican nationals). They generally live on company land in company housing and they seldom rise to any of the skilled trades. There is a long tradition of black and immigrant labor on railroads, dating from the days when Chinese coolies built the western half of the transcontinental railroad for Central Pacific and Irish immigrants built the eastern half for Union Pacific and from the more recent black Pullman workers, who have since been put out of work by the decline in passenger traffic. In southern black and southwestern Chicano communities, railroading traditionally plays a very large role—yet engineers still seem to be all white.

How can it be that workers in the most strategic industry of the country are so underpaid, overworked and so subject to safety hazards, layoffs and racism?

The answer is simple: they don't use their power; they almost never strike. The reasons are complex, having to do with the sordid history of the railroads and the unions and with the importance of the industry, which makes it subject to government intervention.

Militant beginnings

Rail workers were not always meek. In the early days of railroading, they sparked two of the largest and most violent labor uprisings the U.S. has ever seen. With the end of the Civil War and the defeat of the southern aristocracy, northern capitalists began developing the country and their principal means of expansion was the railroad. An expansion-minded and railroad-influenced government donated over 150 million acres of land (larger than France) and millions of dollars in loans to the railroad capitalists, which they used for their own profit. The history of the early stock market scandals by such railroad magnates as Commodore Vanderbilt, Jay Gould, Dan Drew and J. P. Morgan is part of the lore of America. Though they have refined their methods, the railroad companies have never lost their conviction that profits are more important than people.

The booming and corrupt railroad industry marked the beginning of powerful corporations in America and railway workers were the proletariat of early corporate capitalism. They organized into unions and in 1877, eight years after completion of the transcontinental railroad and six years after the Paris Commune—in the middle of a long depression caused by overquick postwar expansion—they struck the Baltimore and Ohio after their wages were reduced. Riots, joined by masses of the unemployed, spread like fire from Baltimore to Pittsburgh, where the Penn Central was struck, to Chicago and San Francisco. In the spontaneous, leaderless uprising dozens of workers were killed by federal troops and militia.

In 1894, during another economic crisis, a more conscious strike by the American Railway Union under Eugene Debs led to the country's greatest labor revolt. The strike, which started among Pullman workers, spread to the entire industry. Against Debs' wishes and possibly at the hands of company agents, some 2000 railway cars were wrecked and burned and property and business losses ran to $50–$100 million. The rebellion was defeated by the concurrence of the three classic means of breaking strikes: government intervention (based on the supposedly anti-business Sherman Antitrust Act) and a court injunction; the occupation of Chicago by 10,000 federal military troops, later raised to 50,000; and the lack of solidarity from the reactionary American Federation of Labor craft unions under Samuel Gompers, who viewed Debs' industrial union as a threat. Present railway union leadership honors Debs' memory, but fails to mention that reflecting on his failure in jail he became a socialist and anti-imperialist.

Union collapses

After the strike, the government built armories in the industrial cities and, together with the rail industry, began looking for ways to prevent the recurrence of such a strike. At the same time, the American Railway Union fell apart. Railway workers have been split into rival craft unions ever since, originally 21 and merged in 1969 to 17. The companies can play the unions off against each other and keep wages depressed in the crafts that employ minorities, which is much harder where there is an industrial union as in steel, auto or trucking.

BEHIND THE RAIL STRIKE, PART 2

Railroads and railworkers were put under federal government control during World War I.

At the end of the war, railroad workers' organizations—which had 1.8 million members and constituted the progressive wing of the entire labor movement—developed the "Plumb Plan" for retaining government ownership of the railroads with control to be shared by industry, labor and government. Rejecting the plan, Congress passed the Transportation Act in 1920, which returned railroad ownership to private interests and put the railroad brotherhoods under the hostile Railroad Labor Board. Workers rebelled in the wildcat switchmen's strike of 1920 and the strike of 400,000 shopmen in 1922. The first strike was broken and the second was defeated because the running trades scabbed on the shop trades, encouraged by reactionary union leaders who supported the Transportation Act.

The defeat of these two strikes cost the unions hundreds of thousands of members as well as their militancy and progressive character. They have been under the control since then of the kind of leaders who accepted the 1923 B&O plan of union–management cooperation, which articulated the corporate capitalist notion that workers would win more by increasing productivity (speedup) than by striking. Since then the railroads have been an almost no-strike industry.

Corrupt railway union leaders also developed labor banking, a racket which lost members of the Brotherhood of Locomotive Engineers $17,000,000 in one of the U.S.'s great financial scandals. To this day the maintenance unions in the rail industry remain probably the most undemocratic unions in the country. Their members have no right to vote on contracts or officers, and apathy and disillusion with the unions are universal among workers.

No-strike clause

The no-strike policy was cemented in 1926 with passage of the Railway Labor Act. This important piece of legislation, as amended in 1932, still governs railway workers' negotiations with companies. It puts them in a class by themselves, subject to extreme federal control and outside the purview of the 1947 Taft-Hartley Act. In exchange for the right to a closed shop and a fairly adequate grievance procedure, the act virtually forbids strikes and forces arbitration. Progress through its sequence of delays, mediation and cooling-off periods can take years for each contract negotiation. The act was pushed by management and union leaders and denounced by Communists, who were then expelled from the railway unions.

By the end of World War II, due to their quiescence, railway workers had seen their wages fall from 1st place (in 1928) to 20th place. In 1946, stimulated by the UAW strike against GM, two of the operating unions, which hadn't struck for 50 years, attempted a strike. But President Truman put the railroads under the control of the Army and threatened the use of troops. Union leaders ordered a return to work after two days.

In 1963 the companies decided to fire 37,000 firemen. An attempt to strike on the issue was thwarted by Congress; in 1967 engineers struck on the same issue but were forced back to work by emergency legislation. The next year workers in the non-operating crafts struck, but Congress passed a law ordering them back to work after a few days and imposing forced arbitration. The arbitration board was headed, however, by liberal Sen. Wayne Morse, who got railway workers the biggest wage increase they had ever had (5%).

The dispute over firemen's jobs is still not settled. Since the conversion to diesel locomotives firemen have not been needed as such; but their union insists they be kept on to secure their jobs and because it is unsafe for an engineer to drive without a partner to watch the other side of the tracks. (There have been numerous accidents and deaths in railroad yards where firemen were removed and engineers started driving with a blind spot.) Ignoring the safety issue, the companies accuse the union of "featherbedding." Like many such issues, this one will probably be solved by attrition. The unions are the only defense workers have against thorough automation, which could probably eliminate 50% of railroad jobs if companies had their way. But the unions worry only about their own members who are still working, not about increased unemployment among the entire working class. So when the last remaining firemen have died or retired, which will be fairly soon, the fireman issue will be dropped.

Half the jobs eliminated

Despite a fairly strong position on work rules by the railroad unions, automation and rationalization in the rail industry have eliminated many jobs.

Just between 1950 and 1969, railway workers have been reduced from 1.2 million to 578,000.

The biggest step toward rationalization was made right after World War II with the conversion from steam to diesel engines. Not only firemen became obsolete, but also steamfitters, blacksmiths, hostlers and all the small towns 80 to 100 miles apart where the short-range steam engines had to stop. Simultaneously, railroads gradually automated the repairing and servicing of cars; for instance they were able to eliminate hundreds of oilers at each yard by installing machines on each side of the track. In the last decade many more yard jobs have been scrapped due to the installation of pushbutton equipment throughout the repair plants and automatic retarder yards, which allow a few workers to control switching and braking of all the thousands of cars in a yard by computer rather than each car being ridden by a worker.

Depending on the economy of an area, the effect of automation has been either to lay off hundreds of thousands of workers, or to keep workers but double their work load. In California, the railroads have simply increased their freight business: Southern Pacific estimates that each new California resident will add one boxcar to business and California's population has more than doubled since the war.

Increased work for the same number of workers means higher productivity, but companies are complaining productivity is being outstripped by wages. They measure productivity by number of carloadings, which has remained about even since 1940 despite the decrease in workers. But productivity figures fail to mention the increasing size of freight cars, a 25% increase from 1950–1969. There are tankers in freight yards today that have three times the capacity of the old familiar ones, dwarfing the other cars like a 747 at an old airport. Automobiles which used to be carried 4 to a boxcar are now stacked 15 to a tri-level auto carrier.

At the same time they were automating the yards and increasing shipping productivity, the railroads were also busily getting rid of their passenger business. Between 1950 and 1969 revenues from freight increased from $7.8 billion to $10.3 billion, but revenues from passenger traffic decreased from $800 million to $440 million. The number of passengers decreased from 486 million to 296 million and passenger miles from 31.7 billion to 12 billion.

Atrophy of passenger service

Railroads have presented the loss of passenger traffic as a disaster in order to get ICC permission to reduce service, but it is quite possible that they planned the loss to get rid of a business that was not as profitable as freight. They left passenger cars in disrepair while increasing average capacity from 75 to 85, cut the number of cars and bought up large or controlling interest in air and bus lines. While creating a public image of large losses due to the American public's alleged preference for road and air travel, the railroads were quietly cutting proportionately far more passenger trains and routes than the drop in traffic warrants. Consequently, the ratio of passenger miles to railroad car miles has increased 50% from 1950 to 1969. Statistics suggest the contraction in service partially preceded the contraction in demand. Service will increase again not when demand increases, but when the government provides the railroads with the large subsidies they want so they can make guaranteed profits off passengers. The quasi-public corporation (i.e., tax money pays, private industry profits) called Railpax [later named Amtrak and formed in 1971], proposed by Congress, is such a step, but it is underfunded. Interestingly, Railpax proposals have eliminated planned subsidies for West Coast trains, where auto, oil and airline companies make their great profits.

In their attempts to look poor, the richest railroads are also apt to complain about competition from trucking. But Southern Pacific is said to own more trucks than any truck company in California; acres of land formerly used for passenger traffic are now filled with fleets of trucks and piggyback units owned by S.P. but bearing many different brand names.

The Southern Pacific is in fact a huge conglomerate controlling many industries besides the railroad. It has a monopoly on hauling many construction materials for booming California; it shares a monopoly on fruit shipping with the Union Pacific; it owns many of the subsidiary industries that supply it. It is run like an efficient and centralized empire. Its holding company owns timbering, agricultural, oil and mining interests, many on land donated by the government.

But for all its riches, the S.P. has virtually abolished passenger service in smog-choked L.A., and it orders its workers to disobey safety rules to save money. And, like the other railroads, it is trying during present labor negotiations to change work rules so it can rationalize further and fire the then superfluous workers.

Plans to eliminate 18,000 jobs

Work rules, not wages, are the gut issue in the present dispute. The four unions whose contracts are being negotiated (representing 400,000 or ¾ of all railway workers) have demanded a 40–45% pay increase over three years. They have been offered 37%. The figure was recommended by the presidential panel appointed to mediate as the last step in the Railway Labor Act's stalling devices. But the panel also recommended accceptance of the companies' demands for work rule changes and the unions flatly refused, although they were very close on wages. Union representatives claimed that although the wage increase would cost management $709 million, the work rules changes would save $782 million by eliminating nearly 18,000 jobs.

The work rules in question affect members of the United Transportation Union (UTU), the 1969 merger of the Brakemen's, Switchmen's and Trainmen's unions. Briefly, the companies want to increase the distance each worker travels on a train and when the road crews (which work unpredictable hours) return to the yards after a short day the companies want them to do yard work. This cross-craft method would be a disaster for the switchmen, who presently have a monopoly on the yards. It is one more manifestation of the basic battle between rationalization and job protection. It is true that the union is holding back "progress," but all this progress would mean is less workers doing more work; it would not mean any improvement in service. Workers will have to fight to preserve obsolete jobs as long as the capitalist system provides no other, more meaningful jobs.

There is another work rule the companies are trying to change but, although it refers to the clerks, it is not at issue in this contract period. They want to establish system-wide seniority for clerks, so they could move business from one place to another without paying severance pay. This would open the way, for instance, for S.P. to make a desired move from many square miles of some of the most valuable land in downtown L.A. to a place 100 miles out in the desert and then to develop the real estate while throwing the L.A. workers out of jobs without severance payments.

Since the emergency board's recommendation was the last step provided in the Railway Labor Act, after 19 months of going through its provisions one by one the rail unions were finally legally able to strike Dec. 10. In record time, Congress passed special legislation outlawing a strike during another cooling-off period, to March 1. President Nixon signed the bill an hour after it was passed, at 2:10 a.m. Dec. 10 but the strike had already started at midnight. At 3:17 a federal judge signed an injunction ordering the unions back to work and at 5 a.m. the heads of the UTU, Brotherhood of Maintenance of Way and the Hotel and Restaurant Employes' Union ordered a return to work—but workers would not cross picket lines maintained all day by the largest union, the Brotherhood of Railway and Airline Clerks. The president of the Clerks' union, representing half the strikers, ordered a return to work in the evening, a few minutes after the judge who had signed the injunction backed it up by declaring a $200,000 fine per day if the union stayed out.

C. L. Dennis, president of the Clerks' union, claimed it wasn't the fine that decided him, but assurances by Assistant Secretary of Labor W. J. Usery, Jr., that the Association of American Railroads was ready to start bargaining in earnest (which the *Wall Street Journal* later stated was just a trick to help Dennis save face with his rank and file) and also that Congress would consider a plan to allow limited strikes in the future.

Revision of Railway Act?

In fact, there is a good chance that the Railway Labor Act will be revised since, restrictive though it is, rail workers still seem to be able to strike. Revision of the Act might well occur in the context of a whole series of new labor laws, prompted by increasing rank-and-file militancy, work stoppages and respectable wage settlements. The barrage of anti-union propaganda from government and the media seems to be preparing measures like the labor law just passed in England. The *Wall Street Journal*, for instance, in its Dec. 11 and Dec. 15 editorials on the rail strike, talks about "unbridled displays of union power," unions that "misuse their power to damage the public," "outrageous union featherbedding practices" and "make-work rules"; it calls the Railway Labor Act a boon to the unions and a "disaster" for the railroads (i.e., their owners); and it concludes that "labor law in general needs to be overhauled to make it clear that government is no more than an impartial mediator between labor and management and not the enthusiastic union supporter that it has so often seemed to be in recent years." (Strikers who have received antipicketing injunctions or been arrested by police who protect scabs will wonder about the *Journal's* assessment of the state's position.)

In passing delaying legislation Dec. 10, Congress granted workers a 5% pay increase retroactive to the beginning of the year, plus increments making a total of 37% in three years (13% as of now). This is because the contract has been in the process of negotiation for so long that workers missed a year of what should be a new contract period. Congress left work rules unchanged for the postponement period until March. So although the unions have not yet won the right to strike, they have not lost any ground so far.

With the militant mood growing, another strike is likely in March and probably so is repeated Congressional action. As determined as the workers are to keep work rules, the companies are also determined to increase "productivity" (i.e., decreasing the number of workers) to pay for wage raises. Of course they have already raised freight rates to cover anticipated wage raises. After being granted an 8% boost by the ICC in November they are planning to ask for 7% more—in addition to two other increases granted this year and two in the two previous years.

There is no question that the railroads can afford to keep all workers on and raise their wages, too. Whether they will depends on the militancy of the workers and on the position of the government in this most regulated of industries.

THE AFFLUENT WORKER (WOMEN AND CHILDREN)

For some segments of American labor, working conditions are getting worse rather than better. A recent study by the American Friends Service Committee and studies of the Labor Department, reported in *The Guardian*, indicate that the use of child labor in agriculture is increasing.[18] Roughly one-fourth of the agricultural work force in the United States, or about 800,000 workers, are children. In general, they are not covered by federal legislation; consequently, working conditions are poor, especially on large farms. For example, in a five-county area in Oregon, 75 percent of the work force are children, earning an average of 40 cents an hour. A bill in the state legislature to set the minimum age for workers at twelve years was changed to ten years after pressure from the Oregon Farm Bureau. The director of research for the Farm Bureau argued that a minimum age of twelve years would cause younger children to "lose this opportunity to learn" and the "responsibility" that working teaches them. In the state of

18 *The Guardian*, June 2, 1971, p. 5.

Washington the working conditions for 4,500 children during two summer months with temperatures of 100 degrees included no hand-washing facilities near outhouses, inadequate drinking water, and DDT in the fields. The tobacco industry is one of the most profitable in the nation. In the South conditions such as these were found: twenty-eight children, from seven to fifteen years old, miss school to work seven and eight hours a day in a cramped area unprotected from the sun with temperatures of over 100 degrees. The area was too cramped for adults. Adult workers do little better; the average annual income of a migrant farm worker is $891.

Child labor is not confined to agriculture, however. *The Guardian* article notes, "A typical violation in the service industry uncovered recently occurred at a Detroit motel-restaurant where the employer had hired 72 children under the age of 16 as dishwashers, laundry workers, and maids." This was about half the work force at that establishment. Hurt by the economic crisis, employers are resorting to child labor. The Labor Department reported a 15 percent increase in 1970 of violations of child-labor laws. Thus capitalism, according to the New Left, both lays off increasing numbers of workers or cannot provide jobs for new ones, and increases the exploitation of labor, including children. Obscure studies by government and groups such as the American Friends Society or reports of legislative activity in Oregon rarely receive much attention in the mass media. Radicals dig them out, however, and spread the word among the faithful. These items help to sustain the image of a callous society dominated by business.

Recently the list of exploited groups has come to include women. While the "think magazines" of the middle class dwell on the problems of the unfulfilled suburban housewife, the New Left has done a little probing into the conditions of women working for the system. A fair number of them work for the telephone company. American Telephone and Telegraph Company is one of the largest, most prosperous, most sophisticated and forward-looking corporations in the United States, as befits a monopoly with a guaranteed rate of return. There have been exposés of it before, similar to the stories on General Electric and Litton Industries reprinted in Chapter 2. One article shows AT&T's actual rate of return to be considerably higher than the official one allowed.[19] The *New York Review of Books* recently published a fascinating and highly sophisticated analysis of female telephone operators.[20] But somehow or other, the brief, fugitive, and hasty piece reprinted here has its own compelling quality. It is an example of the better vignettes that circulate through the underground press. Originally this article written by anonymous telephone operators appeared in an obscure Berkeley, California, paper, *Tooth and Nail,* and was picked up by *The Guardian* and other underground papers.

[19] "Regulating AT&T," *New Republic,* September 26 and October 3, 1964.
[20] Elinor Langer, "Women of the Telephone Company," *New York Review of Books,* March 12 and March 26, 1970.

1970

"LOWER YOUR VOICE—SWALLOW YOUR GUM" [21]

Anonymous

When people come into contact with a phone company employe, usually the operator, they are ready to scream. If the operator were to respond humanly to this rage, and reveal her own rage, total bedlam would ensue. The primary quality required of an operator is maintaining a courteous front at all times, to prevent violent interchange. Over the phone the operator must totally erase herself. She cannot make jokes, show anger, reveal emotion.

Only women can be counted on to be operators, not because we are passive or dumb, but because jobs for women are scarce and—as members of a lowly caste—we are forced to do the shitwork for everybody else.

Physical surroundings

Inside the company office, operators are forced to deny their personalities. Each operator's office contains two long rows of switchboards with 25 "girls" to a row.

The operator must enter her chair from the left and leave from the right. She must face the switchboard at all times, never turning her eyes to the side or looking behind her. She may not swing her arm across the back of the chair. She may not cross her legs. She may not chew gum but may suck quietly on a Lifesaver if she must. If she needs help, she turns on a light above her seat which summons the supervisor, who stands behind the operator and converses with her through the circuits. This method of communication is rude and dehumanizing.

The operator's voice

The operator is always referred to as "she" and the customer is "he." "She" must always be respectful to the customer. Even if "he" calls her a "filthy

21 Anonymous, "Lower Your Voice—Swallow Your Gum," *The Guardian*, March 7, 1970, pp. 5 ff.

bitch" she does not have the right to express anything but courteous acceptance.

An operator may never interrupt a customer who is rambling off "his" name,
address and phone number too fast. She must wait until "he" has finished and
then ask him to repeat it all again. And the operator takes the blame if "he"
gets angry at having to repeat his information.

The operator is expressly forbidden to show any humanity to either the
calling party, the other operators, or the called party (unless, of course, a
mother should break down on the phone because her son has been wounded
in Vietnam, in which case the operator may mumble some condolence, but
not too much).

Correspondence or a friendly word to a familiar operator's voice is grounds
for reprimand. One woman who has been an overseas operator for 30 years
got to know a Saigon operator through letters and occasional greeting on the
job. The Saigon operator married a GI and came here to visit the U.S. operator. Since then the American operator has been forbidden to work the
Saigon circuits.

Repression of any possible humanity is aided by official company language,
consisting of the abbreviations and initials operators use with each other, pat
phrases for customers, and the exaggerated enunciation required—careful,
modulated tones which often lead to the nasal "operator voice"—a fine cover-
up for the rage burning deep inside the average operator.

The hierarchy

The supervisor's job is a little higher in status than the operator's, but she is
in constant danger of being "busted back to the board." A 62-year-old woman
who has been working for the phone company since she was 19 was made
a supervisor after 32 years on the job. After 9 years as a supervisor she was
busted back to the board and it took the union two years to get her back
to supervisor. It usually takes less than a year to become a supervisor.

The company holds out the chance of climbing the hierarchy but normally
only to the position of supervisor or upstairs secretary, since management
rarely comes up through the ranks but comes straight from college.

The highest pay for an operator is $2.15 an hour, or $86 for a 40-hour week.
After 6 months on the job, operators receive a note in the mail: "Congratula-
tions! You will now received $1.00 a week more."

The supervisor monitors her charges' progress by listening in on them un-
announced. Above the supervisor is the ATOM (Assistant Traffic Operating
Manager). The ATOM monitors the supervisor under her as well as the operators under her supervisors. The ATOM relays orders from the TOM (Traffic
Operating Manager) who has some 300 women under her.

Everyone in the office, including the ATOMs, is monitored by the TOM from
her office inside a glass cage at the side of the room. And on another floor, the
Public Utilities Commission is monitoring the customer's phone call.

The TOM is the only woman who meets with "the men"—the executives.

Whenever they come to check the office or bring in visitors, the TOM is the official greeter. As they enter her office, the TOM rushes to tell the ATOMs to tell the supervisors to tell the operators to lower their voices, swallow their gum, hide their Life-savers, and give the impression of quiet efficiency. The operators in pants must hide in the back of the room. One time "the men" came through, the TOM sent four women home for wearing pants.

"The men" come through the office and look around as they graciously chat with the TOM and compliment her on her "good group of girls." "The men" also shop around for particularly attractive and well-groomed girls who might be given the honor of a job "upstairs" as a secretary at higher pay.

The regimentation and terminology reminds one of the army—such as the "induction center" where operators report for orientation. The ATOMs and the TOM are the brass. Work schedules are called "tours of duty." Everyone belongs to "the force."

The phone company also resembles elementary school. The building itself is barren, with entrances policed by two rent-a-fuzz who check passes. Noses are counted every 15 minutes to insure that operators do not play hookey.

If an operator wants to go to the toilet, she puts on her overhead light to signal the supervisor. When the supervisor comes, the operator says, "May I have a minute?" (Saying anything but this euphemism causes raised eyebrows.) If permission is granted, the operator signs out and must be back in three minutes. Operators may not smoke in the john while "on a minute."

Operators must conform to dress regulations. The union won the right for women to wear slacks, but then passed another regulation specifying that the demand did not include blue jeans. Supervisors are told that wearing pants means no promotion.

If she feels ill, an operator must convince her supervisor to let her go home. Once an operator died at the boards—she had been denied permission to leave. "We do make mistakes," an official admitted. There is no sick leave. Every absence is taken out of the operator's pay.

The cafeteria

Operators live in parallel isolation from one another. Since the possibility of relating to the "girl" two inches from her left elbow is slight, the only time to be together is during the two 15-minute breaks and the 30-minute lunch. And any two people do not have the same breaks for any sustained period of time.

The cafeteria is a grim room where inedible food can be bought for outrageous prices. With only a half hour for lunch, the operator is forced to eat there or bring her lunch. On the graveyard shift, the cafeteria is closed and operators must walk to an all-nite plastic diner.

Each office has its own lunch table and the familiar faces talk to each other about the terrible day they're having, the cranky customers, the utter frustration of trying the same calls for two hours, and the nagging bitchiness of supervisors who hate "new girls" for their ineptness. (Almost everyone is a "new girl"—the turnover rate is 60% in six months.)

Since an operator is never allowed to react on the spot, it all builds up in-side. No matter how much she hates telling her little anecdotes during break, she finds herself doing it. She just has to get it out and search for sympathy. She receives a little support from the other "girls" and goes back to the board to begin again.

AT&T has lice in its switchboard. Often operators suffer from lice bites on their faces, arms and legs. Operators must get used to receiving minor shocks when they plug in. Occasionally an operator will scream or fall off her chair from a bad shock.

That women operators are policed and bossed by women makes the work experience even more devastating. Women managers are in a far less secure position than men; they must continually fight to maintain control where men can assume it. Besides, they have to contend with women who act like them-selves when men aren't around.

Operators dress for comfort, are less disguised by make-up, are less shy, less careful about what they say, and, in general, harder to control than if they were typists in an office under men. In order to maintain control, women managers are forced to conduct constant campaigns to humiliate "their girls."

Male bosses are duty-bound to respect the myth of the "mysterious" woman. In the man's world, women are considered empty-headed fools. But no man would dare tell them how to dress, when to go to the bathroom, or take an aspirin. The phone company's military discipline is maintained through women bosses who, by virtue of their sex, are granted the license to investigate and regulate all habits, personality traits, and the normally regarded "private spheres" of an employe's life.

The boss has the right to refuse bathroom permission to an operator, to veto the kind of perfume she wears, to pull her into the glass cage and lecture her about her body odor, her hair style, her vocabulary or her life insurance. The company grants no sick leave to "girls" and a sick operator may be denied permission to go home and rest. The ATOM considers herself competent to diagnose illness and prescribe medicines which the operator is forced to swallow.

Women managers must do these things because, as women, their authority is constantly under question, because with no men around, women do become more "natural" and less willing to be servants.

The motionless sitting in a confined position for long hours, the combined physical and emotional constriction, the para-military organization, the con-stant petty harassment and humiliation (at a wage scale lower than that of most men), all make the operator's job brutal and lobotomizing. The company understands that women from ages 15–25 and mothers who need staggered hours are the only ones who would put up with these conditions.

Understanding the special indignities and degradation working women are subjected to is only a first step. No one has yet figured out how to hurdle the enormous obstacles of building a movement of women workers. Women, the most despised caste within society, have little leverage on the job. Existing unions are controlled by men for men and refuse to fight against women's oppression.

Furthermore, many women who work go home at night to another full day's work of child-care and housework. Burdened by two jobs at the price of half of one, they have little time to spare. Kept out of the world in an isolated and marginal existence, women have little understanding that power relationships exist at all and their egos were long ago smashed by despair.

Women have a tough job ahead, but the rage is there and will someday explode.

When sociologists regularly announce that the United States has become a middle-class nation, they are referring to female workers like these in the telephone company and to the hundreds of thousands of female clerks, sales ladies, and typists working in various service industries and manufacturing concerns. Roughly one-third of the work force in the United States is female, many of whom hold second jobs in families or work for a few years before or after child-rearing. They are middle class only in the statistics of the Department of Labor; their incomes are low, for the most part they are married to blue-collar workers, and the degree of mental rather than physical labor in their tasks is not substantial.

If we subtract the females from the work force and look only at employed males, who after all are heads of households and whose occupational status influences the class attitudes of the family, this is hardly a middle-class nation. The work force is made up predominantly of members of the blue-collar working class. In fact, in spite of the image of a sophisticated technology demanding a sophisticated, highly educated work force that is middle class in character, the occupational class structure of the United States has changed only very gradually in the past sixty-five years. In 1900 the proportion of the male work force employed in blue-collar positions was 70 percent; in 1966 it had declined only eleven percentage points, to 59 percent, despite the fact that the intervening decades were ones of supposedly revolutionary change in business and industry.[22] As the work force has been moving out of mining and manufacturing because of capital-intensive labor-saving devices, it has moved into the service sector of the economy. Thus, were the New Leftists to find ways to mobilize the worker, they need not fear that he is a rapidly disappearing phenomenon in an affluent society.

THE COOLING OF AMERICA?

This sampling of material on the automobile, railroad, agriculture, and communications industries is not intended to be representative of the condition of workers as seen by the New Left. This material is meant to indicate that

---

22 See the extensive analysis in Richard Hamilton, *op. cit.* The figures are from government reports.

the Left is not concerned only about "the student as nigger," the FBI and the CIA, imperialism toward the Third World, and Vietnam. The Left perceives gross injustices among American workers, and certainly, in a theme we have hardly touched upon here because it is so blatant and obvious, among blacks and Chicanos. But the Left also sees the workers as a source of hostility toward the Left, as racist, as pro-imperialism, and as prowar (until recently, when the population as a whole moved toward a position favoring complete withdrawal from Vietnam, with union members favoring withdrawal somewhat more than the general population). The Left piles up and counts the straws that indicate that a new, militant working population with a true consciousness is emerging. The better-organized groups endlessly debate the proper tactics to be used to bring labor around; the less-organized Left hangs back, baffled. Well they might.

In recent years, groups in American society have become increasingly insurgent. The revolt started with minuscule movements in the late 1950's and grew with the civil rights and peace movements of the early 1960's until about 1965. Since then, insurgency has become unprecedented in almost every institutional area—religion, abortion, pollution, consumerism, legal reform, the organization of black ghettos, the organization of Puerto Ricans and Chicanos, draft evasion and draft protest, welfare-mothers rights organizations, college and then high school revolts, strikes by white-collar unions, dissident military groups, stockholders' campaigns, and so on. Insurgency within unions and among workers appears to be a part of this general social movement, although it is still a laggard part.

As models of action and recognition of the legitimacy of dissent and protest become widespread, labor may create its own insurgency without the "help" of radical youth with their dogmatic rhetoric and defiant lifestyles. Mr. Roche of General Motors and his vice president for personnel can serve this cause well with their righteous indignation toward labor. But even if they and others were to cool the scene and adopt a soft-sell approach, the New Left would be likely to be there, digging up the dirt, as the next chapter will show. *Time* magazine, among others, heralded "The Cooling of America" early in 1971.[23] But given the increasing economic militancy of blue-collar and white-collar labor, their participation in the mass demonstrations against the war in the spring of 1971, the increasing militancy of minority organizations, the steadily mounting opposition to the war and the disclosures of the Pentagon Papers, and the fumbling attempts by the FBI and the Justice Department to prosecute popular radicals and the Black Panthers (despite their success in jailing and perhaps shooting them), such predictions may be quite premature. Labor is a part of society, and the society as a whole is changing. The New Left may try to lead the way with their shrill voices, as well as their analysis, but labor may simply go its

23 *Time*, February 17, 1971, pp. 10–19.

own revolutionary way regardless of attempts by the organized Left to sweep it into the fold.

But radical change is not the only paradigm for the future, even if the United States is not cooling off. There is also reform. What about the attempts of business to reform and to display the social consciousness that liberals request and radicals scorn? The following chapter attempts to put into perspective the response of business to the social crisis.

CHAPTER 6

Tidying up the stables, or the social responsibilities of business

Clearly, the situation in the United States could be much worse than it is. We do have a welfare state to some degree, although the level of social welfare is below that of most industrialized nations, and far below some of them. The number of people living below the official poverty level has declined substantially since the Second World War, reaching a low of 24.3 million in 1969, but rising to 25.5 million in 1970. The courts still manage to free political prisoners occasionally, despite the power of law-enforcement agencies. Ground combat in Vietnam is winding down for American forces, although the bombing has intensified during the Nixon years and more people in Laos, Cambodia, Thailand, and Vietnam are involved as combatants or refugees or simply as casualties. The administration does attempt to censor the mass media, but the outlets for radical journalism do not seem to have diminished. Pollution is finally a public issue, and there is some enforcement of new and old controls. Life in the ghettos is, if anything, worse than ever, but business has taken up the challenge of revitalizing the cities, even as business moves to the suburbs. This is a bitter-sweet picture, but if business were as powerful and as cruel as it is sometimes described, the picture might be only bitter.

Most members of the New Left have no problem explaining progressive programs and the maintenance of some traditional freedoms; they see the system as one of *liberal* corporate capitalism. The adjective "liberal" means that capitalists attempt to relieve at least some of the basic social ills of the nation, which it also is in their long-run interests to do. Naturally it is not in their interests to change the system in any meaningful way, but just to ameliorate the impact of the system when expectations rise, exploitation becomes too excessive, a labor supply is threatened, consumption slows down, or the voice of revolution is heard in the land. The amelioration of the impact of the system is referred to as the social responsibilities of business. It might also be described as letting off steam while keeping the lid on, or more simply, as tidying up the stables.

For some members of the New Left, all this theorizing is nonsense. The system is rotten through and through; it does nothing to clean up after itself; capitalists are racists, reactionary pigs out for all they can get; and all liberal changes are illusionary. They might be right, but most Leftists seem to have a more sophisticated view of the system. In dealing with a broad social movement, one should not mistake the ideology of the movement's fringe for that of the mass, any more than one should characterize the tactics of the New Left from occasional bombings and terrorism rather than from confrontations, marches, publicizing, and communicating. By the same token, because one should not characterize the business establishment by its fringe of cretins, this chapter will look at the largest and most important businesses and businessmen.

The social responsibilities of business have been frequently discussed since the rapid industrialization of the United States after the Civil War. Each crisis and each period has produced its own version of these same possibilities.[1] There are some meaningful debates within the business community and among its analysts (primarily economists and lawyers) about whether the good of the nation is best served by assuming corporate responsibility for some social problems or by merely pursuing profits (with some few restraints). Conservative economist Milton Friedman is associated with the latter position, but, at least publicly, most businessmen accept some responsibility for pursuing goals other than just maximum profits, or even satisfactory ones. Most businessmen that we shall hear from in this chapter believe this.

The question of profits is quite complex. As the material in this chapter shows, it is the consensus among businessmen that the short-run costs of curing social ills, regardless of the long-range benefits to business, should be borne by all social groups. Business cannot reduce its profits significantly and thereby promote the general welfare because the general welfare includes the condition that business make profits adequate to attract investments in order to promote growth and efficiency, and thus provide more goods and services and employment.

For the New Left, this line of reasoning is spurious. The vast majority of profits go to a tiny percentage of the population; the huge incomes of top

---

1 See Chapter 5 in Reinhard Bendix, *Work and Authority in Industry* (New York: Wiley, 1956), for a dramatic account of the changing rationale for management's right to rule over the work force since the 1870's.

businessmen are not necessary to attract their talents; and profits depend heavily on production for waste rather than for use. Finally, most social problems stem from the business system itself. If this is the case, the costs of cleaning up the stables should not be borne by taxpayers in general, nor should the risks be borne by the powerless; costs and risks should be borne by the wealthy who benefit most from the system.

Rather than justly apportion costs and risks, the system itself should be changed so that the wealthy neither control investment and production decisions nor benefit disproportionally from them. If investment and production decisions were made by experts freely elected by the people in a society in which business did not control the political system, then the inevitable costs of producing goods and services could be distributed equitably, production for waste eliminated, and social problems solved. Presumably such a system would have to be called socialism. Large corporations would be nationalized. It would be a radically different political system, in which most members of the governmental elite would not come from and return to command posts in business and corporate law firms, as is the case today. In this new system real issues would be presented in elections and clear choices could be made; financial support for political parties would not come from wealthy people in the business system; the mass media would not be owned and controlled by large corporations, but would be freely competitive and subsidized with little or no advertising. Under such a system, presumably, major social ills would be drastically reduced.

In contrast, the business elite attributes social ills to groups other than itself, sees itself as taking an active role in correcting them, and does so in spite of the fact that the mass of Americans is not disposed to do much about them. Business is involved, not primarily because of altruistic motives, which it suspects, but because of long-range enlightened self-interest.

We will examine the response of business to social problems in two critical areas—the urban crisis, particularly as it involves the black ghettos, and in less detail, the pollution issue. Both problems present excellent case studies for the doctrine of enlightened self-interest and the social responsibilities of business. The first problem, the crisis in the ghettos, is particularly instructive because it is a well-delimited phenomenon with a clear beginning—the fall of 1967—and a fairly clear and substantial demise—the spring of 1970.

THE URBAN CRISIS

In a special report published in November 1969, aptly titled "The War That Business Must Win," *Business Week* explores the occasions for three business executives to become involved in social problems.

1969

from THE WAR THAT BUSINESS MUST WIN[2]

The Editors of Business Week

Robert Dehlendorf II, president of Arcata National Corp., remembers the day all too well. It was in August, 1965, and Dehlendorf was in a plane high over Los Angeles. "I couldn't believe what I saw below," he recalls. "It looked like a city being bombed. Pillars of smoke were rising block after block. Tanks moved up and down the streets, their hatches closed and turrets swiveling." What Dehlendorf saw were the violent beginnings of the Watts riots. When the flames and pillage subsided, 34 people were dead, $40-million worth of property was destroyed, and for the first time many Americans had come to realize that there were explosive discontents ticking away within their ghettos.

For Charles Luce, board chairman of New York's Consolidated Edison Co., the day that will long live in memory came in 1966. That June, a special city task force warned: "All the ingredients now exist for an air pollution disaster of major proportions." Sure enough, on Thanksgiving, pollution from two states filled the skies over New York City and poisoned the air beyond endurance. When the thick, sooty shroud lifted, 168 people were dead.

In Cleveland, Walter O. Spencer, executive vice-president of Sherwin-Williams Co., still shivers when he thinks about last June 22. On that day, the oily, oozing Cuyahoga River—a waterway so reeking of filth that it cannot support even leeches, sludge worms, and other common low forms—actually caught on fire and damaged two railroad bridges that span it.

Nationwide concern

Sherwin-Williams' Spencer, Con Ed's Luce, and Arcata National's Dehlendorf are typical of thousands of businessmen who are concerned about the deterioration of our social and physical environment and who are trying—though often with mixed results—to do something about it.

After the Watts riots, Dehlendorf organized the country's first small business investment company chartered exclusively to finance minority entrepreneurs. Partly as a result of New York's killer smog, Con Ed's Luce has mounted a major antipollution effort that one government official describes as a "model" for the industry. Following the Cuyahoga River fire, Sherwin-Williams' Spencer ordered a reassessment of some of his company's water control measures, and made cleaner water almost a personal crusade.

2 *Business Week*, November 1, 1969, pp. 63–64.

Elsewhere, similar efforts are multiplying on a scale that rivals the miracle of the loaves and the fishes. For example:

In St. Louis, businessmen helped clean up decaying waterfronts.

In Pittsburgh, they banded together to reduce air pollution.

In Chicago, Los Angeles, and Rochester, N.Y., they joined in the war on crime.

In Portland, Ore., they helped solve a parking problem.

In almost every big and small city, businessmen are also building or renovating slum housing, improving schools, and rooting out the squalor and blight that helps send the fever charts of our cities soaring. What is more, says Donald C. Burnham, president of Westinghouse Electric Corp., industry is being challenged not only to play a key role in these areas, but to "take the lead."

This is quite a list, and it grew longer early in the 1970's. But one might note at this point that Con Ed's "model" antipollution effort is considerably less than satisfactory; as of this writing, Con Ed is still being cited for failures to reduce pollution. Furthermore, the campaign to finance minority entrepreneurs has been a flop; the Cuyahoga is still a running sore; parking problems such as Portland has are generally solved by removing blacks. As *Business Week* notes, by making traffic studies for large cities, "Ford Motor Co. hopes to help untangle traffic jams—and thus sell more cars." [3] The war on crime in the major cities has meant a war on political leaders of the New Left or insurgent minority groups, with the result that the FBI's Most Wanted list is made up overwhelmingly of political figures, while organized crime seems to grow in power and respectability.[4] Finally, the decaying waterfronts of St. Louis promise the removal of poor citizens, higher land values, and new entrepreneurial activities for business. The specifics do not concern the New Left as much as the consideration that by "taking the lead," the business system further stabilizes and controls the population.

Mr. Dehlendorf was prompted to action in the summer of 1965. But for most of business, the Watts riot was not so impelling. There had been riots before, and this one was fairly isolated, if shocking. Besides, it did not interrupt major industries in Los Angeles that much. Not until two years later, after several cities burned in the summer of 1967, did the real "war that business must win" start. "The first corporate urban affairs programs were launched in the wake of the 1967 riots and the shock waves generated by the Kerner Report," says an authoritative study conducted by the business consulting firm of McKinsey and Company.[5] (The impact of the Kerner Report on violence and racism was probably trivial as compared to the

---

3 *Ibid.*, p. 65.

4 The federal indictment of the Harrisburg defendants—Father Philip Berrigan, Sister Elizabeth McAlister, and others—claims that they are more dangerous to the United States than all of organized crime. Since they want to change the system and organized crime doesn't, the government is revealingly correct.

5 Quoted in Jules Cohn, "Is Business Meeting the Challenge of Urban Affairs?" *Harvard Business Review*, March–April, 1970, pp 68–82; the quotation appears on p. 68.

impact of the riots.) In city after city, businesses found that their plants were shut down because the disorder interrupted the flow of workers, materials, and outputs. It was like a series of strikes, and they are expensive. The president of General Motors noted that it was the sight of "his city" of Detroit burning in the summer of 1967 that propelled him into action. Businessmen I talked with in Milwaukee were completely taken by surprise at the disorders there and repeatedly noted that they lost a great deal of money by having their facilities idle for several days. Workers could not travel out of the black and the white ghettos, for example; roads were closed, and curfews were tight. One executive is quoted as saying that "it wasn't until after the Detroit riots that the automobile makers got busy. If their factories were in East Cupcake, they wouldn't be so energetic about the hard-core." [6]

In any case, the riots of 1967 led to the formation of the Urban Coalition. Its purpose was to organize coalitions in cities throughout the country and to get businessmen to invest in the ghettos, cooperate in solving urban problems, hire more minority workers, promote open housing, and so on. The National Alliance of Businessmen was also formed at this time. This group was tied more closely to the government, receiving funds from the Labor Department for training minority groups. These two groups received a great deal of publicity and constituted the finest hour of business since the Second World War, when companies made record amounts of armaments and profits and employed whoever would work.

The publicity was glowing. Three showcase projects were presented over and over in the business press and in the mass media—the Watts Manufacturing firm set up in the Watts area of Los Angeles by Aerojet-General (apparently a success); the Hough Manufacturing firm in Cleveland established by the machine-tool giant, Warner and Swasey (still losing money in early 1971); and the Roxbury sheet-metal plant set up by an electronics firm in the ghetto of Boston (it folded). Statistics on the success of minority training and hiring programs rolled out of the national press. The programs were impressive in that they went from zero to a few hundred thousand in a few months, but not impressive in terms of the nearly three million seeking work in this country at the time.

The McKinsey survey, made in late 1970 and early 1971, provided a more doleful picture. From among *Fortune* magazine's list of the largest industrial and financial (banking and insurance) firms, 247 corporations were selected. Of that total, 201 indeed had some sort of urban program, but for more than half of these the program simply amounted to new or revised forms of corporate giving. As John Gardner, head of the Urban Coalition, remarked, most businessmen would prefer to "lob some money over the ghetto walls" rather than to set foot inside them and talk to some blacks. Only 16 percent of the firms offered hard-core training and upgrading programs, with a

6 Quoted in *ibid.,* p. 76.

little over half receiving federal aid for these, which ran as high as $5,200 per trainee. Only about 20 percent allowed their managers to apply time and skills to ghetto problems on company time.

Enlightened self-interest was the motive most frequently mentioned for urban programs. David Rockefeller of the Chase Manhattan Bank sounded the liberal line: "Our efforts are aimed at creating the healthy economic and social environment that is vital to the very existence of any corporation." [7] Strengthening the corporate image and reputation was cited by 80 percent of the firms. For 40 percent of them, compliance with federal equal-opportunity requirements was at least part of the reason (and presumably a vital one for the aerospace firms, which were heavily involved, since government requirements for them are more strict). A third of the companies saw the programs as discouraging boycotts, violence, and other threats to company well-being. As Henry Ford II remarked in this connection in 1969,

There is no longer anything to reconcile, if there ever was, between the social conscience and the profit motive. Improving the quality of society—investing in better employees and customers for tomorrow—is nothing more than another step in the evolutionary process of taking a more far-sighted view of return on investment.[8]

Corporate rationale could not be put more succinctly—*investing* in better employees and customers, for a better return. *Time* magazine spoke for the enlightened section of the business community in 1970 and added a crucial thought: "More and more businessmen are becoming aware that social action is not a luxury; they realize that either they have to change, or change will be forced upon them. Their goal is to create social reforms without real revolution." [9] The phrase "real revolution" is probably used advisedly. Social reform is not revolutionary; a "real" revolution would go far beyond that. Preventing forced change is the goal of reform in business.

There is nothing sinister in the motives that business leaders gave in the interviews; this is the way the system operates. Social instability is a threat to any system, and the liberal means of promoting stability, such as training and hiring minority groups, investing in the ghettos, and better housing, are better than repressive ones. Not that repressive means were not used also, but they were more likely to be used by government than by business. Of course, most of the leaders of the Urban Coalition and the National Alliance of Businessmen move freely between government and business, but they are not personally responsible for local police actions in a direct sense.

7 Quoted in Cohn, *op. cit.*, p. 70.
8 Quoted in *Business Week, op. cit.*, p. 64.
9 *Time*, July 20, 1970, p. 63.

Only one-eighth of the 247 corporations cited profits as a reason for their urban programs. Because more than half of them did little more than increase or rechannel donations (which are often tax-deductible), they would be unlikely to cite profits as a motive. Thus one might speculate that at least one-quarter of those companies with active programs acknowledged the profit motive. Other evidence suggests that it was a rather strong incentive. First, the McKinsey survey notes that for some firms, at least, an indirect profit motive was operating because they needed employees. In view of the tight labor market of the late 1960's, "we were willing to try anything," one businessman said. Jules Cohn, author of the report, points out that "adequate training may cost less than the high turnover associated with no training." [10] The recruitment and retention of unskilled employees has been a particular problem for American Telephone and Telegraph, which is not surprising because they may pay wages below the poverty line and provide poor working conditions, as described in Chapter 5. Thus AT&T was quite active in the training programs. (*Time* magazine presents an interesting slant on this: "The Bell System's commendable record of recruiting employees from the slums has contributed to the recent decline in telephone service." [11] Poor working conditions and lack of planning for expansion would seem to be far more significant contributions.)

A more direct profit incentive is revealed by extensive investigations made by the Government Accounting Office and the Senate Subcommittee on Employment, Manpower, and Poverty. They claimed substantial and widespread fraud and undelivered services among those who received government funds for training. The National Alliance of Businessmen (NAB), which runs the Job Opportunities in the Business Sector program with the Labor Department, had contended that the retention rate of trainees was 80 percent; the subcommittee charged that in 1968 it was only 32 percent, and in 1969 only 46 percent. The NAB's statistics were inflated. Numerous instances of apparent fraud and false statistics were cited in the report. Some involved large national corporations, such as the ones that the McKinsey survey included. For example, to quote from a newspaper report,

Woodside Division of Dan River Mills, Greenville, S.C., got a $1,856,000 contract to hire 1,100 trainees at $1.60 an hour (50 percent subsidized). It plans to bill the government for $132,000 for orientation which includes one hour for "welcome to Woodside Mills"; one hour to discuss vacations, one hour to discuss leaves of absence, six hours to tour the plant and two hours set aside for "location of rest rooms." [12]

10 Cohn, *op. cit.*, p. 76.
11 *Time*, July 20, 1970, p. 68.
12 Report in the *Capital Times*, Madison, Wisconsin, May 13, 1970, of a speech given by William R. Bechtel, of the subcommittee staff, before a vocational educator's conference in Madison.

One of the most dramatic and widely heralded actions was made by the insurance companies, who announced that they would invest $1 billion in the rotting inner core of the cities. A new corporation, the National Corporation for Housing Partnerships, created by the Johnson administration and carried on by the Nixon administration, would raise $50 million from private industry for "seed-money" investment in low-rent housing projects. A front-page article in *The Wall Street Journal* concluded with these two paragraphs:

The attraction to the investors is a potentially handsome return. Not only is it calculated that local housing projects will return a basic 6% profit (distributed among the national and local partners in accordance with their participations), but the advance of fast tax depreciation would be available to both local and national investors.

Because of this tax advantage, it's calculated that investors would receive an actual return on their investments ranging from 24.4% in a project's second year to 16.8% in its 10th year. That return, says Mr. Moskof, would be "comparable to the yields sought by most industrial investors" and is required to attract private financing to low-cost housing.[13]

So fraud is not even necessary in connection with meeting the challenge to private industry; legitimate profits can come high enough to attract business into these risky areas. The Office of Economic Opportunity Jobs Corps program was a cost-plus-4-percent operation, passing on the training costs and profit incentive to the taxpayer. Discussing ghetto plants, *Business Week* finds it quite legitimate to ask if they can be "money makers": "Are they entitled to government aid and, if so, how much?" The manager of a Ling-Temco-Vought plant, which opened in a San Antonio slum in December 1968, said: "Let's not kid ourselves, LTV doesn't just open plants for altruistic purposes." [14]

The McKinsey survey was made two years after the unprecedented response by business. Jules Cohn notes, "After the two relatively 'cool' summers of 1968 and 1969, public and governmental pressure on corporations to act to ameliorate the urban crisis has somewhat diminished." [15] That was putting it rather mildly. The economy was booming throughout 1969, and unemployment was only about 3.5 percent in December. But less than three months later, with sales sagging, Chrysler canceled its $13.8 million federal contract to train hard-core unemployed workers. The chairman of Chrysler, Lynn Townsend, was just about to become the chairman of the NAB. Chrysler suspended another program later that year, and Ford

13 *The Wall Street Journal,* February 5, 1969.
14 Both quotes from *Business Week,* March 22, 1969, p. 100.
15 Cohn, *op. cit.,* p. 69.

and General Motors cut back their job pledges despite the personal involvement of Henry Ford II and James M. Roche in the programs. (Mr. Roche was
just about to give his speech proclaiming that "we have a right to expect
more from labor.") Texas Instruments, Pan American Airlines, International
Industries, and other large corporations also curtailed or canceled their
programs. Urban Coalition programs in several cities had become moribund
before the recession.[16]

The hard-core hiring programs never really got off the small plot of ground
that had been announced for them. The Department of Labor asked for $420
million for fiscal 1970 for 140,000 jobs. Congress gave it only $280 million; in
May of 1970, the Labor Department indicated that it would not be able to
spend $105 million of that. It expected to allocate about $175 million, enough
for 75,000 trainees at a substantially reduced rate per trainee.[17]

In its first eight months, the Urban Coalition "could point to few solid
accomplishments," according to *The Wall Street Journal*. "Fresh crisis, apparently, is what the Urban Coalition needed to generate momentum." [18]
That is, burning pays. The fresh crisis referred to was the assassination of
Martin Luther King, Jr., in the spring of 1968 and the disorders that followed
in some ghettos. John Gardner, who had left his Cabinet post as Secretary
of Health, Education, and Welfare five weeks before, agreed to take command of the young organization. There were thirty-three cities represented
in it at the time. After the tragedy and the disturbances (which did not,
however, match the riots of the previous hot summer) many more cities
sought to join the Coalition. On this basis, Gardner predicted that one
hundred cities would be included by the end of 1968. By May 1970, however,
only forty-seven cities remained in the Coalition, with twenty-three of them
considered to be strong. Gardner has since left the Coalition to head
Common Cause, a lobbying group that welcomes, but does not depend on,
businessmen and their corporate donations.

The following summer of 1969 was cool, and so was that of 1970. Business
activity in the urban area, spurred by the riots of 1967 and the disorders
in spring of 1968 following King's assassination, seems to have slowed down
considerably even before the recession that started in earnest in 1970. But
that recession seems to have been the major de-escalation of "the war that
business must win." Government activity, of course, also slowed down under
the Nixon administration.

The business press denies that there has been anything but a slowdown
for economic reasons. *Business Week* recently titled a special report "Business Fights the Social Ills—in a Recession." [19] Aside from anecdotes, the

16 See, for example, *Business Week*, March 22, 1969, p. 41; August 16, 1969, p. 44; January 17, 1970,
p. 29; March 7, 1970, p. 23; and May 30, 1970, p. 31.
17 *Business Week*, May 16, 1970, p. 29.
18 *The Wall Street Journal*, April 17, 1968, p. 1.
19 *Business Week*, March 6, 1971, pp. 51–62.

evidence is hardly persuasive. For example, the highly touted Minority Enterprise Small Business Investment Company (MESBIC) is the backbone of black capitalism. Two-thirds of its funds were to come from the government, one-third (a trifling $150,000) from corporate sponsors. But, "in a period of tight money, many companies simply did not want to invest in new ventures," notes *Business Week*. Instead of the one hundred businesses that were to be licensed by June 1970, only twenty-five had been licensed by March 1971. *Business Week* sums up the whole "social ills" program of enlightened capitalism in the last sentence of its report: "If the recession has proven anything, it is that business-run social programs, however necessary and enlightened, must also be economically viable." [20] Phrased less succinctly, that means that regardless of the imperatives cited by Henry Ford II, David Rockefeller, and others, if the short-run investment will not pay off in profits, or if no surplus profits are available with which to make long-run investments, the social responsibilities of business take a back seat. It is interesting to speculate what urban riots might produce in a period of high general unemployment and lowered corporate profits. Would the response simply be more troops?

For one who is not accustomed to the radical attack on business, the question of profits and "who will pay" is an annoying one. Such a person would argue that business can hardly be expected to go into debt because the country has social problems. Business can hardly be expected to shoulder all or most of the cost, rather than pass it on to the taxpayer in the form of higher taxes and higher costs for goods and services. To do so would violate some extremely simple and stubborn laws of human nature. The New Left would answer this justification somewhat as follows. First, wealth is very unequally distributed, and the very rich are not hurting while the poor are; second, the nation incurs huge amounts of waste through the production of wasteful goods and services; third, business itself is actually responsible for our social problems.

The concentration of wealth and the distribution of income have already been mentioned in this book and need not be discussed again.[21] It should be noted, however, that a loss on the balance statement does not necessarily indicate a poor corporation that is unable to protect the income of the super-rich. Even the Penn Central Railroad found that it was not so poor after all when it decided in 1971 to sell properties in New York City that were estimated to be worth more than $1 billion.

We have looked briefly at the New Left's argument of production for

20 *Ibid.*, p. 62.
21 For a radical review and interpretation of income and wealth data, see the entire issue of *The Review of Radical Political Economics*, 3:3 (Summer 1971). This is one of the most scholarly and responsible of New Left publications. It is published at the University of Michigan by the Union of Radical Political Economists.

waste, which will be examined a little more in connection with the pollution crisis. But at this point, the issue of blame needs a brief discussion. To give full treatment to this topic would require a book in itself, a rehashing of some of the material already covered in this volume and a summary of many volumes critical of the military effort, the creation of artificial tastes, the annual model changes in the automobile industry, and so on. For example, a recent study in the *Yale Law Journal* puts the cost of the annual model change in the automobile industry in 1969 at $1.5 *billion.* The result, according to another survey by a government agency, was a reduction in performance for each 1969 automobile.[22]

It is the third answer, business' response that it should not have to give up profits in order to cure social ills, that is the most interesting. Business is more than willing to celebrate the free-enterprise system and to take credit for the strength, growth, and affluence of the nation. But when business catalogs the social ills of the nation, the sources are found in the malfunctioning of a large variety of nonbusiness institutions and in the practices of nonbusiness groups. The president of the Chase Manhattan Bank, David Rockefeller, has been quoted as saying that the urban crisis is really a witch's brew of crises blended "from all the major ills of our country: inadequate educational systems, hardcore unemployment, hazardous pollution of natural resources, antiquated transportation, shameful housing, insufficient and ineffective public facilities, lack of equal opportunity for all, and a highly dangerous failure of communication between young and old, black and white." [23] That clearly leaves the solution up to a variety of institutions and agencies, and above all, to "the people itself." The New Left, on the other hand, would link each of these major ills directly to business itself, as follows:

1. Educational systems are inadequate primarily in the poor districts. People in those districts cannot afford to vote adequate school taxes because they are poor, and they are poor because wealth is so inequitably distributed because business has vested interests in keeping wages as low as possible and in maintaining a nonprogressive taxation system with large loopholes for business and wealthy families. Furthermore, businessmen worry about the educational system only when the labor market is tight (such as when "only" about three million people are looking for work) and they cannot get well-disciplined workers cheaply, and when disorders in the schools threaten social stability.

2. Hard-core unemployment would disappear with better health measures, with housing and education for the hard-core poor (which could not ma-

---

22 From the review by Robert C. Townsend of *America Inc.*, by Morton Mintz and Jerry S. Cohen (New York: Dial, 1971), in the *New York Times Book Review*, May 30, 1971, p. 1. See also "Annual Style Change in the Automobile Industry as an Unfair Method of Competition," *Yale Law Journal*, 80:3 (January 1971), 567–613.

23 *Business Week*, November 1, 1969, p. 63.

terialize unless they were endorsed by business), and with better job opportunities, which business (and government) can provide.

3. Pollution of natural resources is, of course, primarily a business responsibility.

4. Antiquated transportation is a result of the investments in the profitability of the automobile, oil, and highway-construction industries, as is the cost of the air and water pollution they cause. As *Business Week* notes: "The companies involved in the building and use of highways are led by the automotive and oil industries. And it has been estimated that the so-called highway lobby accounts for more than half of all political contributions." [24] The public bears the costs of building highways (which may easily come to more than $10 million a mile in cities), maintaining them, and policing them. While the poor pay for highways and their associated costs and pollution, they must also pay increasing fares for the antiquated transit systems that they must rely on.

5. Shameful housing can be laid at the door of the private-enterprise system. The United States has little low-cost public housing (far less than most other industrialized countries), but it does have highly profitable insurance and real-estate ventures, slumlords, and banks holding mortgages that pay handsome returns. [25]

6. Public facilities are insufficient and ineffective. One needs little imagination to realize that when business fights the extension of various kinds of public facilities; when it proposes private, commercial alternatives instead; and when it resists attempts to increase the taxes of managers and stockholders, public facilities will be insufficient and ineffective. Actually, public facilities are inadequate only for the poor; they are probably adequate for the middle class.

7. The lack of equal opportunity for all exists preeminently in private employment, and it has taken strong federal action to make a dent in this inequity.

8. Finally, the failure of communication between black and white, young and old, may be attributed at least in part to the failure of the mass media. They have the greatest communicative power to respond to these divisions. The media are corporations, of course, which operate for profit and make very handsome profits. In addition, the profit system requires that advertisers —business again—pay for communication time on television, and they have been more than reluctant to use that time to promote communication between groups.

24 *Business Week*, May 15, 1971, p. 74.
25 The United States Commission on Civil Rights recently charged that the Federal Housing Administration had, in effect, delegated its legal responsibility under a 1968 low-income housing program to the private-housing and home-financing industry, which ignored the civil law and allowed the program to perpetuate segregation and overcharge minorities for inferior housing. *The New York Times*, June 11, 1971, p. 1.

Thus the sources of urban ills, which are generously spread by business, are highly concentrated by the New Left. "Some people," mourns David Rockefeller, "are blaming business and the enterprise system [he left off the adjective "free"] for all the troubles in our society." [26] They surely are. Why shouldn't the rich give up some or most of their riches to help the poor in order to eliminate most of our urban problems? Because this is not the way the system is designed to operate. In the logic of the businessman, the rich must be motivated to do a good job by paying them richly; those with no future, the unmotivated, are a social problem, but they are not a problem of the business system.

DOMESTIC IMPERIALISM

Thus the "impressive beginning," as *Time* called it, made by business to attack our glaring social ills looks a little less than spectacular a few years later. But these efforts can hardly be considered spectacular in the first place, given the magnitude of the problem and the years of neglect. Nevertheless, even though risks were underwritten by the government and modest to immodest profits were assured, perhaps it was better than nothing. Some blacks got jobs; some got started in small businesses; a few blacks mounted the executive ladder (one even got on the General Motors Board of Directors recently); and some housing was built. Perhaps the senseless violence of the urban riots was forestalled, at least for a time. Now there is a national concern with pollution. Viewed in this perspective, this *was* business' finest hour considering that there have been so few hours with any social content.

The New Left would not agree with this rationalization. To view the effort in these terms is to make the same tempting analysis that is made of imperialism in Latin America. The development of a Latin American labor force does provide jobs and thus food, but it also sucks the poor into the basically exploitative system of capitalism. In the same way, building houses and injecting wages into the ghetto does help the blacks, but it helps business much more by providing outlets for construction material as well as utilities and new markets for consumer goods; and it does so by ensuring that blacks will not develop their own construction and materials firms, their

---

26 *Newsweek*, May 24, 1971, p. 74. See also the remark of James M. Roche, until December 1971 the chairman of the board of General Motors, quoted in *The New York Times*, April 21, 1971, p. 47:

> Corporate responsibility is a catchword of the adversary culture that is so evident today. If something is wrong with American society, blame business. Business did not create discrimination in America, but business is expected to eliminate it. Business did not bring about the deterioration of our cities, but business is expected to rebuild them.
> The dull cloud of pessimism and distrust which some have cast over free enterprise is impairing the ability of business to meet its basic economic responsibilities—not to mention its capacity to take over newer ones. This, as much as any other factor, makes it urgent that those of us who are in business stand up and be counted."

own utilities, or their own plants for producing goods. In this way blacks are linked to the giant system of capitalism. This is domestic imperialism, says the New Left, and once profits drop off or the economy temporarily slackens so that it is less profitable to expand markets than to cut costs, the effort will also slacken.

This is the message of the following selections from two articles. Note, however, their divergent analyses. Richard Cloward and Francis Piven assert that business no longer needs racism or blacks; what has happened is that racism and poverty are beginning to exact costs from corporate capitalism. Jill Hamberg and David Smith pursue a more traditional radical line by emphasizing the opportunity that the ghetto affords for imperialistic ventures. Both selections, however, are profoundly suspicious of anything business does that might look human. Perhaps both analyses have as much error as truth. A more moderate observation would be that business was frightened by the impending costs of social disorder (they admit it, as we have seen), but when business went into the ghetto, it had to do so in terms of its system imperatives, which include profits and the expansion of control over every nook and cranny of the nation. How could business do otherwise? Why should it do otherwise? Businessmen readily admit they are not in the ghetto for the sake of humanity; if humane works can be profitable and expansionary at the same time, business will be humane. If good works are likely to be expensive, however, someone else will have to pay. Regrettable as it may be, under capitalism the first responsibility of business is to make a profit for its stockholders and to maintain it over the long run.

Cloward and Piven begin by noting that the response of the general public to the 1967 riots, which had just concluded, was an outburst of racism, while corporate and political leaders were apparently responding with statesmanship. How, they ask, can such discrepant responses on the part of the masses and the elite be explained?

1967

from CORPORATE IMPERIALISM FOR THE POOR[27]

Richard Cloward and Francis Piven

The answer is not difficult to find. First, corporate enterprise no longer has major stakes in domestic racism. Historically, racism helped to perpetuate a caste system that produced a surplus of cheap black labor. That surplus was used against white workers, chiefly to undermine wage levels; more directly, blacks were hired as scabs and goons to impede efforts by whites to unionize. The resulting antagonism between blacks and whites was one aspect of a history of pervasive conflict among ethnic groups in America, leading them to turn upon one another rather than against oppressive classes, thus accounting in good measure for the absence of a cohesive working class. However, antagonism has been most acute between poor blacks and whites. Nor has that conflict subsided: it now extends beyond the labor market, erupting in bitter struggles to control neighborhoods, schools and city government.

With automation and the corporate management of markets, low-skilled and low-paid labor has become a relatively unimportant factor in the profits of much large-scale urban enterprise. Consequently, racism is no longer needed to depress wages and inhibit unionization. The racist attitudes of the working and lower-middle classes persist, but these attitudes, and the ghettos they help to produce have become anomalies—vestiges of an earlier era of industrial organization.

Indeed, racism is beginning to exact some costs from corporate enterprise. Violence in the cities disrupts the civic stability on which huge, bureaucratized enterprises depend. Note, for example, that department store owners are prominent in the spate of local committees and commissions formed in the wake of the riots. Nor is it any accident that insurance companies, faced with huge losses in property damage, are at the forefront in proffering investment funds for redevelopment of charred ghettos.

Now, too, there is the promise of profit to be made in removing poverty. Redevelopment promises to be a huge business, running into billions of dollars—provided that public funds and public powers are employed to eliminate risk and guarantee profit. Far-seeing corporations like Litton Industries and U.S. Gypsum have been alert to these possibilities for some time, undertaking research and demonstration projects (often put forward as

[27] Richard Cloward and Francis Piven, "Corporate Imperialism for the Poor," *The Nation*, October 16, 1967, pp. 366–67.

"civic" activities) to explore cost-saving materials and new building techniques so as to create a product within reach of the ghetto market. Industry's technical explorations have not accomplished much to reduce costs, but that doesn't matter: public subsidies will bridge the gap.

For their part, politicians are in trouble, and the alliance is a way out. Urban disorder has made them vulnerable; they must act to end it or face defeat at the polls. However, they are not free to indulge the outraged sentiments of their working- and middle-class constituents, for repression would alienate blacks all the more and might lead to worse violence. Blacks are also becoming a major electoral force in the cities, a fact which cannot be ignored much longer. Nevertheless, white racism prevents political leaders from securing legislative approval for programs to pacify the ghetto. The corporate alliance solves this dilemma: relatively small amounts of public money can be used to stimulate relatively large private investments. Furthermore, programs carried out under corporate auspices will neutralize a great deal of opposition: this is, after all, "the American way of doing things."

The President, it should be noted, has the most to gain, for he is in the deepest trouble. With rapidly escalating costs in the Vietnamese War already creating pressure for an unpopular tax rise, he risks political disaster by calling for even higher taxes in order to placate rioters. Opening the ghetto for private investment permits him to avoid the antagonism of the electorate toward both blacks and taxes, while continuing to pay for the war primarily from current revenues.

The new program, in brief, is impelled by the threat of disruption and the promise of profit. It will work to curb violence, and to secure gains for political and corporate leaders alike. The ghetto is also likely to be somewhat better off economically for being absorbed into corporate spheres.

Who, then, can reasonably object? Well, clearly peace groups should. If the President succeeds in avoiding substantial tax increases, the task of shoring up weakening electoral support for the war will be considerably eased. Grassroots black activists also have much to fear, for these developments portend a vast extension of corporate power in the ghetto. The economy of the ghetto is now run by relatively small entrepreneurs who are somewhat vulnerable to local pressure, such as consumer boycotts and rent strikes. The new managers of the ghetto will be huge quasi-public development corporations (like the New York Port Authority) insulated from effective political control and endowed with powers to issue bonds, condemn property and form webs of relations with private investment companies, large-scale contractors and management companies. Industrial firms will spin off new subsidiaries to exploit opportunities for subsidized profit in employing ghetto people. And predominantly white unions will absorb these workers, thus neutralizing whatever potential that separate Negro unions might have had as an instrument of ghetto power. The ghetto has nothing much to offer which corporate enterprise needs—skilled labor, entrepreneurial skills or raw materials. It is even too poor on its own to attract corporate products on any large scale. Governments will thus convert the ghetto to a subsidized market, and life conditions will be improved; but no Negro-controlled economic institutions are likely to emerge, nor will the ghetto have the resources to influence the operations of outside corporate enterprise.

The greatest danger to blacks is that the new corporate role will help to erode the power of municipal government, and this at a time when the black is about to obtain control of the city. Lyle M. Spencer, president of Science Research Associates (a subsidiary of IBM), glowingly comments on the new corporate alliance: the "military-industrial complex," he observes, is about to be superseded by a "social-industrial complex." Considering the influence the former exerts in national life and foreign affairs, who can doubt that the latter will possess comparable influence over city government and the ghetto?

Impending changes in the relations of federal and local government will mesh well with corporate intervention, further weakening the traditional powers of city government. The federal government is beginning to use the vast resources of its grants-in-aid programs to create metropolitan-wide administrative agencies to cope with pollution, blight and other urban problems. As agents of federal power, the metro bureaucracies will supersede local government as channels for federal money. Since these new administrative complexes will be largely removed from popular control, the blacks of the ghettos—even as they reach electoral majorities in the cities—cannot hope to influence them greatly. But the metro bureaucracies—manned by an emerging class of planners and technicians—will find congenial counterparts in the corporate world. In other words, just as black majorities come to power in the city, much of that power will be usurped by an alliance of national corporations and political leaders, as well as by federal-metropolitan bureaucracies.

There is not likely to be much opposition to these developments, however. Churchmen and union leaders have already given their blessing. Traditional civil rights leaders have special reason to be pleased, for their symbolic hegemony over the ghetto has been undermined, on the one side by the failure of the Johnson Administration to keep concessions flowing, and on the other by the growing challenge of spokesmen for black nationalism. It was not without reason that traditional civil rights leaders joined with the President and leaders of the insurance business to announce the billion-dollar pledge of corporate funds to the ghetto.

It is possible to imagine that militant leaders in the ghetto will resist the intrusion of corporate giants, but it is much easier to see how their resistance will be overcome. The new corporate imperialism will be mediated through a host of intervening subsidiaries and management structures, many located in the ghetto itself. Advocates of "participatory democracy," "decentralization" and "black control of black affairs" will find these themes turned against them as they are invited to endorse and participate in the new corporate subsidiaries. Even now business leaders in some cities are cultivating black activists, often over the protestations of local politicians befuddled by the curious twist in alignments.

If grants-in-aid were to be funneled through city governments, as in the past, and not through quasi-public and private corporate structures, black municipal leaders could convert these funds into the jobs, services and facilities required not only to improve economic conditions but to consolidate a black electorate as well. Under such circumstances, local government would serve blacks as it has served other groups by providing a base for power in state and national affairs. Once absorbed in local corporate subsidiaries, however, blacks will become instruments of national corporate power. Their economic lot will be improved somewhat, to be sure, but their long-term economic prospects depend on their potential political power, and that will be diminished.

Thus the New Left joins the Nixon administration in proposing direct revenue-sharing to cities. The liberals are very suspicious, because they do not see enlightened leadership in the cities (let alone many blacks in leadership positions), but only ineptness and corruption. But the New Left, in its search for non-Marxist alternatives, has been led to argue for radical decentralization of power. Just as Brazil might suffer for a time if U.S. corporations pulled out, so would Harlem suffer. But in the long run, somehow, a more viable nation and community would emerge, but only if the decentralization took place throughout the nation and the present system of corporate power were broken. We could hardly have socialism in one city.

1968

THE URBAN COALITION IN ACTION [28]

Jill Hamberg and David Smith

The sectors of the economy which appear to be in the vanguard of ghetto investment are: (1) those which have a stake in the central city—e.g., **banks**, insurance companies, utilities, transportation; (2) industrial concerns **with a** direct interest in expanding their markets—aluminum, gypsum, steel, electric appliances, etc.; and (3) defense contractors interested in diversifying as a speculative hedge against military cut-backs (possible but unlikely) when the Vietnam war is over.

In short, the basic motivations underlying corporate America's move into ghetto business are: stability, profits, control of raw materials (labor force) and the expansion of markets.

To see how this works let us look at one of the most interesting local coalitions in action, the Boston Coalition.

28 Jill Hamberg and David Smith, "The Urban Coalition in Action," *Viet Report*, Vol. 3 (Summer 1968), 51–53.

The Boston strategy

"Business with a Conscience" proclaimed the newspaper headlines when Boston's business statesman, led by Louis W. Cabot,* marched resolutely off to do battle against racism, poverty, unemployment, and bad housing. And so began the Boston Urban Coalition. In addition to Mr. Cabot, Coalition members included Robert Slater (President, John Hancock Mutual Insurance Co.), Eli Goldston (President, Eastern Gas and Fuel Assoc.), John Collins (MIT professor and former Boston mayor), and Barnard O'Keefe (President of EG&F and of Boston's Chamber of Commerce).

The Boston Coalition quickly established two prime objectives: first, to provide equity and technical skills to "black entrepreneurs"; second, to make black labor available to business. As for the first, it is often difficult to tell where business leaves off and the city takes over. However, it becomes increasingly clear that hand in hand with the city, the Coalition intends to compete with groups in the black community in initiating economic development measures. A close look at a series of recent events underscores this goal.

For some time now the New Urban League (a militant black-power–oriented organization) and the United Front (an all-black federation on the model proposed by Stokely Carmichael) have been working on a variety of programs for internal economic development of the black community. Among these was a Small Business Development Center (established at the New Urban League during April as a source of equity capital to be administered by the United Front). Then on May 13, Boston's Mayor White and a group of businessmen announced the establishment of the Boston Urban Foundation "to help finance small business ventures," together with a technical advisory center run by a board of directors chosen by the mayor. The response of the black community was immediate and to the point:

> ... this alleged $56 million program is a sham, an insult to the black community. The program you announced is doomed to failure in this community because it was developed downtown. ...

To reach its second objective, the Coalition's major committee, the National Alliance of Businessmen (NAB), is sponsoring a summer job program designed to create three to four thousand summer jobs in Boston. (If the early returns on this program are accurate, NAB is not likely to meet even its own stated goals.) NAB chairman, Louis Cabot, is also receiving special assistance from the New England Telephone Co. for a remedial education program. This kind of collaboration parallels a general move by utility companies to capture a crucial corner of the ghetto market: *Item:* Michigan Bell Telephone has taken over the operation of a black high school in Detroit. *Item:* Time, Inc. and General Electric have formed a corporation headed by Francis Keppel (former U.S. Commissioner of Education) to provide education materials. *Item:* Xerox,

---

* The Cabot family has distinguished itself through its connections with United Fruit, Middle South Utilities, and natural gas reserves. The family holds controlling interests in Mississippi Power and Light and Louisiana Power and Light.

Raytheon and IBM have recently purchased publishing companies. *Item:* New England Telephone, like its sister corporation in Michigan, is interested in moving into the education field, and has made inquiries about taking over one of the Boston Public Schools.

In these instances the corporations control both the medium and the message. That ghetto schools crush and destroy children, is a well-documented fact. It is also clear that it costs money to run elaborate training programs for unskilled labor, black or white, in order to meet industry's needs. Using the community's disillusionment with public education as a lever, the corporations have found an uncomplicated way to meet their manpower needs. No frills, no middlemen, no separate "counselling" is necessary; the corporations simply train young people for what they need. As the *Wall Street Journal* has stated:

It is clear both government and industry will play increasingly active parts in deciding what schools will teach and how they will present it.

While the principal interest of some corporations is the establishment of stability or the control of the labor force, the primary concern of others is profits—a competitive return on investment and the expansion of markets.

Eastern Gas and Fuel Associates (EG&F) is one Boston-based company which has taken the lead in ghetto development. It is not too difficult to get at some of its more pecuniary motivations for investing in the rehabilitation of slum housing. EG&F is a holding company whose subsidiaries include producers and distributors of coal, coke and gas; shipping concerns (barges, tugs, bulk cargo vessels, terminals); and, most significant, the Boston Gas Company, New England's largest utility. EG&F's interest is in expanding its market for gas. This is also how the other firms which enter the low-income and rehabilitation housing field intend to make their profit. Most of these big companies—Alcoa, Armstrong Cork, Reynolds, U.S. Steel, Westinghouse, National Gypsum, Pittsburgh Plate Glass and U.S. Gypsum—are interested in increasing activity in the entire housing industry while also getting a larger share of that market's business by pushing out competitors.

Fanny May's President, Raymond H. Lapin, has pointed out that "the profit earned on a sheet of gypsum board is the same whether the board is used in a low-rent apartment or a $50,000 house." However, because of increasingly high interest rates in the conventional mortgage market (up to 8%–9% currently), the number of housing starts has ebbed off. Firms which depend on volume of construction are looking to government-subsidized programs, such as moderate-income mortgages, to counteract the present trend. Moreover, the major construction financiers will not fund low-income areas without government subsidy. The highly publicized $1 billion nationwide mortgage fund announced by the life insurance companies last fall has not yet become involved in low-income housing. In Washington, D.C., mortgages go primarily to families with annual incomes of over $10,000. Almost all the families are black, but they are not poor. Also, over half the mortgages go to the suburbs and the fringes of the city rather than to the ghetto.

In Boston, EG&F began its foray into the housing rehabilitation business last winter by setting up a subsidiary, Eastern Associates Properties Corporation, which has the equity investment in the program. By using a double declining depreciation basis in figuring taxes, an equity investor in a high tax bracket can receive his full initial investment back within two to three years. This subsidiary bought a half-interest in a privately sponsored and federally subsidized massive rehabilitation program in Roxbury. It was announced in December that $24.5 million was committed for renovating moderate-income and rent-supplemented housing. EG&F in partnership with Maurice Simon contracted for all 731 rent-supplemented units, and more than 1,000 of the moderate-income units. This left 1,000 units to the four or five other developers. The Simon–EG&F contract is being managed by Sidney Insoft, without question the most hated slumlord in Roxbury. However, the selection of Insoft has backfired. His crude eviction procedures (which threw hundreds of families onto the already tight low-rent housing market) produced a steady stream of community protest, delaying the project by several months.

EG&F put up more than $1 million in equity capital for this program. What did it get in return? First, it received commitments that the 1,700 units will use gas for fuel heating, water heating and cooking. Combined with a later project, this constitutes for Boston Gas the largest single increase in gas sales volume in recent years. An article in the January 1968 issue of the *Yankee Oilman* indicates that some of the original buildings in the program were planned for oil heat and, in fact, had oil heating equipment installed. The article also points out that the State Department of Public Utilities does not have jurisdiction over holding companies such as EG&F.

The next move by EG&F was to offer technical assistance to a group of black businessmen headed by Thomas E. Sanders, Boston Celtics basketball star. The utility company did not put up any of the capital, although it did obtain agreement that all 83 units which the group intends to rehabilitate will use gas heat. And it was recently announced that Eastern Properties Associates will sponsor the rehabilitation of an additional 57 units located in vacant buildings in Boston's South End and in Charlestown, with the promise of more to come.

Breaking ground in the ghetto

In 1966 the giant AVCO Corporation (Bay State Abrasives, Universal Pictures, radio stations, and so on) did 69% of its business with the Department of Defense and its earnings soared to an all-time high. In 1967 AVCO received a grant of $1.3 million from the Department of Commerce to subsidize the establishment of a printing plant in Roxbury. The government's largesse was made available to AVCO through the federal TEST program, brainchild of Mr. William Zisch. He is vice-chairman of the board of directors of Aerojet-General, a large west coast defense industry firm. In 1966, Aerojet-General established a wholly-owned subsidiary, Watts Manufacturing, to operate a plant making tents for use in Vietnam. Mr. Zisch also secured money from the Commerce Department to pay for a training program at the Watts plant. Aerojet made money, the military had its tents, and several hundred people received jobs—but at a pay scale well below that in the rest of the Aerojet operations.

Zisch's idea was expanded in the middle of 1967 into a full-fledged government program designed to call upon private industry to join the federal government. "I have no doubt that private industry will respond," said the then Secretary of Commerce Alexander Trowbridge. There was no reason to believe otherwise. The program was designed to "pay unusual costs" associated with hiring the ghetto unemployed, which meant that the federal government guaranteed a profit. Because of Mr. Zisch's concern with a redistribution of wealth in America, his first act as the program's administrator was to send telegrams extolling its virtues to the 500 largest corporations in the country.

Within a month after AVCO received its telegram it had a federal commitment for $1.3 million to set up a printing plant in Roxbury, which it had planned to build anyway. Like Watts Manufacturing, the Roxbury printing plant is operated by a wholly-owned subsidiary, Economic Systems Inc. (ESI). ESI has been engaged in other areas of public-private cooperation such as running a Job Corps center and manpower development training. With the below-market wages it pays, AVCO's 1966 earnings of $32 million will not be threatened; the assistant to the general manager Van Henderson predicts normal profits at the end of the second year. Normal profits for AVCO run about 18% of their sales. When someone boldly suggested that the 18% could be better used by the community if ESI did not own the plant, the façade was dropped: "What do you think we are, a charity?" As for the training program, one disgruntled AVCO job trainee described it as "the biggest brainwashing I ever saw."

In Boston, as elsewhere, the "conscience" of the corporate elite—from Louis Cabot to William Zisch to Henry Ford, II—reveals its major concern: new profits and increased power in social planning.

With federal resources severely overextended in Vietnam, the government is looking to business to pacify the homefront. Washington clearly believes that its money can buy more stability through subsidies than with direct grants which cannot stretch as far. If and when the war is over corporate involvement will already have taken root. Defense spending will not be reduced by very much, if at all, and domestic spending for urban areas increased only slightly. The programs in Boston will continue and the expectation is for more of the same elsewhere.

Physically, the ghetto may be changed—new and rehabilitated housing, new factories—but the position and the lives of the people living there will remain the same. Even a new house cannot provide the poor with the economic or social mobility they need to change their common lot. And the new corporate intervention simply reinforces the growing realization that the only way to transfer power is to seize it.

PACKAGING POLLUTION PROFITS

The pollution issue jumped into the headlines in the late 1960's, but it had been around for more than two generations. There were federal water-pollution laws before the turn of the century, which were resisted by industry and then ignored by both industry and government. Detailed estimates of the cost per household of industrial air pollution were made in 1918; the United States Public Health Service had studies on the reduction of sunlight in New York City in 1927; popular books, such as *Stop That Smoke,* were published in the 1930's; the League of Nations nearly forecast the death of the ocean in a study in 1935, "Pollution of the Sea by Oil"; and the government published in 1939 a detailed, frightening report on the problems of water pollution and the failure to enforce existing regulations.[29]

In the early part of this century, industry evaded existing regulations, fought proposed ones, and argued that the public would not pay the cost. The cost would have been rather small then. Today, industry evades existing regulations, fights proposed ones, and argues that the public will not pay the cost. "Businessmen simply do not believe that, in a showdown, consumers would accept a lower standard of living," says *Business Week* in another of its crusading special reports.[30] But the question might better be phrased, Will the wealthy accept a lower standard of living? Why should the poor and the modestly well-off bear any part of the burden when wealth is so concentrated and the rewards of avoiding pollution costs go to so few? The attitude of business, continues *Business Week,* which should know, may be summed up by Joseph S. Whitaker, who, as coordinator of environmental health at one of the major polluters, Union Carbide Corporation, should also know. "Industry," he said, "will do whatever people ask us to do and whatever they will pay us for doing." [31] The president of a major job-training company remarked, "Whenever a human problem is solved, it's always because somebody has found a way to make a buck on it." [32] Industry has found that selling pollution-abatement equipment is profitable, and the firm that purchases it can pass on the costs. "Executives," *Business Week* notes, "do not want to dip into dividends to meet these costs. Even when profits are good, companies need to keep investors interested." That is to say, they need to keep the wealthy wealthy. "Lower profits just are not the answer, they say." Another large polluter, the Monsanto Company, has a newly formed organization, Monsanto Enviro-Chem Services. Its president concurs, "We are living in a fool's paradise if we think that industry will do

---

29 These are cited from K. William Kapp's pioneering study, *The Social Costs of Private Enterprise,* originally published in 1950 and republished in paperback by Schocken Books, New York, 1971.
30 *Business Week,* April 11, 1970, pp. 63–78.
31 *Ibid.,* p. 63.
32 *Business Week,* November 1, 1969, p. 65.

anything until it is forced to." [33] The forcing has not been marked for some seventy years; it may be increasing now.

Of course, industry is not the sole polluter; municipalities, universities, hospitals, and so on also contribute a great deal. So does the executive branch of the federal government. The Citizens Advisory Committee on Environmental Quality (Laurance Rockefeller, chairman) noted that the discrepancy between what Congress authorized and what the administration actually appropriated from 1964 to 1969 was $2.6 billion in water-pollution control grants to states, and figures in the hundreds of millions of dollars for water conservation, air-pollution control, solid-waste management, and highway beautification. [34] The industry panels that make recommendations for the administration are staffed by industry personnel. Apparently they are reluctant even to have the taxpayer's money spent.

Surveys indicate that the voters put air-pollution control at the head of the list of items on which the government should spend more money. In one study, 64 percent chose air pollution, 62 percent chose education; only 8 percent chose space exploration and 7 percent the war in Vietnam. [35] But no one is listening. We have the space shuttle program announced at $5.5 billion, and the war goes on. "Industry will do whatever people ask us to do and whatever they will pay us for doing." The people are asking. They have no choice but to pay, either. They do not set prices, and the industries in which pollution is the greatest are highly concentrated industries with administered pricing, so that the risks of competitors taking advantage of the socially responsible firm that spends money on pollution, while others do not, are not great.

Industry has responded aggressively to the pollution crisis in another way. As a friend once remarked to me, reading corporate advertisements with a clear head is an intensely radicalizing experience. Jerry Mander, who is in the business (he is the president of Freeman, Mander, and Gossage, a San Francisco ad agency) agrees, as the following article indicates.

[33] *Business Week*, April 11, 1970, p. 66.
[34] *Business Week*, November 1, 1969, p. 71.
[35] *Business Week*, April 11, 1970, p. 73.

1970

SIX MONTHS AND NEARLY A BILLION DOLLARS LATER, ADVERTISING OWNS ECOLOGY [36]

Jerry Mander

A few months ago, my partner and I were treated to a meeting with an experienced advertising man, about to open a new agency. His idea was to run a full-page newspaper ad (which he has since done) announcing that right from the first day, his office was going to devote 20 per cent of its total time to "good" causes. He was going to raise money to fund this agency on that basis, and would I like to invest in this wonderful thing?

I asked him how he decided that 20 per cent was exactly the right amount of time to give to saving the world, instead of, say, 16 per cent or 28 per cent. I don't think he got what I was driving at because he didn't leave, so I let it drop, but the point was that he was using "do-goodism" as a gimmick to raise money for an otherwise normal advertising agency and that whatever he did, do-goodwise, was bound to be phony.

It shouldn't have surprised me, really, because advertising people in general have an inordinate fascination with "image." They assume that by *seeming* a certain way, the world will come flocking around, tearing at their clothes. My late partner, Howard Gossage, used to say he preferred the word "identity" to "image"—the former having to do with the way one *really* is—which made him a lonely man in the advertising business.

Well, at one time, the difference may not have been all that important except for the psychic good health of advertising people and those few people whose idea of fun is to spend their day reading collections of ads. But the way I perceive it right now, at this point in history, the difference may be more like life and death.

Industry saves environment

With the sudden, immense outpouring of words from business and industry during the last six months concerning all the wonderful things they are doing to solve the pollution problem—most of these words being expressed in ads—

36 Jerry Mander, "Six Months and Nearly a Billion Dollars Later, Advertising Owns Ecology," *Scanlan's*, June 1970, pp. 54–61.

it's worth having a look at what's being said; of course, when seen close up, it's all image and no identity.

Most of industry still sees pollution and environment questions as more of a public relations and advertising problem—in other words, an image problem —than as anything fundamentally related to the way they are doing business. Shell Oil Company, for example, recently ran a four-ad series showing: 1) how they saved the lives of a lot of fish by *not* polluting things as much as they had been; 2) how they are feeding starving millions by producing more and better pesticides (which on the other hand are killing the fish they just saved); 3) how they overcame a lovely little Connecticut town's fears that their new gas station would prove a blight because it would replace a number of lovely trees, by showing the townspeople that the station would itself be a lovely gas station; and 4) how they were against littering.

I'm sure that the president of that company feels that this position makes him a conservationist, because until recently it was unusual for an oil company even to mention pollution or ugliness. Now that there's public goodwill in conservation, now that it's a hot topic, it's "good business to think of the environmental *implications* of industrial action," as a major chemical company executive recently suggested.

Another example: a recent copy of the *New York Times* carried a Pan American Airways ad which announced "the latest breakthrough" in relieving airport congestion. I was ready to be told they had reduced their total number of flights, or scrapped the Boeing 747, or cancelled their SST orders. But it turned out that what they had done was to build a second terminal at Kennedy Airport in New York, so they could handle up to twice as many passengers with less congestion—inside. Getting the planes onto the ground without bumping each other is another matter, and getting passengers into New York City from the airport was somebody else's problem.

And we've all seen more than our share of power company ads. Usually they bring us one—or more—of four urgent messages: 1) use more electricity; 2) the folks at your neighborhood power company are working like crazy developing new and creative means for winning the War on Pollution (a recent headline from Pacific Gas & Electric: "We Put a Smile on Mother Nature's Face"); 3) we need more power plants to fill our growing power needs, atomic ones; they're as safe as chocolate ice cream; 4) they need a rate increase to finance the research.

I had thought I had already reached the pinnacle of my own shame and disgust concerning utility advertising—what are they doing advertising at all if they are a *public* utility—when by chance I came across an old congressional record and found a speech by Senator Lee Metcalf which somehow has gone unnoticed by the press and by conservationists.

Senator Metcalf pointed out that during 1969, public utilities spent nearly $300 million on advertising, *more than eight times* what they spend on research, all the while proclaiming *in the ads* their feats of anti-pollution research. Metcalf also noted that about a fourth of all the power companies in this country actually did no research at all, yet they spent millions in advertising to *talk* about research and to sell us all on using more electrical power at the same time as they tell us there's a power shortage. If advertising dollars are going to be spent by utilities, one would think—considering this so-called power shortage which makes the introduction of nuclear plants "inevitable," in the words of *Newsweek*—that the ads would be appeals to use *less* power.

It's also worth noting that like other utility industries, power companies work on a cost plus basis. That is, they add up all their costs and then they can charge you and me, say, 7.5 per cent of the total and that's their profit. Advertising is included among the allowable costs and so you see they actually make more money by running more ads and artificially building up their costs.

The joys of nuclear power

Westinghouse Corporation has *really* jumped onto the ecological bandwagon. As one of the major suppliers of the technology needed to build nuclear power plants, Westinghouse has been running four-color ads everywhere, extolling the anti-polluting virtues of atomic power. The picture shows a beautiful girl sunbathing upon a lake which has one of those dome-shaped neo-modernistic nuclear plants in view. "Nuclear power plants are good neighbors," says the ad, "reliable, low-cost . . . neat, clean, safe."

And in a corporate brochure called "The Infinite Energy," we read about the pollution problems of conventional power systems and the marvelous advance that nuclear power represents. As for fears of radiation hazard, those are overstated, says Westinghouse. Even the sun, after all, produces radiation! "Sunshine is a gold blanket of radiation," reports the brochure. "The sun is actually a giant nuclear furnace operating much like a nuclear power reactor that is used to generate electricity. Overexposure to some of these rays is dangerous, just as overexposure to the sun's rays can be dangerous."

Simply ignored are the extreme dangers of "nuclear excursion"—of which there have already been several fortunately minor instances. A "nuclear excursion" is a leak in a reactor which could potentially cause the radiation effects equal to an atomic explosion, without any of the visual appeal. All buildings and inanimate objects within range would remain; only people and other living things would be done in.

The likelihood of such a disaster is great enough that Dr. David Lilienthal—a former director of the AEC—when asked his opinion of a proposed nuclear power plant in Queens said, "I wouldn't live in Queens if there was going to be a nuclear power plant there." And Dr. Edward Teller—no trainee in nuclear physics, and no bird watcher either—has said,

A single major mishap in a nuclear reactor could cause extreme damage, not because of the explosive force but because of the radioactive contamination. . . . So far we have been extremely lucky. . . . But with the spread of industrialization, with the greater number of simians monkeying around with things that they do not completely understand, sooner or later a fool will prove greater than the proof even in a fool-proof system.

Westinghouse doesn't include *that* point of view while telling us of its concern with the environment. Nor does it, or any power company, while extolling the virtues of nuclear power, mention the radiation danger involved in the disposal of radioactive wastes. Nor do they mention that nuclear power plants produce another spectacular kind of pollution which is, if anything, *more* dangerous to the natural system than radiation, and that is thermal pollution: the water will be heated to the point where the ecological cycle will be disrupted, some species of fish or other living organisms will be killed, and whatever depends upon them for sustenance may not survive and so on up the line.

So much for Westinghouse's "non-polluting" power system.

"Plant a lawn in a deep freeze"

Atlantic Richfield diverts us from their destructive Alaska Pipeline project by telling us that they are planning to seed the tundra areas done in by the pipeline. The fact is, they are going to *try* to plant grass, but no botanist outside the company thinks it's likely to work. And anyway, is planting grass a suitable solution for the terrible disturbances which the pipeline will cause to a very fragile wilderness?

Potlatch Corporation, a lumber company whose slogan is "the forests where innovations grow," has taken to running ads with pictures of trees and birds and rivers to show us that, as lumbermen, they have an intimate feel for the natural order. So while they are cutting down the innovations, we ought not to worry; they know what they are doing.

Coca-Cola ads tell us that it does offer "deposit and return" bottles but, on behalf of its customers who "demand" the no-deposit-no-return version of the bottle, they are continuing to put out that kind too. But just don't litter, they say, and everything will be all right.

Advertising is destroying the word "ecology" and perhaps all understanding of the concept. A few weeks ago, PG&E ran a headline advocating "a balance between ecology and energy." But ecology is not a thing that is balanced against anything else. The word describes a science of the interrelatedness of *everything*. Energy is a detail which only Man has decided to make a fuss over. That is what must be remembered, and it is getting increasingly hard to do so with this immense outpouring of diversionary, false and deadening information.

A billion dollars of reassurance

I am prepared to make the case that the $300 million in advertising spent by power companies (which, by the way, is about a third of the entire federal anti-pollution budget in Mr. Nixon's budget message), combined with the millions spent by oil companies, chemical companies, auto companies, industrial associations, the newly burgeoning anti-pollution industries, and so on —nearly a billion dollars, I would guess—is actually producing a net *loss* in this so-called War on Pollution. It's called cooptation in other circles, and I believe that it's operative here, perhaps not deliberately, but nevertheless.

All of the government rhetoric, magnified by industrial assurances, has the effect of destroying the power of the ecology message. People's eyes are already beginning to glaze at the sight of still more jargon about saving the world. It's awfully hard to out-shout roughly a billion dollars of advertising money. Especially when you consider that last year's total offsetting advertising expenditures by for-real conservation organizations were only roughly $200,000 —or two-hundredths of one per cent of the industry output.

The net effect of all this media spending and the government's cultivated image of activity is to encourage a society already dazzled by technology to be further assured that technology is solving the problem—people want so much to be assured—and so it's back to the television set. Perhaps even worse than the fact that the ads are misleading—even lying in many instances—is the fact that they divert the reader from a more basic understanding of what's really going on: that technological society is beginning to reach its limits, economic expansionism is going to end, and endless consumption is going to end, and we're all of us going to begin adopting some of the techniques of peoples who live on islands, say, and for whom a finite system, such as island Earth, is a given.

If we don't develop that understanding of the limits of things, of the islandness of Earth, of the fact that we are wildlife, too, then all the anti-pollution messages and money will be useless. Suppose our technology does manage to develop a pollution-free car engine? Will *that* make it acceptable to cover the landscape with highways and automobiles?

Advertising a dying industry

A short while ago I made some of these remarks to the San Francisco Association of Industrial Advertisers. I even went so far as to tell them that I personally believe advertising is a dying industry. Tied as it is to an expanding economy and given that we live in a finite system, on an island in space, advertising is doomed, eventually, at least in the form we now know it. If you don't need to sell more of a thing, then you probably don't need advertising.

If advertising has any future at all after, say, the next ten years, it will probably be more in the area of propagandizing for issues of one sort or another, basically issues which help expand the individual rather than the economy; or perhaps we'll have advertising of products that are related to issues—such as for a company which really has found a way to harness the sun's energy as a clean power fuel; or, it will be purely informational in nature: "We have eight old Fords here today."

I had expected, frankly, to be attacked by this industrial group—for having attacked them and for the nonsense about a no-growth economic system which didn't include advertising the annual style change. Instead, the response, after the first few minutes, was giggling, chattering under the breath and staring at the ceiling. Nobody was the slightest bit upset. Nobody *was listening.*

It was a very depressing evening. I eventually went out and got drunk with a *Wall Street Journal* reporter interested in the implications of the no-growth system. He had seen the no-response and remarked that for the first time, he really believed the world *was* coming to an end.

Business and advertising and public relations have gotten so adroit at imitating honesty that many of us have gotten out of the habit of just leveling, taking the good with the bad and hoping that since the basic intentions are good, things will work out. We can't avoid trying to steer the world back in our own direction. So the truly gratuitous act rarely takes place. Yet I believe a San Francisco dressmaker, Alvin Duskin, could be elected mayor of San Francisco with a little bit of effort, and it's only because he gratuitously committed himself publicly on a subject of concern—not turning over Alcatraz to H. L. Hunt—and at the end, he didn't try to sell anyone dresses, or finish up his stand with some catchy slogan like, "Always Interested in Beauty, Whether on Ladies' Dresses or in Your Bay."

But that kind of gratuitous behavior is very rare indeed. It is, in fact, discouraged as being unjustified by profits, whereas ads which self-serve while seeming to be taking up controversial questions in the public interest, are given extreme praise for their image of involvement.

For example, the most prestigious of all advertising awards are those given annually by *Saturday Review* "for distinguished advertising in the public interest." But what *they* call "public interest" is not exactly what you'd call public interest. Here is the way *Saturday Review* defined the way to think about the award-winning ads:

> Although corporate advertising does not have as its primary objective the direct sale of specific products to the consumer, it certainly does create and maintain a favorable selling climate among customers and prospects. It skillfully cultivates the image of quality.... Insofar as a corporation communicates a feeling of company responsibility, good neighborliness, and an awareness of public service, the sort of campaigns submitted in *SR*'s 1970 competition must pay off not only in community relationships where the company operates but among its citizen customers.

It should therefore not be very surprising that this year, out of 40 awards, 16 (40 per cent) went to power companies, oil companies, chemical companies and mining and extracting companies, all of whom have a lot of "good neighborliness" needs to get across. Only three awards went to what you could call "do-good" institutions, if you are prepared to think of the American Institute of Architects, Blue Shield, and the Advertising Council as "do-good" institutions which are something beyond sophisticated lobbies. (Howard Gossage once said of the Advertising Council that it was willing to advocate causes, "but only those that would be thought of as controversial by people who are for cancer or against safe driving.")

As for *Saturday Review*'s "18-Year Honor Roll" of award winners, it shows 20 winners, 11 of which are companies engaged in extracting—Weyerhaeuser, Shell Oil, etc.—and three of which are chemical companies in need of communicating "a feeling of company responsibility, good neighborliness and an awareness of public service."

Human chauvinism

Whereas corporate "institutional" advertising used to show pictures of labor and capital shaking hands, now it's "business and ecologists working together to control the environment," as a bank ad recently put it. Technology will take care of everything. Man's ingenuity will win out. Even the Ford Foundation says so.

I recently approached Ford about a project which had the possibility of countering the glut of industrial eco-advertising: an advertising foundation, funded by Ford and managed by a coalition of militant though "respectable" conservation groups. The ad foundation would be manned by the literally hundreds of ad men who have made known (to me, and also publicly) their interest in working solely on this subject—even at half salary. They would create ads which reveal the half-truths and omissions in industry ads; fight on specific issues as they come along; and undertake to educate the public as to truly basic, not cosmetic, solutions to the environmental crisis. They would take up such questions as life-styles, consumption patterns, the need for a no-growth economy in a finite system, the requirement that technological innovation ought to be scrutinized from the point of view that it is guilty until proven innocent, not vice versa.

It didn't take long for this Ford man, a certain Mr. Felling, to dismiss the project as hopelessly naive and to go on describing Ford's work in teaching young children how to "better manage the environment." The meeting broke up when I told him that that sort of education—"managing the environment" —would do far more harm than good. We are already *managing* the environment, and that's why we are in the mess we are in; it is a further example, borrowing from Women's Lib, of what let's call *Human* Chauvinism.

It hardly matters whether one believes that we were given dominion over other living things or we just took it, but in any event our excuse is that we've got the brains and can use machines, giving us some kind of de facto royalty status. As a result, however, we have removed ourselves from the processes that formed all the other living things; we forget that the fabric is all connected and we are just a thread of it.

Every ad that espouses a new technological intrusion into natural systems, even as a solution to pollution, encourages us to forget that fooling with one stitch alters the whole fabric.

Controls on advertising

We already see many signs that what began with cigarette advertising is likely to become the model for all advertising within industries which drastically affect the environment. Cigarette advertising, after all, is demonstrably less of a menace to society's survival than the advertising of pesticides or detergents or lumber or power.

Friends of the Earth, in concert with other conservation groups, has begun proceedings to apply the results of the Fairness Doctrine case against cigarette advertising to advertising of polluting industries. If they succeed, as I believe they eventually will, all radio and television stations will be required to provide a conservation organization with time in which they may present a counter message to an ad. If an automobile company runs a one-minute spot advertising its new model, Friends of the Earth could indicate what the implications of the annual style change are. Or they could talk about the pollution from cars, or the raw materials that go into building them, or the problem of disposing of them. And the roads needed to run them on. When a Standard Oil ad for its F-310 appears, calling it "the most long-awaited gasoline development in history," they will be able to put it in perspective by showing that the gas represents only a 5 per cent pollution improvement, leaving 95 per cent, and that the ad is filled with deliberately misleading information.

So far, I'm afraid, that sort of government interference strikes me as the only way to mitigate the effects of the millions of ad dollars which are being spent to tell just one side of the story. The only other alternative is for ad people to get on the firing line and influence what kind of message is going down. It might be that a new period of laying it on the line would then ensue and we'd all be better off.

Advertising people are, by and large, intelligent; it's a question of commitment. I hope that more and more find themselves in the position of Mr. James Webb Young, who retired himself from the business one day to work for some worthy foundation. When asked why he did it, he said, "One morning I woke up and I didn't give a damn whether they sold more Quaker Oats than I sold Cream of Wheat."

For the New Left, this article represents only a detail. There are more important issues than advertising; indeed, to focus only on the ecology movement is to cop out. True to the development of New Left thought outlined in the first chapter of this volume, the real point is that ecology is not an isolated phenomenon that can be corrected by vigorous law enforcement. The Environmental Teach-Ins of 1970 were only a con game. In the foreword to a collection of articles reprinted from *Ramparts*, David Horowitz says that to the authors of the articles,

the destruction of the living environment is seen to be an integral part of the general social crisis in America. . . . Like the race crisis and the Vietnam War, the ecological impasse is not merely the result of bad or mistaken policies that can be changed by a new Administration or a new will to do better. It is, rather, the expression of a basic malfunction of the social order itself, and consequently cannot be dealt with on a piecemeal, patchwork basis.[37]

[37] David Horowitz, "Foreword," in *Eco-Catastrophe*, by the editors of *Ramparts* (New York: Harper & Row, 1970), p. v.

The editors of *Ramparts* see the clear distinction between the liberal, reformist position and the radical position in the issue of ecology. Most liberals take heart at the publicity ecology has received, the outpouring of volunteer citizen effort, the pressure brought to bear on industry, and the signs of the beginning of a national commitment (no matter how weak at first, it is at least something). They link this movement to such insurgent programs as the Vietnam teach-ins.

The editors of *Ramparts,* on the other hand, view this parallel as "obscene." Those who organized the Vietnam teach-ins and voiced the first open opposition to the war "worked at great odds and against the lies and opposition of government, university administrations and the media." They raised their own money, and they laid their bodies on the line. The ecology movement, however, has worked out of facilities lent by the Urban Coalition, has received the blessings of the Department of Health, Education, and Welfare in the Nixon administration, has received donations from business, and has produced official brochures and a handbook. The ecology workers see the problem as one of regulating business and securing public commitment. We have heard all that before, argue the editors, in the Kennedy-Johnson War on Poverty. President Nixon has promised to clean up America, but "even TV's *Laugh-In* knows the punch line: 'If Nixon's War on Pollution is as successful as Johnson's War on Poverty, we're going to have an awful lot of dirty poor people around.' "

Ramparts' editors argue instead that socially useless, ecologically disastrous waste products make up nearly half of the gross national product. "No businessman, alone or with other businessmen, can change the tendencies of this ultimately ecocidal process unless he puts the system out of business. Regulation is not the answer. What we do need is a *redistribution* of existing real wealth, and a reallocation of society's resources." [38]

THE HEALTH INDUSTRY

Economic concentration, racism, exploitation of workers, imperialism, and war are standard themes of the Left, both Old and New. The issues we have considered in this chapter, urban ghettos and riots, hard-core unemployment, and ecology are distinctively modern topics. They represent, for the New Left, the advanced stage of corporate capitalism, the transition from problems of production to problems of consumption, from a production economy to a service economy, from a concern with widespread poverty to a concern with the quality of life. With these changes in the economy the power of the economic elite has increased because of greater rationalization, centralization, and interdependency. While economic hardship was more widespread in the first forty years of this century, the system was

[38] "Editorial," in *ibid.,* pp. vii–x.

looser. Now the grip of the elite is tightening as problems and challenges emerge within the service sector, involving education, pollution, urbanization, and, most recently, health. The service sector must be rationalized and controlled, if for no other reason than that there are handsome profits to be made and new areas for investing capital.

Thus, it is not surprising to find that the New Left, starting about 1970, began to look seriously at the organization and distribution of health care in the United States. Once again, liberals provide the foil. Liberals who concern themselves with this issue agree that the delivery of health services is woefully inadequate. The problems are complex. The American Medical Association restricts the number of doctors trained; medical schools encourage exotic specialization and research careers; the government and private foundations pour billions into the study of rare diseases and the prolongation of life for the well-to-do while inexpensive, known cures for diseases that plague the lower class are not made available; duplication of services and rarely used but prestigious facilities abound in hospitals; practicing doctors are concentrated in wealthy areas; and municipal hospitals are understaffed, unclean, and inhuman. The liberal indictment of health care is forceful, but it misses the point, according to the New Left.

In the liberal view, health care in the United States is a classic case of a nonsystem requiring rationalization, consolidation, centralization, and new governmental resources. A recent annotated bibliography in the area of health care testifies to the frantic search for the means to merge hospitals or basic services such as laundry and for ways to increase the effectiveness of local health councils and of the federal government's tardy regionalization plans.[39] Automation, new equipment, new payment plans, the training of medical-care managers, and sporadic forays into the ghettos are discussed.

Recently a group of radicals in the health area took a broad view of the problem and found, predictably, that far from being a disorganized patchwork of practices and facilities, medical care is a well-organized system.[40] The system was changing and further rationalization and centralization were indeed in the offing, not primarily in the interest of better health care, but of increasing already handsome profits.

The radical paradigm proposes that we examine the interlocking directorates of such groups as the following:

1. The drug industry (consistently one of the three most profitable industries in the United States, it spends an average of $3,000 a year to influence each doctor);

2. The hospital-equipment and hospital-supply industries (rated as the fastest growing and most profitable industries by investment services);

[39] The bibliography is being compiled by a group at Johns Hopkins University under a contract from the National Center for Health Services Research and Development of the United States Department of Health, Education, and Welfare.
[40] Barbara and John Ehrenreich, *The American Health Empire: Power, Profits and Politics* (New York: Random House, 1970).

3. The Blue Cross and Blue Shield bureaucracies and the insurance companies, which have enormous financial stakes in shaping the system;

4. The American Medical Association, declining in power as the influence of the commercial groups mentioned above increases, but still a powerful voice for private entrepreneurs whose income is extraordinary and who resist attempts to train more doctors;

5. The professional associations of hospital administrators, nurses, and technicians, which are not powerful but which must be taken into account lest their domains and interests suffer and they embarrass the system;

6. The prestigious university medical complexes that absorb hospitals, the best personnel, and the federal research dollar, but that make only token moves into the unhealthy ghettos that now surround them, and that concentrate either on exotic medical therapies for diseases concentrated among the well-to-do or on therapies too expensive for anyone else;

7. The large foundations that finance the planning and rationalizing of the private interests involved; and

8. The appointed and elected officials in the swelling health bureaucracy in Washington.

When one realizes that there is evidence for interlocking directorates among these interests, and ample evidence of their profitability, growth, and prestige, and when one considers that health care in the United States is below that of most industrialized countries and that it is the only system that provides substantial private profits, it is not hard to see that the radical paradigm deserves investigation. It seems doubtful that liberal academic institutions or the liberal foundations would come up with the view that the health system is guided by profits for business and by prestige and power for educators. The suggestion of exploring coordination at the top in this fashion is not that novel or radical in itself; economists did this long ago for industry and banking. But the prevailing viewpoint is not one that attempts to link such diverse phenomena, because the prevailing paradigm is one of pluralism. The importance of the view that business is a system, and a system that dominates and incorporates all important aspects of our lives, is suggested by this brief example. One may disagree with it, but it deserves at least as much systematic investigation as is given to the need for coordination and rationalization at the local level. For the New Left, the experts on health have failed to define the key elements of an intact subsystem of capitalism; they have wrung their hands over trivial competition and dependent groups that illustrate powerless pluralism.

But nevertheless, in matters of health as in many other respects, the stables are tidier than they were even a generation ago. They must be, in order to forestall massive disruption and to prevent the emergence of contradictions in the system. But for some on the Left, the contradictions cannot be suppressed or tidied; capitalism is facing imminent demise. We will turn to this final vision of the New Left in the next chapter.

CHAPTER 7

The formal theory

So far I have spared the reader examples of the technical, formal theorizing that is characteristic of the more explicitly Marxist members of the New Left. I have done so because I feel that the detailed, descriptive, and evocative pieces carry more force. However, formal analysis is a key part of the radical attack on business, and it should be examined. The selection to be used places many of the themes explored earlier in this book in a more inclusive context. Without the previous material, this piece by James O'Connor would appear outrageous; only after one has examined the arguments in detail, as we have done, does it make sense. The article does offer some new observations, in particular about the taxonomy of classes in the United States and their role in the coming demise of monopoly capitalism, on which I will comment in passing. Most important, however, the argument here is in a tighter form and more interdependent than those of previous selections. It requires close reading, but the effort will be repaid; it summarizes an important part of radical thought.

Because the writing leaves something to be desired, however, I have generously larded the piece with clarifying statements and reworked some tortuous sentences (with some help from the author in two cases). I have also added critical comments designed to raise questions or point out omissions. This is my way of saying that the formal analysis of contemporary capitalism, while it is interesting and provocative, has a long way to go before it can be compelling.

Throughout this book I have distinguished between the formal and the informal aspects of the New Left. Many members do not commit themselves to socialism or to a Marxian analysis with all its baggage of "the means of production" and other terms. These radicals see a destructive system, but one whose nature is so apparent in so many ways that formal analysis is hardly necessary. They work for specific changes, seek out opportune pressure points, and try to raise the level of consciousness of groups in general without feeling the need for a guiding theory that could become a Procrustean bed. Other Leftists, however, feel that sheer action, muckraking, and gut reactions are hardly enough, and they believe that a guiding theory of revolutionary potential is necessary.

James O'Connor belongs to the latter group. He and others are trying to develop a compelling theory of the coming demise of capitalism that would indicate where the action should be. That the theory may have holes in it he would no doubt agree; most theories do. That there are obvious objections to parts of it he might also agree, but he would add that these objections can be made only because a separate essay or a long discussion is not included to meet them. But because an interpretative framework for action by the New Left is essential, part of the movement must therefore devote itself to hammering one out, imperfect though it may be. The movement also debates this framework, sometimes very vigorously or even violently. Factions of the New Left appear to expend great energy in the fruitless task of trying to convince opposing sects or wings of the movement and attempting to hammer out a consensual interpretation that has some content. Rather than argue that this is an infantile disorder of the Left, I would suggest that some part of any revolutionary movement must attend to these problems.

In O'Connor's piece, for "corporate bourgeoisie" one can read members of the upper class who are not simply idle rich or rentiers, but who are involved in corporate affairs, including, of course, banking and corporate law. For "state power" one can read the national government, particularly those aspects of it that control the means of violence, control economic activity through fiscal and tax measures, control investment policies (such as deciding whether or not to invest in education, military power, the cities), and control military and foreign relations.

1970

SOME CONTRADICTIONS OF ADVANCED
U.S. CAPITALISM [1]

James O'Connor

The situation in the United States at present is the following:

Politically, the old corporate liberal power, expressed in the "consensus governments" of Wilson, Roosevelt, Truman, Eisenhower, and Kennedy, organized under the leadership of the large corporate bourgeoisie and incorporating small business, farmers, and professionals (as well as organized labor and organized minority groups), is breaking down. In domestic affairs, the national corporate bourgeoisie is liquidating the independent influence of other classes. In foreign affairs, the corporate bourgeoisie determines all United States policy.

State power in the United States is passing completely into the hands of the corporate bourgeoisie. The national state no longer regulates the relations between the classes, but is rather an instrument for, by, and of the corporate bourgeoisie.

The reasons that the national state power is passing into the hands of the corporate bourgeoisie at the expense of local and regional bourgeoisies are the following:

In general, the large corporations have established hegemony over economic society, at home and abroad. The corporations have reduced all but small, local bourgeoisies to a dependent status, emerging as the only important economically independent section of the capitalistic class. Within the capitalistic class, the corporations have established not only economic but also ideological hegemony.

In specific, there are fewer and fewer capitalist interests independent of the interests of the corporate bourgeoisie. Agriculture is being rapidly corporatized. Small business is being integrated into the structure of the large corporations. Bank capital is no longer independent of industrial corporate capital, nor does it stand above industrial capital.

This is the current Marxist view regarding the role of finance; it finds its clearest expression in Paul Baran and Paul Sweezy's *Monopoly Capital*.[2]

---

1 James O'Connor, "Some Contradictions of Advanced U.S. Capitalism," *Social Theory and Practice*, 1:1 (Spring 1970), 1–11.
2 New York: Monthly Review Press, 1966.

This view has recently been severely challenged by data released by the "Patman Report"—the "Report on Commercial Banks and Their Trust Activities," of the House Subcommittee on Banking and Currency—and brilliantly interpreted and expanded by Robert Fitch and Mary Oppenheimer in a series of articles in *Socialist Revolution*, called "Who Rules the Corporations?"[3] They argue that a few large financial institutions have obtained control of the corporations. Their work is long and technical, but extremely thorough and well written. I highly recommend it. O'Connor has written an angry rebuttal.[4]

The banks which have not been historically integrated with the industrial corporations are being transformed into financial instruments of the corporations. Corporate capital thus indirectly establishes more control over small business, utilities, and other capital dependent on, or owned or controlled by, the banks. The corporations employ a larger portion of the professional classes. The colleges and universities place less emphasis on training governing elites, and more emphasis on preparing labor power for the corporations. The giant corporations increasingly become conglomerate corporations, operating in many branches of industry; today's merger movement is the strongest in industrial history, and the largest share of mergers are of the conglomerate type.

The single remaining important intra-capitalist class conflict is between the corporate bourgeoisie and local propertied groups, such as realtors, landlords, etc., a conflict reflected in the so-called crisis of Federalism.

No doubt O'Connor assumes that his readers need no more examples, but "realtors and landlords" are hardly large groups that would promote much intraclass conflict. One would expect other sources of intraclass conflict to be far more important, such as disagreements between those industries in favor of free trade versus those favoring high tariffs, or those dependent on war spending versus those hurt by inflation and the upward pressures on the salaries of engineers, scientists, and technicians caused by war spending. Nevertheless, it is remarkable how competition among groups has been moderated by conglomerate forms of organization (for example, rail and trucking need not compete if a railroad such as the Southern Pacific can be a major factor in the trucking industry; oil, gas, and coal interests merge in the major energy firms; automobile manufacturers move into transit systems; and so on). The hegemony of the financial interests reported in

---

[3] Robert Fitch and Mary Oppenheimer, "Who Rules the Corporations?" Parts 1, 2, and 3, *Socialist Revolution*, 1:4, 5, 6 (1970).

[4] James O'Connor, "Question: Who Rules the Corporations? Answer: The Ruling Class," *Socialist Revolution*, 2:1 (January–February 1971), 117–49. Robert Fitch replies in the same issue.

the Fitch and Oppenheimer article mentioned above provides even more substantial evidence of declining intraclass conflict.

Similarly, in the international economy, the U.S. corporate bourgeoisie dominates the world capitalist economy through its instrument, the multi-national corporations. Due to acquisitions, mergers, and other forms of concentration between European capital and U.S. capital, and due to the lack of big mergers between European national capitals, the elements of disassociation within the E.E.C. [European Economic Community] are stronger than the elements of association, and E.E.C. is becoming a U.S. economic stronghold.

It is not clear how the New Left treats the startling growth of the Japanese economy and its competition with United States industries. Businessmen see it as a threat, but Harry Magdoff appears to treat it lightly.[5] Japan expanded its economy under the military umbrella of the United States and is assumed to be a tool of the United States' world capitalist domination. I would think that an interpretation of the world capitalist scene as one of greedy national capitalists devouring one another in ruinous competition and struggle for raw materials would be an acceptable thesis for the New Left. I have not found it, however.

Economically, the situation facing the corporate bourgeoisie is as follows:

The accelerating development of the forces of production, in particular, science and technology, has basically modified the relations of production.

In the first place, the development of science and technology has increased the total overhead costs of production, and revolutionized their character. Enormous amounts of capital are required in petrochemicals, transportation, and other expanding branches of production. Capital also increasingly takes the form of technical, administrative, and scientific brain-power. Increasingly, economic development depends more on science and technology and less on the number of machines and men in production. Labor power takes a different materialized form—that is, skilled, technical labor power replaces raw labor power.

Science and technology, being truly social productive forces [that is, rather than material productive forces], require far-reaching forms of social integration. Capitalist private-property relations have not provided for these, and the corporate bourgeoisie has turned to the state.

In short, the corporate bourgeoisie increasingly uses the state power to socialize the costs of production, in particular, the costs of transforming raw labor power into technical and administrative labor power and the costs of research and development. Capital is acquired from the state—that is, the people, through taxation. The state pays for the great mass of education and training costs and provides over 60 per cent of research funds.

5 Harry Magdoff, "Does the U.S. Economy Require Imperialism?" *Social Policy*, 1:3 (September–October 1970), 20–29.

This is not to say that the radicals would not want the state to pay for education; the complaint is that education is designed to provide training for private enterprise. I shall discuss this distinction further below.

There is thus a large and growing new stratum of the working class, the productive indirect corporate employees—teachers, administrators, scientists, technicians, etc.—all are employed in the state bureaucracy.

This is the first of several classes named in the article. Note that teachers, administrators, and scientists are labeled "working class." In Marxist theory, this is technically correct; those whom this book calls working class should be referred to only as blue-collar workers.

There is also a related stratum of "publigopoly" employees in the military and related industries, which are in the private sector of the economy, but whose employers are subsidized by the state, and hence subject to political, as well as business norms.

The second way in which the relations of production have been modified is that

the development of science and technology and the productive forces in general has reached the stage at which all economic needs can easily be satisfied. Commodity demand based on the economic needs of producers and formed by the forces and relations of production rises only slowly, or not at all. Socially necessary labor steadily declines. Consequently, the corporate bourgeoisie is compelled to lay out larger and larger portions of profits on selling expenses in order to maintain and expand the volume of purchasing power by discouraging savings. In short, commodities are both use values and waste.

"Use values" involve the actual consumption of a commodity; "waste" involves advertising and many other selling expenses, such as packaging, built-in obsolescence, superfluous decoration for marginal differentiation among identical products, and so on.

Increasingly economic waste replaces use values, and socially unnecessary labor replaces socially necessary labor. To acquire use values to meet economic needs, the working classes are compelled to consume waste—that is, pay for the expenses of selling. The interpenetration of sales expenses and production costs, or waste and use values, is the basic method employed by the corporate bourgeoisie to maintain the level of private purchasing power.

That is, if the prices of commodities were not inflated by waste values, there would presumably be more saving and thus smaller profits.

The corporations compel the working class to purchase waste by embodying waste into use values, and by evoking needs which can not be satisfied by commodities and promising that these needs can be satisfied by commodities. The corporations strive for hegemony over the consciousness of the working class itself.

In short, the worker alienates his consciousness, as well as his labor, and constantly reproduces the conditions for his own socially unnecessary exploitation, a process that requires the active intervention of the state.

The corporate bourgeoisie uses the state power to develop, reinforce, and accelerate the process of the accumulation of waste, and the appropriation of the workers' consciousness, which is the necessary pre-condition for the appropriation of labor power and its realization as surplus value and profits. The corporate bourgeoisie has developed programs for "full employment" (i.e., a large volume of economic waste and socially unnecessary labor), transportation (i.e., highways to expand the demand for automobiles), housing (i.e., insurance and guarantees in the field of mortgage credit, subsidies to private single-unit housing), etc.

There is, thus, a large and growing stratum of unproductive indirect corporate employees, employed by and in the state bureaucracy.

Presumably there is an equally large stratum of unproductive employees managing the production of commodities in socialist states also.

The third reason for the modification of the relations of production is that

... the development of science and technology and the inexpensive reproduction of technical-scientific knowledge (and hence labor power) leads the corporate bourgeoisie to employ a capital intensive technology, despite the relative abundance of raw labor power. It is more rational to combine technical-scientific labor power with capital-intensive technology than to combine raw labor power with labor-intensive technology in production, due to the fact that the costs of training technical-scientific labor power are met by taxation falling on the population at large.

It is true, as we have noted in earlier chapters, that the costs of training are met by taxation, but this can only be an objection if one is opposed to the whole system, as the New Left is. There is no ground for intermediate reform here, for if people were trained for other things in the schools, they would not have access to the bulk of jobs in society as it is presently organized, and thus they could not earn a living. Furthermore, to ask industry to pay for the training of technical-scientific labor power would simply raise the prices of goods under a capitalist system, even as taxes went down. Taxes would not go down very much because the government itself buys a large part of the industrial output (for example, from the aerospace and defense industries), and would pay contractors more to reimburse them for their cost of training, and thus would have to tax people for the money to buy these goods. Finally, the training, which might start at the junior high school level, would be completely in the hands of industry; consequently, not even a pretense of providing a general education would be needed and no ideological checks would exist at all. Major reform of the educational system would thus have to wait for the reform of the ownership of the means of production.

There is thus a large and growing stratum of unskilled, untrained workers, chiefly blacks and other minorities, who constitute a post-industrial proletariat.

This proletariat constitutes a new class in post-industrial society. It figures heavily in radical analysis because once these workers become aware of their powerlessness, they can be mobilized. The term "post-industrial" is not exclusively a New Left term, but one that has come into general usage. It refers to the period since the Second World War or the Korean War, when the volume of tertiary (service) economic activities came to exceed the primary (mining and agriculture) and secondary (manufacturing) activities. The post-industrial period is characterized by heavy emphasis on research and development, automation, and the concentration of economic power as state regulation expands.

The relative size of this stratum does not regulate the level of wages; thus it does not constitute a true reserve army of the unemployed. Raw labor power does not compete with technical labor power, in the context of capital-intensive technology.

State capital, not corporate capital, also employs these workers, when they are able to find employment at all.

The economic situation facing the corporate bourgeoisie at present is extending the basic contradiction of capital (i.e., the contradiction between the social character of production and private ownership of the means of production), which permeates not only economic society, but also the political sphere.

In short, the class struggle has been *displaced:*

In the first place, on the one hand, the corporate bourgeoisie uses the state power to socialize and thus lower costs of production and to subsidize and hence raise the level of effective demand. Furthermore, state capital is employing a larger and larger part of the post-industrial proletariat, in particular, the blacks. The corporate bourgeoisie thus heaps more and more financial burdens on the state.

On the other hand, the corporations reserve all directly productive economic activities (i.e., money-making activities) for itself. Profits are appropriated by the few; the state remains a pauper state, as it relies altogether on tax and loan revenues. Even though there is a sizeable surplus over economic needs in the hands of the people, the surplus is not a taxable form, as it consists of waste embodied in commodities which are needed to meet economic needs.

This combination of phenomena produces the present fiscal crisis of local and state governments and, increasingly, the growing crisis of the national tax state.

The corporations want fresh recruits for the technical labor force (partly in order to avoid re-training older workers, necessary due to the rapid changes in technology), but realize that the training work force (not to speak of the students) can not by itself create surplus value. The state, that is, the people, must therefore pay. But the corporate bourgeoisie keeps the state poor, on the one hand, by monopolizing the directly productive activities, on the other hand, by transforming the economic surplus into waste. High employment intensifies the fiscal crisis of the state because an expansion of state expenditures ceases to automatically generate more revenues—that is, in the absence of unemployed resources, state spending does not help to pay for itself via an expansion of production, employment, incomes, and hence the tax base.

The state thus can not simultaneously ameliorate the economic and social conditions in the ghetto cities and in the depressed or under-developing regions, increase the standard of living of the state employees, meet the economic demands of the corporate bourgeoisie, and wage imperialist wars.

For these reasons, a struggle is shaping up between state employees and the state administration. Strikes against the state numbered 142 in 1966, and are rising at an expanding rate. At present, the public school teachers are in the forefront of this struggle, the issues being a mixture of economic and non-economic issues.

In short, the socialization of costs and the subsidization of demand has displaced the class struggle from the sphere of direct production to the sphere of administration,

or nonproductive, indirect labor performed by the state in the interest of the corporate bourgeoisie. Presumably this labor includes education, social services, municipal services such as police and fire protection and sanitation, operation of courts and legislative bodies, and tax collection, to name a few. Some of these tasks are performed by private enterprises when some surplus value (profit) is discerned—private mail services, private police protection, proprietary hospitals (now forming into chains controlled by conglomerates, and skimming off the profitable cases that once subsidized the unprofitable cases handled by charity hospitals), and school systems that pay industry for its services on a performance basis.

The second way in which the class struggle has been displaced is that

the substitution of waste for use values and socially unnecessary labor for socially necessary labor has led to the development of a post-capitalist stratum, a growing number of youth who reject the "affluence" of corporate capitalism and drop out of the established civil institutions. In essence, they are living proof that the class struggle has also been displaced from the sphere of production to the sphere of consciousness, in particular within the family. They are in revolt precisely against the appropriation of consciousness—that is, they do not believe as their parents do that commodities can substitute for affection, a loving family, sexuality, and other non-economic needs. They face the choice between alienating their labor to acquire waste and use values and becoming rootless, separated from the sphere of production. They choose the latter.

This stratum originates in the middle income families, that is, precisely where the contradiction of commodity production is most real, due to the volume of waste consumed in these households, and the inability of this waste to generate affection, loving, and useful surroundings. As corporate capitalism accumulates more waste, this revolt will filter down into the lower middle income families.

The post-capitalist stratum is freeing itself from socially necessary labor, beyond the bare minimum—that is, it is a free stratum. It is neither an exploited or exploitative class; it does not constitute a reserve army of unemployed; it is not needed in the state administration. Historically, the free stratum is an altogether new phenomenon.

Standing outside the economic society, this stratum nevertheless comes into conflict with society in every sphere of civil society except the place of production and in the political sphere, particularly with the workers in the districts which they colonize

As we have seen, there has been little evidence of successful "colonization." (Incidentally, the preceding four paragraphs sum up the interpretation of the rise of the New Left that prevails in liberal circles.)

From the standpoint of the corporate bourgeoisie, as a category they are unimportant, except as a source of ideas, styles, etc.—that is, as a source of ideas for new forms of economic waste, the quantitative impact of which on the economy as a whole being relatively small.

This is a recurrent theme in the New Left literature—how the new lifestyles of the free stratum have been used to stimulate consumption among the straight middle class, and how the free stratum itself is subverted by business. Rent-a-hippie agencies, which supposedly provide hippies for upper-middle-class parties, are a caricature of this. Rock music, clothing styles, hair styles, and psychedelic drugs are all exploited by legitimate and illegitimate businesses that feed off the innovativeness of the free stratum. Although there may be some general gain in consciousness-expansion and defiance of tradition, basically the Left seems to feel that the economic exploitation of its life-styles is just one more indication of the system's ability to adapt, despite its contradictions. For an ironic view, see Irwin Silber, "The Growing Market for Free Ideas" in the November 22, 1969, issue of *The Guardian.*

In brief, the free stratum has no important relations of production with the corporate bourgeoisie or other classes, and hence there is no open or covert struggle for control over the means of production. Like the bourgeoisie in feudal Europe who made the bourgeois democratic revolution, the free class is in the forefront of the ideological struggle for a "popular democratic revolution." Like the bourgeoisie, the free class is neither the main exploited nor exploitative class. Unlike the bourgeoisie, the free class is not contending for control of the means of production (which it sees as waste), and hence can not directly use the means of production to rule or subjugate other classes.

The free stratum is a progressive force but can not lead the political struggle, even though many of the values, ideas, styles of life, etc. permeate other classes and groups.

This is a key point. The hippie culture, or the counterculture, cannot make or lead the revolution; it can only provide ideas, values, and so on. The New Left, as a political group, draws to some extent on this culture (and may even exploit it), but it must mobilize other strata.

The third way the class struggle has been displaced concerns the post-industrial proletariat.

This stratum does not have an economic base, excluding service functions such as post office work, public maintenance work, etc. Monopolizing the menial, low paying state jobs, they are subject to the same salary schedules, etc. as the other state employees, even though their functions are peripheral to the needs of the corporations.

Suffering high unemployment and underemployment, the post-industrial stratum, especially the blacks, are developing community organizations, seeking self-determination and the abolition of racism, as well as putting forth material demands on the state (e.g., in the areas of unemployment, housing, community services, health facilities, better schools, etc.). Understandably, the struggle of this stratum also manifests itself directly in the sphere of consumption, as in the massive seizure of consumer goods during urban uprisings.

This struggle is "understandable" because the workers lack access to widely advertised consumer goods.

As for the industrial proletariat engaged in directly productive activities: it is on the decline numerically, it is relatively well-paid, its unions are led by individuals who in effect act as hiring agents for the corporations. In this stratum of the working class, the class struggle manifests itself chiefly within the unions, pitting militant workers who agitate against shop conditions, work rules, "managerial prerogatives," etc. against the established union leaders who concentrate on wage demands and fringe benefits, attempting simultaneously to please the corporations and the workers. The class struggle is reflected, on the one hand, in wildcat strikes, spontaneous slow downs, etc. and, on the other hand, in intra-union revolts against the established leadership of the large industrial unions.

As for the remaining large stratum of the working class: the growing army of sales, administrative, and other nonproductive personnel will in the future outnumber the industrial proletariat. The labor power of the "sales stratum" is not exploited, as they live on the labor of the productive work force. Neither poor nor exploited, their pay not subject to the fiscal crisis of the state, largely immune from the ideas and values of the post-capitalist class, auto-manipulative, withdrawn, and passive from the political standpoint, this parasitic group forms a neutral element, due to their peculiar relation to the means of production (i.e., the means of marketing and sales).

Thus we have the following classes: the corporate bourgeoisie; the petty (or local) bourgeoisie (e.g. small businessmen, landlords); the nonproductive working-class stratum (sales and administrative personnel); state workers (who can be either productive or nonproductive); post-industrial workers (largely members of minority groups, who are unskilled and work primarily for the state); and the "post-capitalist stratum," or the free stratum (middle-class youth who have cut their ties with the economic system). The growing complexity of industry, capitalism, and society has made the two-class system of earlier Marxism out of date. The analysis of the New Left also rejects the social-science division of classes on the basis of income, education, and a simple-minded scale of occupations. This classification hides the dynamics to which O'Connor refers.

To summarize, the development of the forces of production under the control of the corporations leads to the passing of the state power to the corporate bourgeoisie. The developing forces of production, together with corporate hegemony over the civil society and the state, have changed the character of the relations of production and determined new relations of production. There are three broad new strata which must look to the state for that which they can not provide for themselves—the state workers, the post-industrial workers, and the post-capitalist stratum.

Socially, culturally, and politically, the new strata and the old live side-by-side. Their values mix, their ideas merge, their institutions borrow freely from each other. It appears to be a confusing situation. In all economic societies, past and future live side by side; there is always confusion. In corporation capitalism the future (i.e., the post-capitalist group) borrows much from the past (i.e., the post-proletariat), in music, life styles, etc. The post-proletariat attempts to alienate labor, but does not know how. The post-capitalist stratum knows how to alienate its labor, but refuses to do so. Meanwhile, the present (i.e., the industrial proletariat and the sales stratum) becomes more fearful, more troubled, and more confused.

Politically, the decisive stratum in the immediate future are the state workers.

Like the industrial proletariat, the productive state workers are exploited; like the post-industrial proletariat, they can not expect a rising material standard of living; like the post-capitalist stratum, they are acquiring the new personal values, in particular, those of social usefulness and service. Finally, by gradually exercising control over the indirect means of production, they can exercise decisive influence over the direct means of production. The state workers, and in particular the productive state workers, thus have the potential numerical strength, technical ability, motive, and vision to be not only a leading political force, but also a leading force in the classless society.

Unfortunately, we are not to learn more about the membership of this "decisive" group. Other Leftists also look toward a vague category of technicians, engineers, and subprofessionals as the "new working class" that is most likely to have the values, vision, will, and ability to bring about a revolution. They sometimes dismiss, as does O'Connor, the traditional working class as the prime movers.

How is the corporate bourgeoisie using the state power internationally?

Abroad, the state power is employed to defend militarily the global economic interests of the corporate bourgeoisie, not from attacks arising from competing bourgeoisies, but rather from attacks by popular forces. In their drive to integrate the economic resources of the world capitalist system into their own corporate structures, the corporate bourgeoisie requires the active participation of the state. Prior to the attempt by the U.S. corporations to dislodge and take over the colonial empires, the corporate bourgeoisie (e.g., Hoover) actually opposed the demands of finance capital to acquire the active participation of the state in international economic loans, etc. At present, the state is employed at every step in the accumulation of capital abroad—the acquisition of minerals and raw materials, the creation of investment opportunities in manufacturing, distribution, and so on, the creation of cheap labor havens (Puerto Rico, Formosa, South Korea) for final assembly operations, etc. The state guarantees foreign investments, stabilizes the monetary systems under the reign of the dollar, provides infra-structures for private investments with public funds, subsidizes exports, bribes local, client bourgeoisie and armies, creates tariff agreements based on the principle of reciprocity (i.e., the principle of the status quo), dominates commodity organizations, exercises economic, political, and military control over unstable areas (i.e., all under-developed areas), forms military blocs, etc.

In brief, the state defends and promotes the economic interests of the metropolitan power; the only significant metropolitan economic interests abroad are in the hands of the corporate bourgeoisie.

Politically, the significance of the international economic hegemony of the corporate bourgeoisie is as follows:

In general, the imposition of higher forms of social integration (multi-national corporations, etc.) on areas with relatively underdeveloped forces of production via the process of world capitalist integration, displaces the class struggle, setting region against region, country against country, etc.

In specific, prior to the early 1950's, the United States had a regional, not a global foreign policy. Prior to the late 1950's, the United States had a nuclear counter-strike military strategy. Since that date, it has added a counter-insurgency military strategy.

Also prior to the late 1950's, in particular, during the period 1944–1950, the United States actively or passively supported or defended anti-colonial national liberation movements in India, Indonesia, Ceylon, Burma, and most of Africa, including Algeria.

This is a rare assertion for the New Left. For most radicals, what the United States did before the Vietnam War, or at least the Korean War, is not of much importance. For those who dwell on these things, Marxist theory does not easily accommodate a view such as the one O'Connor puts forth in this paragraph and defends in subsequent ones.

At present, the United States is attempting to destroy any and all national liberation movements in Vietnam, Angola, the Congo, and other parts of Africa, not to speak of bourgeois democratic governments in Latin America (i.e., the Dominican Republic, Brazil).

That is, United States foreign policy is totally reactionary, having been previously based on support of democratic movements (even if cynically). In short, the U.S. corporate bourgeoisie has negated its own classic bourgeois principles of free elections, free press, etc.

The reasons for these profoundly important changes are:

The transformation from a regional to a global foreign policy corresponded to the transformation of the U.S. corporations from national corporations with some export markets, foreign investments, etc., to multi-national corporations, as well as being a response to the "loss" of China in 1949.

The transformation of a policy which supported bourgeois democratic forms of government, norms, etc., to a policy that smashes democracy wherever possible is due to the successful insinuation of the U.S. corporate bourgeoisie into the old empires of Japan and Europe. Until the middle or late 1950's, the support, or tacit acceptance, of national liberation movements on the one hand helped to dislodge the imperialist rivals of the United States and on the other hand won favor with the leaders of the national liberation movements.

This is to attribute considerable sophistication, even for the Left, to monopoly capitalism.

The transformation of military strategy is due to the failure of local bourgeoisies in the underdeveloped capitalist countries to rule, develop the local economies and societies, etc., together with the armed struggle of the people against imperialism and its local client bourgeoisies, itself organically connected with the first.

In short, local bourgeoisies and the corporate bourgeoisie are deathly afraid of the mass of people in the underdeveloped countries; rightly so, because the people have suffered the failures of, first, national bourgeois economic development, and second, imperialist-directed economic development. The United States has thus even dropped the pretense of championing bourgeois values, ideas, and institutions.

To be sure, outside of Vietnam, there is the appearance of the victory of the corporate bourgeoisie and its clients over the people following the counter-revolutionary period of 1960 to date. Apparently, everywhere, also, the popular revolution is dormant.

It is doubtful that many theoreticians would agree that the popular revolution, even in the early 1970's, is everywhere dormant.

Soon, however, the revolution will spring to life. The reason is that the workers and peasants of the underdeveloped world were incorporated in the post-independence period into consensus governments in all three underdeveloped continents. In Asia and Africa these were popular front governments, formed due to the popular front nature of the independence struggle. Similarly, in Latin America, national economic development under the auspices of the national bourgeoisie, which made progress in the 1930's and 1940's, required a political alliance between the urban working class and the national bourgeoisie itself. Popular organizations thus grew up in a sheltered atmosphere; the workers and peasants only in a few places independently forged their own instruments, unions, associations, etc.

Only recently have the people in the underdeveloped world begun to understand that they have been cynically used by their "national democratic" bourgeoisies. Only recently has it become clear that "national economic development" is impossible in the context of the imperialist systems.

Thus the active struggle with the people forming their own independent organizations, is just beginning. In the 1970's the masses of people in the underdeveloped countries will truly be on the move, taking their own initiatives, formulating their own demands, etc.

Note that in this review of Third World developments and possibilities, no mention is made of the nightmares of most liberals, including foundations such as Ford, Carnegie, and Rockefeller—overpopulation leading to (nonpolitical) food riots, famines, the plague, and ecocide. Perhaps it is too much to grant that as a part of the system of capitalist domination and exploitation, public-health measures were introduced that vastly increased life spans and reduced infant and child mortality rates, debilitating adult diseases, and murderous epidemics. Of course, this victory of capitalist technology appears to be brief and hollow as the earlier scourges are revived in altered forms, and perhaps the New Left would also say that healthy natives produce more for the capitalists. The problem of overpopulation has always been sticky for the Left; measures of population control are aimed at the poor and exploited, and thus smack of genocide; middle-class programs for the United States appear to be measures of convenience for those who already have so many other conveniences; the involvement of foundations such as the Rockefeller Foundation in population-control measures, is, on the face of it, suspect. See the often tortuous analysis by Steve Weissman, "Why the Population Bomb Is a Rockefeller Baby." [6]

The basic contradictions of U.S. monopoly capitalism developing at present are the following:

1. The contradiction between the state expenditures and state taxes, the former ever-rising, the latter reaching a ceiling. Militant unionism, "free" collective bargaining, strikes, etc., will therefore be increasingly suppressed in the state economy.

2. The contradiction between the development of the forces of production and the volume of employment, pay scales, etc. available to the post-industrial proletariat. "Accumulation of consumer goods" and the struggle for self-determination—that is, urban uprising—will therefore be ruthlessly suppressed.

3. The contradiction between the needs of the post-capitalist stratum (i.e., in general, the values of this class) and the ability of the means of production, privately owned, to supply the material pre-conditions for the satisfaction of these needs. The new life styles in the colonized districts can not therefore develop fully, or truly flower, leading to increasing frustration, denial or access

6 Steve Weissman, "Why the Population Bomb Is a Rockefeller Baby," *Eco-Catastrophe*, by the editors of *Ramparts* (New York, Harper & Row, 1970), pp. 26–41.

to public facilities, involuntary material poverty, due to the pressure of larger numbers of youth on economic resources, etc.

4. The contradiction between the ideals of bourgeois democracy abroad, and the actual practice of reaction, suppression, and the use of brute force by U.S. imperialism. This contradiction can only deepen.

In addition, the broader contradictions shaping up in the future are:

1. The contradiction between democracy and efficiency in the state sector. State capital by definition encompasses both economics and politics; the state is a synthesis of base and super-structure, due to its double character. On the one hand, the state socializes costs and subsidizes demand, and thus is subject to the business norm of efficiency, profitability, etc. On the other hand, the state governs politically, and thus is subject to the political norms of debate, open hearings, free elections—in short, formal democracy. The tendency is for the latter to give way to the former, and for the crisis of bourgeois democracy to deepen still further.

This tendency is also apparent in most socialist countries. It is not, however, so apparent in some small European democracies, such as Belgium and Sweden. The New Left has not attended to these very much. Are they socialist? Hardly, by most criteria. Are they truly democratic? There appears to be a good measure of democracy. Are they capitalistic? There is certainly private ownership of some of the means of production, and some of the larger multinational capitalist firms are located there. These countries appear to support American foreign policy in general, but not in the specifics of the Vietnam War. Sweden is a major supplier of international arms. Yet, income is not highly concentrated, social services are excellent, political freedom is apparent, and the mixed economy (state and private) is prosperous. Surely many of the sins of capitalism (racism, exploitation, and others) can be found in Sweden, but many of the sins of United States capitalism cannot. Might it be possible to reform and liberalize capitalism sufficiently to narrow the income spread, provide full employment and decent social services, and so on? Or must the capitalist system in its entirety be ended?

Indicative of the fact that the state increasingly makes political decisions on the basis of business norms, and hence restricts bourgeois democratic rights, is the U.S. Court of Appeals decision (April 16, 1968) limiting the right to free speech for government employees because of the "increasing indispensable services rendered by government employees." According to the Court, "uninhibited public speech ... by government employees may produce intolerable disharmony, inefficiency, dissension, and even chaos."

Modern liberalism in effect redefines democracy, elevating the market-place ideas of "equality of opportunity," "efficiency," etc. to the status of political principles, thus reducing the great classic ideas of liberalism to the most mundane.

2. The contradiction between the requirements of the home political economy and the international economy. On the one hand, the subsidization of demand by the state, the synthesization of demand by the corporations, etc. leads to a policy of "full employment" at home. No longer is there a reserve army of unemployed to keep wages behind or in correspondence with productivity. Inflation has substituted for the reserve army, as inflation prevents militant "economism" on the part of organized labor from seizing the profits share of income at times of full employment.

On the other hand, U.S. imperialism places great burdens on the U.S. balance of payments. Historically, the outflow of dollars has been offset by a surplus of U.S. exports over imports. But inflation in the U.S., among other factors, more and more ruins the foreign market for U.S. commodities, hence the intensified pressure on the dollar, gold-buying, the new two-price system, etc.

How will this contradiction be resolved? In precisely the same way that it is being resolved in Great Britain—that is, by a long-term glacier-like movement toward compulsory arbitration of labor disputes, the abolition of piecework wages, wage guidelines, state-enforced arrangements to ban "restrictive practices," etc., and, finally, bans on strikes and the abolition of "free" collective bargaining. At this point, organized labor will begin to play an ever-growing revolutionary role, but this point will not be reached in the immediate future.

3. The contradiction between democratic and dictatorial forms of class dictatorship. On the one hand, elections and other bourgeois democratic institutions are losing even their democratic appearance, due to the economic and political hegemony of the corporate bourgeoisie, and the absence of independent sections of the capitalist class contending for power on the basis of alternative progress. The corporate bourgeoisie try to solve problems outside of the sphere of politics, within their private organizations (e.g., C.E.D., Business Advisory Council, etc.), within the state bureaucracy (e.g., Executive branch of the Federal government), and within the supra-municipal and State authorities (e.g., Port of N.Y. Authority).

On the other hand, the rhetoric of democracy, cynically used by the corporate bourgeoisie, intensifies and increasingly alienates people from it.

In the people and, most important, the youth, there is a growing realization that bourgeois democracy was always a form of class dictatorship—that is, the ideological hegemony of the ruling class is fast being rolled back.

In summary, all signs point to one, new developing process—a crisis of bourgeois democracy. The dominant section of the ruling class—the corporate bourgeoisie—is historically not only unable or unwilling to defend the historic values and ideals of liberal democracy, but increasingly subjects them to attack. The corporate bourgeoisie is now following a totally undemocratic reactionary policy abroad, which is increasingly being applied at home.

This is apparent in the immediate political crisis at home. The present political crisis is not a reflection of an underlying struggle between opposing sections of the capitalist class, one representing rising economic power, the other representing a declining economic power. Unlike historic political crises, which were resolved in favor of the rising economic power (e.g., the crisis at the time of the Populist and Progressive movements), which were temporary in character, the present crisis is permanent.

The political conflicts today take place within the corporate bourgeoisie, not between the corporate bourgeoisie and other sections of the capitalist class. Widely conflicting ideas held by national leaders in connection with Vietnam and the black ghetto, not to speak of dozens of lesser questions, are not fundamentally based on different class or sub-class interests.

Quite the contrary, these opposing ideas do not have any significant material basis—that is, they arise due to contradictions which the corporate bourgeoisie faces, but which it can not resolve. Hence the corporate bourgeoisie and its apologists are at present becoming *hysterical*. Neither side in the disputes concerning whether to extend the colonial war in Vietnam or liquidate it, whether to spend billions to reconstruct the ghetto cities or spend millions to repress them, etc., has a *workable* program. Whatever way the corporate bourgeoisie turns, it faces dilemmas—and, ultimately, defeat.

The political crisis arises from the permanent economic crisis. If the corporate bourgeoisie withdraws from Vietnam, its world-wide economic interests —its thousands of branch plants and subsidiaries, markets, raw material supplies, cheap labor havens, local, client, dependent bourgeoisies, etc.—will, it is believed, come under increasing attack by popular forces. One prop of the economic prosperity of the United States metropolitan economy will be decisively undercut.

This is New Left support for the old domino theory. If Vietnam falls, can the rest of Southeast Asia be far behind? The domino theory was denounced by liberals who do not feel that Marxist revolutions would topple one country after another or, at least, that they would not be under the control of Peking or Moscow. The Left, however, feels that the power and prestige of the United States can only be hurt by failures such as Vietnam, and that popular revolutions, no doubt receiving support from Peking, will follow.

If the corporate bourgeoisie significantly extends the war in Vietnam, their government will be compelled to fully mobilize the metropolitan economy. This option is highly unlikely, due to the fact that the resistance to full mobilization by workers, students, blacks, etc. will grow at an accelerated rate. No government in the history of capitalist society, *in a country in which bourgeois democratic institutions were established*, was ever compelled to mobilize the population for a colonial war. The political leaders of British imperialism never were required to face this possibility, which they would consider impossible on its face.

If the corporate bourgeoisie spends billions to reconstruct the ghetto cities, the interest of tens of thousands of landlords, small realtors, small and middle bankers, retailers, suburbanites, etc., will have to be liquidated and local state power will have to be totally subjugated to national state power. This would represent an economic crisis of the first order for the large remnants of the petty bourgeoisie and professional classes, and a final blow against home rule. This option is highly unlikely, due to the poverty of the state and the other fiscal burdens the corporations heap on it—that is, "full employment" means that resources for urban reconstruction are scarce and costly. In the event that the state were able to acquire the resources, the *social* and *political* antagonisms would remain.

If the corporate bourgeoisie spends millions to repress the ghetto cities, the economic crisis of the cities, the fiscal crisis of the cities and states, and increasing poverty, social underdevelopment, and economic backwardness in the cities will intensify.

American capitalism has thus entered its final crisis period—that is, the pre-revolutionary period. There is no way for the ruling class to continue to ameliorate the class struggle.

Unfortunately, the history of Marxist predictions undermines the credibility of O'Connor's concluding statement. He may be correct, but it is worth noting that many others have predicted the end of American capitalism since the time of Marx and been wrong.

Another possible script can be proposed: Disaffected workers will be bought off with even more of the gadgets and entertainments that the system is so clever at developing. Social scientists will finally convince most employers that they risk their positions of power and wealth if they do not make more jobs interesting, physically safe, and economically secure. Most of what goes by the name of organizational theory is just such a humanitarian effort to whitewash the walls of the dark, satanic mills. We are learning how decisions can be decentralized when they involve the trivial aspects of competition and efficiency, thus promoting a sense of participation, while controls over the important aspects of the system are tightened for those at the top. The truly militant, disaffected groups in society, such as the Black Panthers and other movements still to come, can be suppressed through ever more effective surveillance and harassment. The ingenuity of the system here is shown in the current use of the grand jury system, turning it into a middle-class citizens' FBI with the power to compel answers to vague, leading questions or to administer indefinite prison terms for refusal to answer. More effective or compulsory birth-control methods would reduce the welfare burden in a generation or two. Psychological research will tell us more about entertainments, therapies, and conditioning that will relieve anxieties and boredom in an increasingly programed society. Tranquilizers and stimulants are already the major part of the narcotics industry. The New Left will splinter even further without a base to build on, and its radical fringes will turn on one another, even as the Progressive Labor party recently physically attacked peace demonstrators in Chicago.[7]

Meanwhile, famines, civil war, and plagues abroad will help reduce the population problem in the Third World and allow the United States to intervene at the proper moment when a country is in shambles and American

[7] See the account of this incident in *The Guardian*, August 2, 1971, p. 2.

economic interests can be served. The Japanese boom will level out as wages rise and radical sects from the four corners of their political spectrum disrupt society. The Common Market, including Britain, will continue to squabble about agricultural prices and imports from foreign dependencies, while United States capital penetrates further. The ocean will not quite die and the air will manage to sustain life as the regressive tax system pays subsidies to industry to reduce pollution without reducing profits.

If American business is a system with any resiliency and even a modest degree of intelligence, it should be able to manage the disturbances to its equilibrium created by internal contradictions with appropriate ruthlessness and delicacy. One cannot be as confident as O'Connor is. A threat to business more proximate than the internal contradictions of the system is the growing awareness of the nature of the system, which will make it increasingly difficult for business to manage its contradictions as well as it has in the past. To be effective, this awareness must seep into the trained minds of the articulate, active liberals in our society. There are many more of them than there are radicals; the liberals are close to the centers of power (because they serve the establishment); they are intelligent; although they operate under a different paradigm of the nature of the system, they can substitute a new paradigm; and their well-educated, well-bred offspring can change even more easily.

THE SYSTEM AND THE LEFT

The New Left was born and grew in activism. With demonstrations, marches, confrontations, and violence it fought for peace and civil rights, and for the reform of major institutions such as the universities. This activism has not perceptibly changed the nature of our social system in fundamental ways. The military budget remains grotesque, and violence and destruction continue in Vietnam, Cambodia, and Laos with the help of United States materiel and direction. Hopes for real progress in civil rights are sodden under presidential rain. The universities and academic dissent seem ready to flounder in the compromises born of an academic depression. The welfare system is clogged; the cities are mired in poverty, crime, and drugs. Income distribution remains grossly unequal, with no sign of changing. Economic concentration, and thus the power of business, surges ahead. Smothered in rhetoric and distraught by their own terrorism, some in the New Left proclaim the disintegration of their own movement.

New abominations may bring forth new activism and new youthful leaders. But more important than the fruits of activism *per se* are the fruits of the New Left's analysis. The analysis is not that novel; much of it goes back to Marx, and some has accumulated over the past century. But capitalism has changed over the past century, and most considerably in the past thirty years, demanding new analysis. In a few hectic years the New Left has increased the scope of its analysis, embraced more institutions and more complex ones in the framework, improved the documentation, and increased the availability of the analysis through improved presentation. The dissemination of its viewpoint, while still very limited in a vast country, has broadened significantly and has been directed into strategic channels.

The influence of the intellectual insurgency of the New Left, then, does not promise to wane, at least for a time, even if its political and social insurgency has done so. In the long run, because the New Left's tiny band cannot make a revolution by itself and because the workers are not yet disposed to be attentive, it seems likely that the New Left's intellectual insurgency will count the most. It has been strengthened and tempered by activism, and it will continue to need this. But their analysis can move the liberals, and thus trickle down to the moderates and to labor. The New Left offers a paradigm that is, for once, accessible, reasonably comprehensive, and still humanitarian.

The paradigm is still being formulated, explored, and expanded. But it is remarkable that in a few years it has managed to illuminate, at least to the satisfaction of the Left, so much of our world. This paradigm rests on some simple, even crude assumptions: in the last analysis, economic power is the force that organizes and drives our nation in its present state; this power is exercised through elites that draw their power and resources from business, but that also control or occupy government, the military and intelligence apparatus, education, and other key institutions; their interests are worldwide. The system is resilient because the elites have managed to avoid extreme policies that would precipitate revolutionary change at home; and to a considerable extent they have stayed revolutionary change abroad. They need not conspire, but only act intelligently in their own self-interests. Most important, they have evolved and propagated a doctrine of pluralism, competition, free enterprise, and individual self-determination that will withstand much commonplace scrutiny in the everyday world of consciousness, even though more careful analysis indicates that pluralistic groups are powerless, competition is trivial, independent enterprise is precarious, and autonomy is an illusion. In this fashion, the elites have gained the grudging admiration of the populace, including even the liberal intellectuals. To expose the system and lay bare the paradigm is the first task of the Left.

Such a system as the New Left describes must encompass much of our life and operate wherever substantial economic gain can be realized (although I have yet to see organized crime fully integrated by the Left). In this book we have traced its operations in the traditional areas of economic concentration, foreign trade, foreign policy, and labor. We have seen the radical analysis incorporate the emerging areas of the service economy in mature capitalism—education, urbanization, hard-core unemployment, ecology, and health. No significant area of public life and need can remain outside the system if it is to be the dominant system.

One of the many things that distinguished Karl Marx was his attempt to "put it all together," to define every significant area of life in terms of the relationship of classes of men to the factors of production. Since Marx, profound thinkers have been pulling it all apart. The work of Sigmund Freud is sometimes seen as a subliminal, cosmic debate with the Marxian thesis, derailing the analysis of the roots of social power. The impressive sociology of Max Weber, who wrote at the turn of this century, was sometimes explicitly a dialogue with Marx. Weber insisted that status was independent to some extent of class, and so was power. He pulled it apart. Society is a system, of course, but there is no overriding case that economic processes define it. Contemporary social science has made the disintegration of a one-factor view of the system a virtue and called it pluralism. But Freud, Weber, and contemporary social-science theory have been rejected by the New Left; the Left is putting it all together again.

Will they succeed? I have argued that there are some serious difficulties with their analysis, and with the task in general. Even a sympathetic critique, such as this has been, suggests that (1) too often they assume a coherent, integrated, and rational system where there is only a loose, shifting, and partial system; (2) too frequently they neglect the proven resiliency of the system with misleading announcements of its imminent collapse; (3) problems of overwhelming importance are left unexplored, particularly the problem of overpopulation and the related problem of the destruction of the ecosphere; (4) the assumption that United States capitalism dominates the noncommunist world economy is probably true, but a socialist revolution in the United States would leave much of capitalism intact in Europe and Japan, so the system net must be cast more widely than it normally is, and this makes analysis more demanding and technical, and the hopes for a socialist revolution even more distant; (5) the vast differences among capitalist countries make it imperative to distinguish what is particularly American and what is particularly capitalist about our own system; (6) the existence of competition and conflicting interests in strategic areas at high levels in the system, though overestimated by the non-Left, requires more analysis; (7) the nature of the working class and the "new working class" of college-trained technicians and experts is insufficiently analyzed and conceptualized; (8) and the problems of the expertise, centralization, and bureaucratic control and coordination apparently required in industrialized nations have not been sufficiently confronted by the New Left.

But in the last analysis, it is presumptuous to expect a small group of scholars and activists, working largely without research grants or institutional encouragement, to have solved such problems in the short space of a decade. What is striking is that they have so markedly advanced the analysis of monopoly capitalism and its far-reaching impact on human existence, and so vigorously propagated their vision. It is quite likely that the New Left has been partly responsible for the renewed activity of liberals since the 1950's; has channeled the activities of the generation of young people that so shook up the 1960's; has helped to precipitate a massive delegitimization of business, government, and liberalism; and has helped to legitimize and fuel the middle-class insurgency of Ralph Nader, Common Cause, consumerism, ecology, cultural experimentation, and antiwar movements. The New Left would hardly take it as a compliment, but at least up to this writing it appears that where the Left goes, the liberals cannot be too far behind. Perhaps the editors of the *Harvard Business Review* and the General Electric executive, who were quoted at the outset of this volume, have even more reason for alarm than they thought.

Index

A
B
C
D
E
F
G
H
I
J